PRAISE FOR *THE STRATEGIC WORKFORCE PLANNING HANDBOOK*

David takes a subject that usually feels distant and makes it close, real and practical. His clarity, practicality and uniquely human lens make this an outstanding contribution for anyone shaping the future of work.
Priyanka Anand, India HR Leader of the Year

David's eclectic experiences and astute observations illustrate the relevance of SWP. With wit and practicality, he demonstrates how caring for and investing in people continues to be a cornerstone of successful organizations. This is not a handbook but a user's guide.
Dave Ulrich, Rensis Likert Professor Emeritus, University of Michigan, Partner, The RBL Group

This book offers a rich vision of what HR can be, through the lens of strategic workforce planning. David Edwards brings his wealth of unique experience, personal stories and strolls through London and beyond, to create marvellous observations and analogies that encourage and inspire the community of strategic workforce planners to play their important role in shaping the future of work and HR.
John Boudreau, Emeritus Professor and Senior Research Scientist Centre for Effective Organizations and Marshall School of Business, University of Southern California

David combines deep knowledge with a sharp sense of humour, making tough topics easy to grasp. His willingness to share this expertise enriches the entire network, inspiring everyone to adapt and improve further in today's fast changing context.
Alessandro Alessandrini, SWP Director, Airbus

David Edwards adroitly demystifies strategic workforce planning, transforming a topic often perceived as abstract or overly technical into something genuinely accessible, practical and, most importantly, human. This book serves as a vital bridge, showing leaders how to master the transition from the *what* of people analytics – those crucial insights – to the *how* of strategy, turning mere data into powerful foresight that shapes the future of the organization. Given that we are now fully entering the Age of AI and unprecedented workforce disruption, *The Strategic Workforce Playbook* is not just timely; it is essential reading. Highly recommended for anyone serious about building a resilient, future-fit workforce.

David Green, Co-founder and Managing Partner at Insight222, co-author of *Excellence in People Analytics*, **host of the** *Digital HR Leaders* **podcast**

I picked up this book as an SWP neophyte. Not only have I learned about the scale, reach and benefits that SWP can deliver. But more than that, I believe this book offers insight, learnings and tools for anyone looking to effect positive change in a corporate environment and navigate the complexities of functional and hierarchical structures. All HR professionals seeking to move beyond transactional into strategic leadership would do well to learn the lessons from David's extensive experience.

Paul Milner, former MD international infrastructure group

This handbook is everything a treatise on Strategic Workforce Planning usually isn't - clear, practical and refreshingly funny. Drawing from his years as a practitioner, David blends real stories, clever analogies and just the right amount of humour to make the concepts easy to understand and apply. His care and steadfast commitment to excellence in SWP is obvious, but rather than keeping hard-won wisdom to himself, he is sharing it with us in the role of seasoned guide – teaching, inspiring and lightening the load while elevating this essential craft.

Jane Datta, ex-Chief Human Capital Officer, NASA

Brilliant and funny, David has produced a work of art – albeit more René Magritte than Johannes Vermeer. In *The Strategic Workforce Planning Handbook*, he expertly blends his own leadership experience with the successes and struggles of the practitioner community to create a must-have survival guide. Friends and fans will instantly recognize his irreverent, unique voice shining through this highly accessible book, which I wholeheartedly recommend to both newcomers and seasoned practitioners. Even the most experienced amongst us will uncover genuine gems of wisdom – and more than a little catharsis along the way.

Adam Gibson, author, *Agile Workforce Planning*

At a time when workforce planning is more consequential, and more misunderstood, than ever, *The Strategic Workforce Planning Handbook* arrives to bring clarity. David Edwards has created more than a guide; he's curated a global conversation among the brightest minds in Strategic Workforce Planning, weaving together his expertise with their collective wisdom into something both practical and profound.

Cole Napper, Vice President of Research, Innovation & Talent Insights at Lightcast, author of *People Analytics*, and Host of the Directionally Correct Podcast

David Edwards has written the rarest of things: a book on workforce planning that's as engaging as it is essential. His informal, passionate style makes even the most complex strategic concepts feel approachable and actionable. This isn't just informative—it's genuinely inviting, drawing you into a subject that too often feels technical and distant. David proves that rigorous planning and human insight aren't opposing forces but powerful partners. An enriching read for anyone who believes people should be at the heart of business strategy.

Toby Culshaw, Vice President of Strategy – Talent Intelligence, Lightcast

Finally, a book for those who would rather do literally anything else than read a workforce planning book. David proves that rigor, personality and humour can coexist. His writing is engaging and accessible without compromising on complexity. And 'anseriformes' is the best (nerdy, taxonomically correct) way of saying 'getting your ducks in a row' that I'll be stealing immediately.

Stela Lupushor, Chief-Reframer, Reframe.Work Inc., co-author of *Humans at Work* and *Humanizing Human Capital*

This isn't just an HR book: it's a new standard text for anyone thinking seriously about the future of work. Grappling with AI, risk, global volatility and skill shortages, leaders will feel a weight fall from their shoulders reading this. Bringing each theory to life though real-world stories from practitioners, humour and data, David transforms theory into something tangible and useful. It's a rare gem in the world of strategic workforce planning – equal parts insightful, practical and genuinely enjoyable to read.

Betsy Summers, Principal Analyst, Future of Work & HCM, Forrester Research

While SWP might not sound the most thrilling endeavour, David's storytelling and conversational tone really takes you by the hand and kindly guides through the intricacies of what we believe is a way to prepare better for the uncertain future ahead. Equally welcome as light reading for your commute and as a comprehensive guide to what might be the most complex and important work of HR and People profession.
Alise Rupeka, EDHEC Online

You make what we do human.
Liz Jurcik, CEO, Workforce Strategy Partners

The Strategic Workforce Planning Handbook

Design, implement and measure workforce plans to drive business results

David Edwards

KoganPage

First published in Great Britain in 2026 by Kogan Page Limited

Kogan Page
Kogan Page Ltd, 2nd Floor, 45 Gee Street, London EC1V 3RS, United Kingdom
Kogan Page Inc, 8 W 38th Street, Suite 90, New York, NY 10018, USA
www.koganpage.com

EU Representative (GPSR)
eucomply OÜ, Pärnu mnt 139b–14 11317, Tallinn, Estonia
www.eucompliancepartner.com

Kogan Page books are printed on paper from sustainable forests.

ISBNs
Hardback   978 1 3986 2360 6
Paperback   978 1 3986 2359 0
Ebook   978 1 3986 2361 3

British Library Cataloguing-in-Publication Data
A CIP record for this book is available from the British Library.

Library of Congress Control Number
2025045698

Typeset by Integra Software Services, Pondicherry
Print production managed by Jellyfish
Printed and bound by CPI Group (UK) Ltd, Croydon, CR0 4YY

To Finony

CONTENTS

PART FOUR
Where it's heading

LIST OF FIGURES AND TABLES

FOREWORD

In a world marked by rapid technological change, shifting demographics, geopolitical tensions and evolving societal expectations, the way we think about work and the workforce must fundamentally change. Strategic Workforce Planning (SWP) has evolved as a key discipline and a vital pillar of any organization's forward planning to align people strategy with business strategy. Every organization must think ahead to the capabilities, culture and workforce needed to respond to a fast-changing context and deliver on the anticipated business goals and outcomes. This book arrives at an important time, offering valuable insights into how organizations can prepare today for the workforce and capabilities they'll need tomorrow.

For many years, workforce planning was often confined to headcount forecasting or budget alignment, focused on short-term staffing rather than long-term capability. But the context has changed. Organizations must become more agile, proactive and intentional in how they shape their workforces, and the options to fulfil their capability needs.

What makes SWP truly strategic is its forward-looking nature. It requires organizations to anticipate future skills, roles and ways of working. It encourages scenario thinking and long-range planning, blending data with judgment, and analytics with human insight. This is not simply a function for HR, but it is a business-wide imperative. The organizations that will lead in the future are those that view their people not as a cost to be managed but as an asset to be nurtured, developed and deployed strategically.

Yet while the need for SWP is clear, the path to doing it well is not always straightforward. Many organizations struggle to move beyond tactical planning. Others lack the right data, governance or strategic clarity to make it work effectively. And perhaps most critically, some lack the cultural commitment to put people at the heart of strategy.

This book helps demystify that path. It offers both the 'why' and the 'how' of strategic workforce planning. Drawing from real-world examples, practical frameworks and expertise from a wide range of interviewees, it guides the reader through each stage of the process – from understanding business drivers, to mapping future capability needs, to designing and implementing workforce strategies that are sustainable, inclusive and future-focused.

Importantly it recognizes the need to look at workforce in a very holistic way and what has been coined as do I buy, build, borrow or bot. Employees (working in increasing varieties of ways), contractors and contingent workers, outsourcing or partnering, and where to innovate and understand how technology and AI can deliver capabilities and better outcomes, for both people and the organization.

Key questions now are about balancing automation with the human touch and what skills will matter most in an AI-driven economy, alongside rethinking inclusion and diversity to be part of workforce planning, and how to build organizational resilience in the face of continuous change.

These are not just technical questions. They are questions about the future of our organizations and workforces, creating better work that engages and retains our people, supporting wellbeing, fairness and inclusion. Strategic workforce planning is, at its heart, about shaping the kind of organization you want to become, to deliver on business goals but also becoming a responsible and sustainable business for the future.

A key strength of this book is that it recognizes the human dimension of workforce planning, underpinned by good data, insight and evidence. That also means engaging with employees, co-creating the future of work and ensuring that workforce strategies reflect both the head and the heart of the organization.

As someone who has worked across business and policy to advance good work and responsible leadership, I believe SWP has a crucial role to play in building better organizations and ultimately better work and a better society. Done well, it can help close skills gaps, improve job quality, support inclusive growth and ensure that no one is left behind in the transition to the future of work.

Whether you are a business leader, an HR professional, a workforce analyst or a policymaker, this book offers the tools and insights you need to act strategically, and responsibly, in shaping your workforce and organization going forwards.

This book is a timely and important contribution. David writes in an engaging and personal style that makes this important subject very approachable. I hope it informs your thinking, challenges your assumptions and ultimately helps you to lead with greater clarity and purpose.

Peter Cheese
CEO, CIPD
July 2025

ABOUT THE AUTHOR

David Edwards is one of the leading global voices in Strategic Workforce Planning, known for practical, impactful approaches that connect people, data, and strategy. He's renowned for combining hard-won practitioner insight with a sharp wit and a deep sense of how organizations really work – and often, how they don't.

David's career spans leadership roles across technology, banking and consulting. At NatWest Group, he led a strategic workforce management programme – one of the earliest of its kind – that subsequently reduced costs by hundreds of millions through smarter fulfilment, workforce mobility and planning innovation. His background is an eclectic one, having also worked in finance, consulting and operations in organizations ranging from the UK National Health Service to startup software ventures. He is currently Global Head of Workforce Planning at Ericsson.

He has experienced triumphs and disasters and treasures both for what they've taught him. A passionate advocate for making workforce planning practical, human and actually useful, David has spent much of his career helping businesses bridge the gap between ambition and execution. His work focuses on helping leaders make better long-term decisions about people, skills, cost and capability – without drowning in process or jargon.

He is a member of the Workforce Planning Institute's Global Standards Committee and a regular co-chair of its London conference. A sought-after speaker and writer, David's writing is known for its clarity, wit and refusal to accept lazy orthodoxy, with a distinctive voice that is part strategist, part storyteller and part bewildered onlooker.

Originally from Suffolk, David is a lifelong supporter of Ipswich Town FC and claims (with some justification) that the club's fluctuating fortunes have grounded him in hope, realism and improbability.

He sings soul and blues when anywhere near a microphone and remains unsure how his professional life ended up involving talking about fish cakes.

David lives in Hampshire UK with his wife of 40 years, Fiona, and his yappy dog Dylan.

GLOSSARY

Most of the abbreviations in this book are explained as I go along, but here are a few pointers for those new to the subject or to me.

Dylan A small, furry, yappy dog.

Finony Pronounced Fi (as in pie) No (as in Know) Ny (as in Knee). My soulmate of almost 45 years, so-called because my Auntie Peggy was completely unable to pronounce Fiona, her real name.

ACKNOWLEDGEMENTS

The author Percival Everitt has described writing a book as 'knowingly entering a bad marriage'. I've no experience of a bad marriage, just one fabulous one, and in writing this book I've been blessed with a superb coterie of wedding guests, without whom the book – and the experiences that informed me enough to write it – would have been impossible.

I must thank everyone at Kogan Page for turning my wildly unwired thoughts into the thing of beauty it has now become. Lucy Carter felt she could see something in me that was potentially book-worthy and I'll be forever in her debt for encouraging me to take my first steps into writing. Whether my Development Editor, Joe Ferner-Reeves, will be similarly grateful is another matter entirely. He has endured months of drafts from me, accompanied by frequently impassioned defences of some of my more maverick patches of prose, while trying to maintain a professional decorum throughout. That he succeeded tells you everything you need to know about him. Emma Dodworth, my marketing support, has been brilliant in sieving my many ideas and identifying those that were not entirely hare-brained.

Two people kindly and heroically worked their way through the chapters and lived to tell the tale. My good friend Paul Milner acted as the 'know-nothing' bystander and kept me away from being too esoteric and full of self-pity, while NASA's former CHRO Jane Datta gave me an unimpeachable CHRO view and suggestions I wish I'd thought of. Both of them, in their separate ways, kept me honest and are both the dearest of friends.

I'm indebted to Adam Gibson of EY, Professor Nick Kemsley of Henley Business School and to The Royal Airforce Museum, Hendon, for their kind permission to use diagrams they had created. The book is enriched and enhanced by their presence.

I'm especially grateful to and more than a little starstruck by the guitar great Steve Hackett who gave me permission to use his *Supper's Ready* anecdote.

I have tried to reflect points of view from as broad a spectrum of interested parties as possible but will have missed many more than I managed to pin down. To those that I did miss I can offer only apologies and the consolation that they didn't have to endure 30 minutes answering my tedious questions. Next time (if there is one), they won't be so lucky.

Of those who I did ensnare, several preferred to remain anonymous. Their contributions are no less relevant for their anonymity, given the towering figures they are in their respective fields; they all know just how grateful I am to them.

Those who have contributed and unwisely waived their right to anonymity are Alessandro Alessandrini of Airbus, Jen Allen, Director of Beyond the 8 Ball and formerly of Police Scotland, Vincent Barat, CEO of Albert, Tobias Bartholome of Lufthansa, Kouros Behzad of Anaplan, Andreas Berger of Swiss Re, Donna Biggs, CHRO, Mercer UK, Sadhana Bhide of Pearson, Jean Blackstock of JBC, David Boyle of Altria, Professor John Boudreau of the University of Southern California, SWP Professional Donna Breadmore, Olly Britnell of Phoenix Group, Sue Brooks of Imagine Talent, SWP Professional Lindsay Clarke, Pilar Cortés, former Chief of SWP at The World Food Programme, Toby Culshaw of Lightcast, Jill Dobbe of Orgvue, Sheri Feinzig, Adjunct Professor at New York University, Florian Fleischmann of hrforecast/TalentNeuron, Adam Gibson of EY, Alejandro Giordanelli of Merck KGaA, David Green, Managing Partner at Insight222 and host, Digital HR Leaders podcast, Paul Habgood of Mercer, Sheena Hales BEM, Chris Hare, co-CEO of eQ8, Joe Heppenstall, Skills Director at QinetiQ, SWP Professional Matt Higgs, Olly Holbourn, CEO of the UK National Wealth Fund, Benoit Hudon, UK CEO of Mercer, Mark Jackson of Nationwide Building Society, Dirk Jonker, CEO of Crunchr, Oliver Kasper of SwissRe, Professor Nick Kemsley of The Henley Business School, Nick Kennedy, CEO of The Workforce Planning Institute, Shiva Kumar, CEO of the Chartered Institute of Workforce Management USA & Canada, Charlotte Lloyd of Rolls-Royce, Peter Louch, CEO of Vemo, Daniel Mason of Insight Software, Viv Meredith of V Meredith Consulting, former HR Leader at AstraZeneca, GSK & AngloAmerican, Jeff Mike of Flextrak, Amit Mohindra, CEO of People Analytics Success, Jeff Mullen, Strategic Advisor, Workforce Intelligence, Nahal Mustafa of Volvo Cars, Cole Napper of Lightcast, Jordan Pettman, Head of Culture at Rolls-Royce, Alicia Roach, co-CEO of eQ8, Naima Robenhagen Burgdorf of Ramboll, Gergo Safar of BT, Neeta Saggar of Coca-Cola HBC, Steve Scott of Standard Chartered Bank, Global People Analytics leader Dibyendu Sharma, Oliver Shaw, CEO of Orgvue, David Shontz, formerly of Nokia, David Slovak, formerly Head of SWP, FIS, Ashleigh Steele of Rabobank, Amy Stoddard of Humana, Alan Susi of S&P Global, Jo Thackray of TalentNeuron, Matt Tuttle of Verizon, Professor Dave Ulrich of the

University of Michican and Principal, The RBL Group, Ton van Dijk of Capgemini, Jaap Veldkamp of ABN AMRO, David Wilkins of TalentNeuron and Chris Woodward of Cello Consulting.

My thanks also to Ericsson, my current employers, and in particular to my manager Eden Britt, who encouraged me throughout and tolerated my almost daily lapses into author mode.

The author and scholar Marc Sokol rang me one day as he was about to board an aeroplane just to offer me encouragement. At my age, I forget many things but won't forget that kindness in a hurry.

Nobody does these things on their own. My experiences are the culmination of many people's efforts and I want to acknowledge the talent, commitment and endless invention of Tom Carrigan, Gemma McNair, Nicola Cannon, Wendy Cunningham, Marc O'Donnell, Damian Sellers, Wincie Wong, Mel Craig, Craig Findlay, Sarah Kleczkowska, Gail Lynas, Clare Wallace, Sandra Wright, Lorna Shaw, Michael Wood, Enda Magennis, Alan Whelan, Sarah Howatson and countless more besides. Their ideas far exceeded my own in quantity and quality. All I did was stitch some of them together.

I must reserve my greatest thanks to my long-suffering wife of almost 40 years, Fiona (Finony as she is called). Her gifts dwarf mine and her support throughout this project in so many ways has constantly lifted me up when I felt down. She has put up with my many moods, stresses, other worldliness and hermit-like behaviour with none of the irritation that it surely deserved. She is extraordinary and, uninspired by SWP as she might be, this book is dedicated to her nevertheless.

I'd also like to thank our dog Dylan, but I can't. He just spent the last seven months asleep on the carpet, doing nothing of any use whatsoever.

Hartley Wintney, UK
July 2025

Introduction

'It's going to be a very short book.'

I'd just suggested to Finony that one of the titles I was considering for this book was *SWP Without the Boring Bits*.

She laughed. She always laughs at her own jokes, especially the ones she's pleased with, and she had a right to be pleased with this one. I laughed too, but we both knew that there was more than a grain of truth in it – that glazed-over look which appears when you tell someone what it is that you do, closely followed by their retreat to their smartphones to check out their weather app.

SWP may seem to be similarly unenthralling to many. On the face of it, it's dry, overly complex, hopelessly theoretical, all of these things and more.

SWP has been the coming thing for 15 years and still hasn't arrived. It's therefore not unreasonable to ask whether if it's so good, why it is that everyone isn't doing it. Our populations are ageing, our world is increasingly unstable, technologies and their pace of change are increasing exponentially. The talent pool is shrinking, and everyone is after the same people with the capabilities needed to keep businesses competitive. SWP ought to be the No.1 priority for every company with an interest in still being around 10 years from now: why? Because when it works, it works brilliantly, with massive financial benefits and benefits for employees that can be equally seismic and tangible.

But, while there are those who can speak proudly of having reached this Nirvana, the abiding story of SWP is one of failure and abandonment; and for those who are responsible for trying to make it work in their companies, it is all too often a tale of epic struggle to overcome inertia and indifference. The number of companies in which SWP has been successfully implemented is dwarfed by the numbers where it either has not or has not even been attempted.

For over a decade, organizations have wrestled with its challenges – why it matters, how to implement it, how to make it work in the real world. If these were the only challenges, then this really would be a short book. In theory, SWP is the ultimate tool to align workforce capabilities with organizational strategy, ensuring long-term success. But theory and practice are often worlds apart, the gap between them riven with challenge. Perhaps we can close the gap a little with what I intend to say.

So, this is not your typical business book, or at least I don't expect it to be. It's not a retread of the books on the subject that already exist. Indeed, I encourage you to read at least one of them first, whether it be Tracey Smith's brilliantly concise and clear explanation, *Strategic Workforce Planning: Guidance & back-up plans*, Marc Sokol and Beverley Tarulli's fabulous collection of writings from some of the very best practitioners in the field, *Strategic Workforce Planning: Best practices and emerging directions*, Ross Sparkman's aptly titled *Strategic Workforce Planning* or Adam Gibson's hugely influential and insightful work, *Agile Workforce Planning*. This is not that kind of book, and it doesn't set out to teach you things you will find there instead. You may find some of the definitions and methodology mentioned here as well, but they are not the intended centrepiece.

People are not a by-product of SWP: they *are* the product, and they are messy. They come in different shapes, sizes, needs, abilities, prejudices and opinions. They have quirks, competing priorities, motivations and fears. They don't just have jobs; they have livelihoods, dependents, debts, dreams and ambitions. We lose sight of the people impacted by what we do at our peril.

If SWP is to succeed, it must resonate in the world that these people – be they employees, their managers or their leaders - inhabit.

So this is a guide: you might even call it a survival guide. It's a conversation, a collection of some seemingly unconnected stories, and it's more than occasionally a soapbox. But it's also a celebration of people and their spirit; the lives they lead, the passion and desire they have to make things better for people; of their humour, their care for others and of their ingenuity.

It's written for those people, those frequently lonely people, who are trying to make SWP work in their company despite the odds. For those people who have spoken to me at length about their experiences, their frustrations, sometimes even the damage getting it to work (or not) has done to their own mental health. They may recognize something about themselves or their situations here. But that's not the only audience: this is for all HR professionals, finance planners, operations leaders, business leaders and executives, sceptical or otherwise. It's for anyone who has ever rolled their eyes at an overcomplicated workforce plan, who has wondered why it's so hard to hire people; and it's for anyone who's still wondering what all the fuss is about. It's for anyone who is sitting, staring blankly at the ocean of ripples that SWP can create in a company and who doesn't know where or how to start.

So let's start.

PART ONE

Why it matters

01

Why I love doing this

What got me started and why I care

You can probably hear it in my voice, but I'm constantly excited about this work and people think I'm crazy, but I love it. It's really interesting.

ALAN SUSI, S&P GLOBAL

A history lesson

In Bucklersbury Passage in the City of London, a beautiful Art Nouveau-style enamelled plaque, framed in green and blue in the centre, records that this was, from the 11th to the 13th centuries, the site of the Loriners' Trade.

This has absolutely everything to do with Strategic Workforce Planning.

The very name, Bucklersbury Passage, reeks of history. It speaks of dark alleyways, of medieval Londoners bustling up and down a cramped path of uneven cobblestones, polished by centuries of feet belonging to tradespeople, rapscallions and other curiosities that Charles Dickens specialized in describing. It conjures up visions of bucklers working hard in tiny candle-lit rooms, crafting away at casting and finishing buckles of magnificent precision and beauty for shoemakers, beltmakers and, as it happens, for loriners.

It is nothing of the sort.

My son is older than Bucklersbury Passage. It was built in 1997[1] as a route to the Atrium of No 1 Poultry, a large, pink and yellow limestone-faced building that has been described as one of the ugliest buildings in London but which is now a listed building.[2] There is nothing false, however, about the loriners whose trade the blue plaque commemorates.

They were an old City Guild, granted ordinances in 1261; they made bridle bits and other metal work used for horses and the Worshipful Company of Loriners persists to this day; indeed, since 1858, there have been 37 Loriner Lord Mayors of London.[3]

Loriners ceased to ply their trade over seven centuries ago, yet their fate serves as a stark reminder that nothing ever stays the same. Trades evolve, they disappear. The things people do are as permanent as the people themselves – which, as you discover when you get into your sixties, isn't very permanent at all. And in case this feels like some kind of distant example of no present-day relevance, consider the humble Christmas card.

It's personal

Finony and I were walking Dylan along a local pathway last December; I say walking, but really it was more an exercise in taking a few steps until Dylan found something ghastly to sniff and stick his nose into, before allowing us to move onto the next excrescence that took his fancy.

'Have you noticed that we've received far fewer Christmas cards this year?' she asked me, knowing that I probably hadn't because I never really notice anything. 'People are giving up on cards because of the waste of paper, the effect on the climate, the cost of postage and so on' (so on covering the possibility that there might be something else worth mentioning but unsure if there is).

'I think it's time we did the same,' she continued. 'We'll all be better off for it.' Coming from someone who had religiously written, sealed, stamped and sent about 100 cards a year for as long as I could remember, this was all pretty seismic, inasmuch as not sending Christmas cards any more could be more seismic than, well, pretty much anything.

'That's very worthy,' I said back, 'but surely there are unintended consequences here. Postal workers aren't going to be better off because you've done this. And if everyone does the same, then those postal workers will be out of a job.'

'No they won't,' she said with the confidence of someone who really has been right for most of her life, 'They'll just do something else.' And without pausing for any discernible breath, she followed up with something that actually was rather seismic:

'That's where you come in.'

This may not seem terribly revelatory to any practitioner reading this, but it was quite something to hear Finony encapsulating what I do and why I do it. Not only was she totally right, but she affirmed the purpose behind what I've been doing these past 13 years. There it was in five words – the essence of SWP, boiled down, stripped of jargon – seeking beneficial impacts for people, helping them to avoid job loss and evolve into something new, innovative, necessary, just as many Loriners who made spurs eventually joined the Company of Blacksmiths in 1571.[4]

She reminded me that individuals are not merely an outcome of business decisions but help to determine them. Small decisions, rippling out, coalescing microeconomic shifts into macroeconomic consequences for someone they've never met, maybe just sitting down to Christmas dinner with their family, blissfully unaware that, somewhere in the company they work for, their name is on a coldly efficient spreadsheet list that will lead in a few months' time to their losing their job, their livelihood and destroying the certainty that next Christmas will be better than the last one.

It happened to me once. More than once actually, but the first time was absolutely the worst. Around midday one February 15th, I was asked to join a call in one of our conference rooms, only to find the company's chief legal counsel sat in front of a conference phone with my boss on the line from the US, terminating my employment. There had been no hint of anything wrong, nothing.

I cried my eyes out for 40 minutes while the legal counsel sat awkwardly waiting for either the ground to open up and swallow him or for him to find some kind of words to soften the blow. Neither happened. Twenty-four years on and it haunts me still.

Now before you say anything, I'm not advocating that SWP or anything else for that matter can magic away the threat of redundancy, but here's one small example of how it can make a difference.

Several years later, I found myself helping, with a wonderful colleague, to establish what was then called a Clearing House for people who were at risk of losing their jobs. We were trying to create a process that alerted us to potential redundancy situations and helped us to find suitable alternative work for the people in other parts of the company where their capabilities made them a good fit and where they would not themselves have known to look. I'll return to the mechanics of what we did and how we did it later but suffice to say that, when we were doing this, it was not remotely data-driven and was highly constrained by a lack of resources, enthusiasm and belief on the part of many.

What gave me the greatest satisfaction and sense of personal achievement was making that process work for someone. It wasn't about the money or the number of people we saved (although they were important), but it was about the messages of thanks and appreciation that we'd get from individuals whose livelihoods had been restored. We'd even get them from people who we couldn't save and not being able to save them was the source of my greatest frustration.

The personal possibility

Picture an employee's career as a seemingly endless tube of sweets. Each sweet represents a phase of someone's career – right up to the very last sweet, which is when redundancy strikes, the unforeseen end of the tube. It's a fraction of the thickness of the rest, just a thin slither of time to try to find another role in the company they've served loyally for years but happen to be in the wrong place at the wrong time, with a bunch of capabilities that will take other people years to learn. And guess what: the chances are that those roles, even if they exist, won't be found in time to save them.

There's danger in taking the metaphor too far – after all, not everyone has a sweet tooth – but what if you could foresee that final sweet and replace it with a fresh pack before the tube runs out? For most people, the moment of likelihood of job loss occurs when it is imminent. If that moment arose much earlier, you'd do something to avoid it. Moreover, if someone else identifies that moment for you earlier, they might seek to avoid it for you, so that you don't have to experience the seven psychological stages associated with redundancy, the first three of which are pretty unpleasant – Denial, Shock, Anger.[5]

Let's put that into a slightly more structured form.

Figure 1.1 illustrates these phases and inflexion points:

1 **Unthreatened Tenure:** A stable, uninterrupted career trajectory where roles and employment remain secure over time.

2 **Moment of Likelihood:** The point at which it becomes apparent, either to an individual or collectively, that a role or set of roles is unlikely to be required in the future. Collective awareness usually precedes individual awareness and some individuals may not recognize this moment if they are successfully identified for new opportunities during the **Window of Opportunity**.

FIGURE 1.1 Creating the time to do things differently

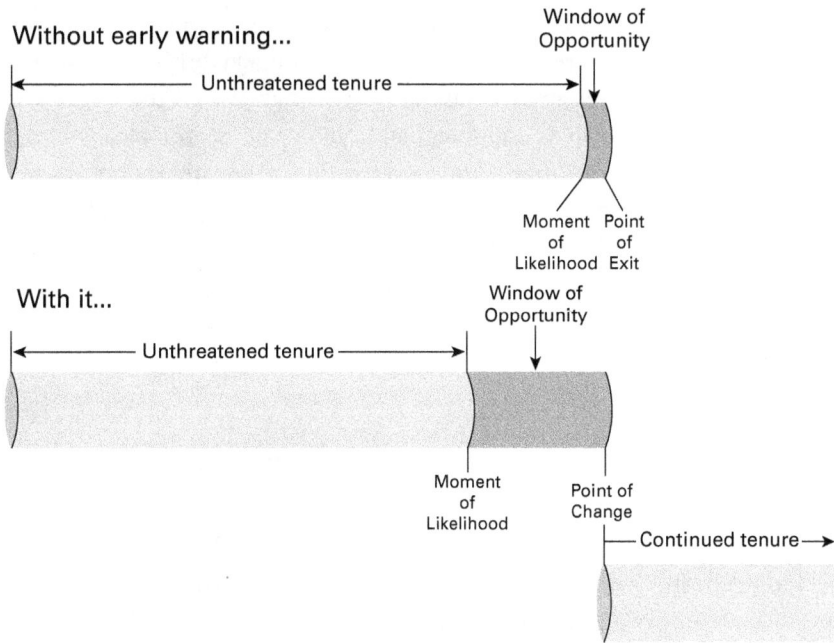

3 **Window of Opportunity:** The period following the Moment of Likelihood but before the **Point of Exit,** when an individual has the chance to secure a new role. A longer window provides more time for solutions, such as reskilling.

4 **Point of Exit:** The moment at which an individual's redundancy is executed.

5 **Point of Change:** The point at which an individual transitions to a new role.

6 **Continued Tenure:** A restructured or redeployed situation where the individual's tenure continues after a period of uncertainty or transition.

If only you had more time. With more time and with earlier awareness, you could do things differently: avoid trauma, enhance someone's career instead of damaging it, reduce the cost to the organization and the negative effect on not only an individual, but also on the morale of their colleagues, the drive of their department or even their division. SWP buys you that time and gives you that awareness.

A wider context

But let's now broaden our perspective. I've focused on the plight of the individual and how SWP creates an opportunity to alleviate that plight. But there would be nothing Strategic about SWP if that was all that it did and little of relevance to you as an individual if you've never lost your job. But the consequences of SWP, like so many other things, are all around us.

If, in the summer of 2022, you'd thought it would be a splendid idea to cast off the shackles of the isolation caused by the Covid pandemic of 2020–2021 and head off to somewhere sunny and warm, you would not have been alone. Unfortunately, nor would your baggage, because it was having a holiday of its own along with several hundred of its mates in London Heathrow Airport's Terminal Five, either before you went on holiday, afterwards or even while you were there.

Can we say exactly why it happened? Well, during the pandemic, airlines and airports (including Heathrow) had laid off or furloughed large portions of their ground-handling and security workforce. Rehiring efforts lagged behind the post-pandemic travel surge because, in many cases, those laid-off people had gone off to do something else instead.

It's way too simplistic to say that this was down to an absence of SWP. But SWP is a way to look at future scenarios and, by so doing, identify approaches that could reduce the risk of things going wrong. It's one isolated example, but one which you could at least argue illustrates how workforce planning, or its absence, can affect people with no direct relationship to it.

The macro opportunity

Business consists of a jungle, often a cutthroat one, of corporate entities of thousands, tens or even hundreds of thousands of people where sentiment is maybe virtuous but unaffordable. If SWP is of no value to them, then it's unlikely to be of any interest.

But the value is there. With earlier awareness and greater foresight, what other things can be done differently, at the macro level as well as the micro? In learning my craft as an SWP practitioner, I came to see that the possibilities, while not endless, were nevertheless enormous, the benefits for an organization potentially vast and not just financial.

We live in an age where age itself has become hugely important. In the European Union, we are already in an era where there are more people aged over 60 (21.3 per cent in 2023) than there are aged 0 to 14 (14.9 per cent),[6] where the generational differences in attitude are stretching conventional organizational norms and wisdom to their limits.

To this we can add almost limitless threats – for that is how I see them – that make that ageing workforces seem rather trivial. Populist movements throwing globalization into reverse; protectionism of jobs and supply chains presenting companies with tough choices; a world returning to a volatility and level of threat not seen since – well, since I was young and thankfully unaware of it; where fact and fiction have become almost indistinguishable thanks to the speed of communication and the willingness of actors, good and bad, to exploit it; and the accelerating pace of technological development that challenges established norms and perceptions in ways we're still trying to comprehend.

In the fall of 2000, I attended a user conference at which David Siegel,[7] a seer of the time who foresaw how the internet would change things, asked us who our biggest competitor would be in five years' time, which elicited various company names who were, at the time, on everyone's lips. 'The answer,' he continued, 'is that they're probably not even in your industry yet.' He was right, of course. Most of the companies we named that day no longer even exist and there's no reason to suppose that we're not in the same situation today, except the timespan could now be as little as two years, maybe even one. Which household names of today will disappear?

The role of Strategic Workforce Planning in helping to mitigate some of these risks is underappreciated, although, as we will discuss, it's not going to solve every business problem there is. Nor is it going to solve anything on its own. Morris Chang, the founder of Taiwan Semiconductor Manufacturing, once said, 'Without strategy, execution is aimless. Without execution, strategy is useless.'[8] The plan and its execution are mutually dependent and that execution demands participation of multiple agencies.

For participation, also read collaboration, and change, and re-organization. Introducing SWP and making it work well is a world of difference to introducing it and watching it limp along. It requires a raft of changes in existing processes and structures, as well as changes in behaviours and mindsets. It is not easy to do and the obstacles to its ultimate success are many and unexpected. There is no one way to do it, no one has all of the answers and what works in one organization may fall flat on its face in another. Not everybody wants to do it and the reasons for not doing it pile up on each other. People who are charged with leading its introduction frequently find themselves struggling for consensus, acceptance, approval, airtime, resources and progress. They seek help and frequently don't know where to find it. And that brings me back to the Loriners.

Pilgrim's progress

It's a walk of about half a mile from their plaque to 200 Aldersgate, which stands directly opposite the Museum of London, which charts the city's history from its earliest beginnings, before Loriners were even a thing. Each year, in November, this building hosts the Workforce Planning Institute's annual Strategic Workforce Planning (SWP) Conference.

Like pilgrims from distant and barren lands, practitioners trudge through London's November gloom, emerging into the slick venue's kaleidoscope of interior design, corporate catering and technology vendor swag. Many of them hug each other like old friends, having spent much of their year talking to each other like some secret society.

They listen excitedly to the High Priesthood of SWP – veteran practitioners, leading thinkers, people who've got something to sell – in search of the nuggets of wisdom that will solve some of the dilemmas they face in making SWP work for them and they draw comfort from hearing those same conundrums being shared by their fellow travellers.

They are pilgrims, but they are also disciples. Like me, they believe in the potential for transformative good that SWP has both for an organization and for its people but they are also, like me, daunted by the many obstacles they find blocking the path to its success. Through the smiles, the bonhomie and the shared relief in not having to explain to each other what they do, tales unfold of situations and challenges that have left them bewildered, frustrated or demoralized. Their resilience is a given in these surroundings, but it needs justification, an outcome that can render the personal toll worthwhile.

Does that sound melodramatic? I don't think so. In a snap LinkedIn poll which I conducted recently,[9] only 17 per cent of the 65 practitioners who responded said they had never experienced anxiety or depression while trying to get SWP successfully implemented.

And yet, they persist. Through isolation, setbacks and moments of doubt, these practitioners return each year to seek not just answers but reassurance: that the challenges they face in SWP can be overcome, that their work matters and that real progress is possible.

The conversations they hold, whether they're about frustrations or breakthroughs, all point to the same conclusion: SWP can work – but only when it's approached with clear purpose, practical strategies and a willingness to adapt.

That's why this book exists. SWP is complex, but it's not impossible. Whether you're facing resistance, uncertainty, or simply don't know where to start, I want to show you how it can be made to work – not in theory, but in practice.

Because when it works, SWP does more than align workforces with strategy. It strengthens organizations, unlocks potential and creates tangible value for employees and leaders alike. But to get to that hallowed place, we need first to dig a bit.

REFLECTIONS

- Workforce change is a constant.
- Workforce changes affect individuals and their circle.
- Unmanaged workforce change can have macro implications.
- Strategic Workforce Planning offers possibilities for organizations and for individuals.
- SWP is hard to do, but it can be done.
- We love doing it.

Notes

1 Mansfield, I (2023) *London's Alleys: Bucklersbury Passage, EC2*, IanVisits, https://www.ianvisits.co.uk/articles/londons-alleys-bucklersbury-passage-ec2-62654/ (archived at https://perma.cc/G9NC-G2VR)

2 Sarrett, L (2023) One of London's ugliest buildings now has listed status, *Time Out London*, 17 August, https://www.timeout.com/london/news/one-of-londons-ugliest-buildings-now-has-listed-status-081723 (archived at https://perma.cc/G6GD-4SR9)

3 The Worshipful Company of Loriners (2020) *Company History*, https://www.loriner.co.uk/the-company/company-history (archived at https://perma.cc/8ZEY-ZDDR)

4   David (2022) An Accountant, Hall, Church and Shakespeare – City of London Blue Plaques. A London Inheritance, https://alondoninheritance.com/london-history/an-accountant-hall-church-and-shakespeare-city-of-london-blue-plaques/#Loriners-Trade (archived at https://perma.cc/UWL8-UHJF)

5   Stevens, M (2023) Double jeopardy: The surreptitious consequences of redundancy, *The Psychologist*, 36(12), 28-nn, https://www.bps.org.uk/psychologist/double-jeopardy-surreptitious-consequences-redundancy (archived at https://perma.cc/HGV4-MFD9)

6   European Union (2023) *Population structure and ageing: Statistics explained*, Eurostat, https://ec.europa.eu/eurostat/statistics-explained/index.php/Population_structure_and_ageing (archived at https://perma.cc/HTP5-87BC)

7   Siegel, D (1999) *Futurize Your Enterprise*, New York: Wiley.

8   Powell, J (2024) *Building the Bridge Between Strategy and Execution*, Forbes, https://www.forbes.com/councils/forbesbusinessdevelopmentcouncil/2024/02/21/building-the-bridge-between-strategy-and-execution/ (archived at https://perma.cc/MX7E-DFFU)

9   Edwards, D (2024) *So, 65 votes is hardly a definitive decision....* LinkedIn, https://www.linkedin.com/posts/dsehw_so-65-votes-is-hardly-a-definitive-activity-7262094010868019200-ezoB?utm_source=share&utm_medium=member_desktop (archived at https://perma.cc/4DG8-NN9V)

02

And what do you do?

The many different things an SWP Practitioner needs to be good at

*Strategic workforce planning requires quite a unique set of attributes…
You need to have a strong understanding of HR, but you need to
understand data, be comfortable with ambiguity, and have a level of
resilience. You make people uncomfortable, and you have to be
comfortable with that.*

PRACTITIONER LINDSEY CLARKE

Questions, questions

I've never met royalty, so I've never been asked 'And what do you do?' by any of them. I'm not sure if 'Well actually I'm a Strategic Workforce Planner' would even register with a royal. Yet when anyone – royal or otherwise – does ask me, it's never easy, especially if someone is unwise enough to ask what that actually means.

I will often mutter something like, 'Well, I try to work out what kind of workforce we're going to need in the next three years, compare that to what we've got, and then try to work out how on earth we're going to bridge the gap.' When you think about it, that essentially sums it up.

Except there's another question I've been asked.

I was speaking at the inaugural SWP Conference in London in 2022. It was a particularly problem-strewn speech, and we were running well over time. A poor assistant at the back was reduced to a sweaty mess, waving the message 'TIME', so I cut everything short and invited questions from the floor in the hope that the audience was either too bamboozled or bored to want to ask me anything.

One hand went up. 'Could you tell us please,' they said, 'what kind of skills you need to be a strategic workforce planner?' After my lower jaw flapped about for a bit with no discernible sound coming from me, I began to list various jobs from my past, leaving out only my time working tumble dryers in a psychiatric hospital laundry.

People were beginning to talk about skills at this time, but I'd never given this a second thought. I had evolved into being a SWP practitioner and, being a new profession, most of the other practitioners I knew had kind of evolved into the role too.

It's clearly not unusual for new roles to emerge – without that kind of emergence, our jobs would be a lot easier as well as quite a bit more dull – but in the case of SWP practitioners it does beg some questions that seem to have lagged behind the arrival of the role itself:

- What should an SWP practitioner do?
- What should an SWP practitioner be?
- Is there more than one SWP practitioner role?

This is more than just idle curiosity, and it goes to the heart of a topic I shall return to, which looks at who or what should own SWP as a function.

If you were to put 10 practitioners in a room for an SWP discussion, you'd probably get at least 15 points of view, so passionately and varied are they about the topic. I spoke to about 60 fellow practitioners and other players in all. Just like Sherlock Holmes had his 'unofficial force'[1] of eyes and ears on the ground, known as his Baker Street Irregulars, these good people were mine. At this stage of the development of the practice (Profession? Trade? Craft? Pastime?) of SWP, there was a refreshing desire to contribute freely (well – in some cases a little less freely after they read what they said) to the debate. Had Holmes had as many irregulars as I had contributors, he would have needed a medium-sized workhouse to house them. What follows then is not only what I think, but what they think too.

What should an SWP Practitioner do?

I don't want to argue over definitions – besides, I'd lose. Here's an example. Rob Tripp of Ford says that SWP is 'a disciplined business process that ensures that current decisions and actions impacting the workforce are aligned with the strategic needs of the enterprise'[2]. Great stuff – but for the average practitioner (and for many more besides, to be honest), this needs practical meaning.

SWP can be given many different purposes but, for me, it exists to do two things:

1 Identify the nature, scale and direction of workforce change needed to address existing workforce risks and to deliver the company's strategic objectives.

2 Give those making the workforce changes as much guidance as possible so they can optimize them.

How is that different from what Rob Tripp said (apart from being twice as many words)? Well, while a 'disciplined' process might be nice to have, my own sense is that SWP is characterized by a considerable lack of it, largely because it's still very much in Tuckman's Storming phase – that early, often chaotic and fluid stage of team development.[3] In any case, much of SWP deals with uncertainty, surely – unclear futures, assumptive fundamentals, hoped-for outcomes. It might be truer to say that SWP is a fluid process in which practitioners apply a *variety* of disciplines to the strategic issues that present themselves to ensure that the workforce is fit for its business purpose.

And then there's the word, 'ensures'. While there are very few SWP practitioners I've met who wouldn't love to have the authority the word implies, I've met equally few of them who feel sufficiently empowered. The best they feel able to do is to highlight how those decisions and actions might or might not align with those strategic needs. The word 'current' also implies a clarity that is often absent and takes no account of the future.

Finally, there's an absence of this pivotal role the practitioner plays in pulling information in, assembling it, assessing it and then passing it out again in a form that can be acted upon. And if that sounds complicated, history gives us a clear example of how it can work brilliantly – the Dowding System during the Battle of Britain.

Hugh Dowding led the airborne defence of Britain in 1940 when it was facing invasion. Now, I'm a history geek, so I'd love to take you through all the ins and outs of the Battle of Britain, but other people have written excellent books on that, and I want to focus instead on the system Dowding created. It ensured that the mass of information about incoming attackers that came flooding in from radar (a new invention then) and telephone reports from observers could be made sense of and passed back to fighter units in time for them to intercept the attackers before they reached their targets. That system is shown in Figure 2.1.

It's a marvel. The key to its success was not necessarily radar – the opposition knew about that and had their own version – but, as one of the battle's aces, Peter Townsend, put it, they 'never dreamed that what the radar "saw" was being passed on to the fighter pilot in the air through such a highly elaborate communications system'.[5] It was the processing of the information, its efficient sorting, packaging and rapid redistribution that made it critical to winning the battle.

Those same principles of gathering disparate elements, making sense of them quickly and enabling responsive action bear a striking resemblance to the work of an SWP practitioner.

For now, I'm concentrating on the SWP Practitioner role, but we'll return to this diagram and how it translates into the world of SWP when we talk about visions and operating models in Chapter 5.

One other important difference to Dowding is that those receiving functions don't necessarily have to act on what they're being told. That can be frustrating, but the essence of the job is about telling the horse where it will find water, not making it drink.

Taken together then, I'd recharacterize Rob's definition thus:

> SWP is a fluid process in which practitioners apply a *variety* of learned disciplines to highlight how current and planned decisions and actions impacting the workforce might (or might not) align with the strategic needs of the enterprise and then inform others who have to execute those actions what to expect, in order that they may act more effectively.

Something like that.

What should an SWP Practitioner be?

Now, if anyone is considering at this point that this all seems a bit vague, then I might just go dancing down my street singing, because being able to embrace vagueness is one of the most essential skills a good SWP practitioner needs in their toolkit.

Although we'll be looking in more detail at the dichotomy between precision and estimation in Chapters 4 and 6 when we talk about metrics, analytics and reporting, I really want to lean into this for a moment, because it's pretty fundamental to the art of SWP.

FIGURE 2.1 The Dowding System[4]

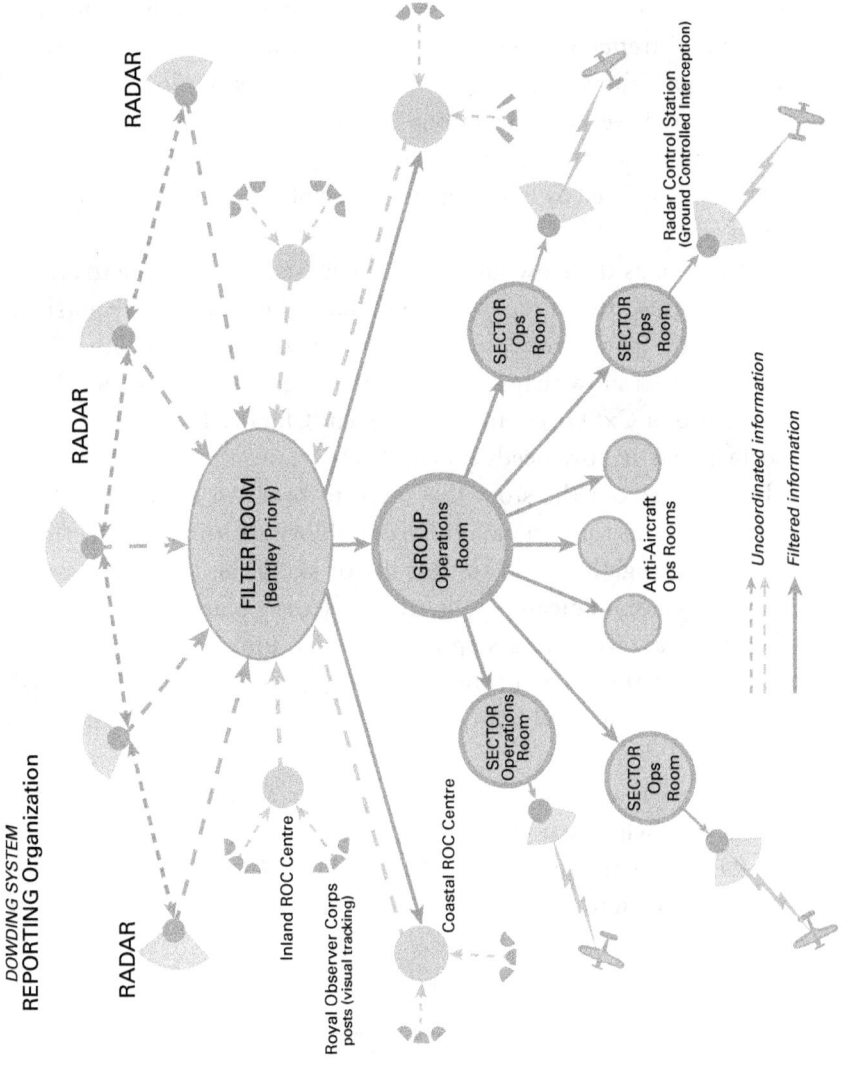

DOWDING SYSTEM
REPORTING Organization

RADAR

RADAR

RADAR

FILTER ROOM
(Bentley Priory)

Inland ROC Centre

Royal Observer Corps
posts (visual tracking)

Coastal ROC Centre

GROUP
Operations
Room

SECTOR
Ops
Room

SECTOR
Ops
Room

Anti-Aircraft
Ops Rooms

SECTOR
Operations
Room

SECTOR
Ops
Room

Radar Control Station
(Ground Controlled Interception)

Uncoordinated information

Filtered information

You're peering, as best as you can, into the future. You're trying to take a large jumble of different expectations and assumptions, connect them to data of varying quality and create some kind of magic trick in which they all come together in an answer so immaculate as to be reliable for the next five years. Actually, you should always bear in mind that well-known and catchy saying, 'Kein Operationsplan reicht mit einiger Sicherheit über das erste Zusammentreffen mit der feindlichen Hauptmacht hinaus,'[6] Translated and heavily paraphrased, it means 'no plan survives its first contact with the enemy'[7] and we know from our own experiences that even the best-laid plans can go awry when challenges emerge. Dealing with uncertainty and remaining unfazed by it throughout is one of the more critical skills this role demands.

Another, as the Dowding System suggests, is being able to craft clarity from what is often difficult to see. 'What's the weather like outside?' asks a character from a very old BBC radio show, *The Goon Show*. 'I can't see for all of this snow that's falling,' comes the reply.[8] So much is happening in front of a CxO (the range of different Chief Officers which is growing so fast that it now needs its own abbreviation) that others need to be able to tease out the story they need to hear. An ability to ask probing questions and the (arguably) harder ability to listen is essential to pull that story together. Add to that list of skills the ability to consolidate, distil and communicate – to be able to see the bigger picture through the fog of data. 'We take a step back and we look at that picture and go, "now what are the best things that we can do in all of these areas?" and we like to do this and hold it all together,' SWP Professional Matt Higgs told me.

So, does that make an SWP practitioner a CxO advisor, an influencer even? Well, while that idea sounds appealing, the reality is mostly different. In another totally unscientific poll, I asked SWP practitioners which level they reported into in their organization, and the results were sobering.

TABLE 2.1 SWP Practitioner reporting levels[9]

Reporting into	Which makes them a	Percentage
The CEO or CEO-1	CEO-1 or CEO-2	17%
CEO-2	CEO-3	23%
CEO-3	CEO-4	43%
CEO-4 and below	CEO-5 or lower	17%

It's quite something, isn't it? Eighty-three per cent of practitioners aren't within even touching distance of the CHRO while many of them will be buried within a hierarchy. At levels like that, it's highly unlikely that most practitioners are going to be CxO advisors; however, that doesn't mean that they cannot still be influential as communicators, or as high-quality data manipulators and interpreters. These skills hold good, regardless of corporate stratum. It's nevertheless striking that many practitioners sit a considerable distance away from the leadership levels that would benefit from their understanding.

Is there more than one SWP Practitioner role?

This wide dispersion of levels suggests that there are probably at least three kinds of practitioner currently in existence:

- **The Advisor-Influencer:** This genuinely strategic advisor navigates across disciplines by virtue of their experience and expertise, translating workforce data into actionable business strategies, often advising senior leadership directly.
- **The Technocrat:** The skilled engine-room operator who is indispensable for generating, analysing and presenting workforce plan data, primarily enabling others to strategize.
- **The HR Careerist:** Deeply embedded in HR disciplines and culture, drawing on their extensive knowledge of practice to partner business leaders through the planning process.

Let's boldly take a deeper dive into what each of these means.

The Advisor-Influencer

For many practitioners this is the pinnacle; the door to the office of the CHRO, or even the CEO, is always open or at least ajar. The insights drawn from data, the intuitive knowledge and understanding of workforce dynamics, the ability to swap languages without thinking from one of HR-speak to finance and then business. You're making a mark, and you've proven your worth. 'You come in,' says one, 'and you go, "the contract we've signed says our headcount needs to be x but actually our demand is going to be over 1000 FTE more than that, but don't worry. We can close most of that gap."'

It is your credibility, the trust that you have built up, that gives you the authority to say things like this and to be listened to.

It's not untypical for people to evolve into this kind of position through several experiences and disciplines – HR, Business Operations, Finance, Consulting and more besides. This was my path – a kind of spiral career shaped more like a collection of random squiggles – and it equips you well for the many faces you need to wear, depending on who you're working with. Only recently have more senior positions begun to emerge where the potential importance of SWP as a discipline has come to be recognized. The potential downside is that, as the role ascends the seniority ladder, you lose track of what might have got you there in the first place and become more abstract in your advice instead of being guided by evidence.

The Technocrat

A Technocrat produces the evidence. They may well be more junior, but that doesn't make them any less important. Because an understanding of the data and a curiosity to identify patterns and revelation from them is so fundamental to unearthing issues of organizational health and trends, the emergence of big data and the means to make sense of them has enabled something like SWP to even be a thing. It follows, therefore, that someone who immerses themselves in doing that is going to be a vital component of making SWP work.

The technocrat will often originate from business operations or, more recently, from mainstream data and analytics or people analytics. Old-school practitioners like me will have got started taking spreadsheet extracts from server-based HRMS (HR management system) tools like PeopleSoft (often having to file requests for extracts that would take days to be received) and would combine them with other spreadsheets looking for those patterns. As Alan Susi of S&P Global, put it: 'I came into... analytics first without having run analytics. I was just dangerous with data.'

It's simpler now, but the key requirements remain – an innate understanding of the fluid dynamics of people data, the connections that are possible and the stories that can be woven from them.

There are subtypes. The first, a relative minority I suspect, are dedicated solely to the crusade to mine data for findings and present it in as clear a way as possible. The second, the seed pods for Advisor-Influencers, are those who understand the significance of what they see and who draw inferences from it. They develop a passion for the topic and advocate for doing more in the space to understand what is going on in their organization and what it might mean.

The HR Careerist

You can be forgiven for thinking that this is a slightly negative term: it's not intended to be. This individual is likely to be a senior HR Business Partner (HRBP), professionally qualified) and a possible secondee at some point in their career into some of the specific Centres of Excellence (CoEs) that can benefit from SWP being deployed. It may be seen as a gateway from a transactional role to something that takes in the bigger picture and draws upon their multiple HR experiences.

One practitioner expounded on this.

Sat in what looked like the inside of a New England log cabin, with varnished panels, antique furniture and a patina that you could almost smell through the screen, they described how they had started out as an industrial-organizational psychologist and had done various stints in learning and development, talent acquisition and others besides. 'SWP kind of represents the culmination of all that... I was doing before, but then also add strategy and add more business relationships and business acumen and partnerships and, you know, seems like it would just propel me to the next level.'

Some HR careerists will take to this like a duck to water, especially if they have a sound understanding of the business of the business. Others may find the transition away from the transactional really hard to manage. Others still will be more strongly influenced by the environmental, social and behavioural aspects that have hitherto been the focus of their HR career journey.

None of the characteristics in any of these practitioner types is invalid; an amalgam of them all is probably close to perfection.

I said earlier on that there are at least three kinds of SWP practitioner in existence: the genuinely strategic advisor, the more technocratic support agent, and the HR careerist. Perhaps there's a fourth, perhaps the most prevalent of them all. This is the **Frustrated Practitioner**. Cast your mind back to the SWP conference and I'd wager that the majority of the attendees fall into this category (or one of its synonyms).

This person may have begun as a technocrat or as an HR careerist but is now aspiring to be an advisor. They may be an advisor or even a theoretician who finds themselves having to double as a technocrat: there are several permutations.

What unites them is their passion for the possibilities, yet their combination of responsibilities without adequate institutional authority to act that leaves them in a state of professional limbo. Other words I've heard used to describe them (by them) include unsupported, bewildered, undermined or even ridiculed. Remember that quote I included about the kind of thing you can say if you're an Advisor-Influencer? Well, things are not always what they seem. Let's finish the quote:

'I was fully expecting to be [greeted with], "Oh, hallelujah, you're here," but [instead] it was a 45-minute telling off. People don't want to be told their view is wrong, even if it's better for them.'

Causes of failure in the implementation of SWP can often result from a setup which causes an SWP practitioner to join the Frustrated group; but wait a moment.

Before we wallow in too much moribund self-pity and rail against the injustices of a world that seems to be against us, we need to recognize that, by failing to read the room or appreciate why senior people don't immediately fall at our feet begging for our help, Frustrated Practitioners may be architects of their own misfortune. Why did my good friend fail to win over an audience they expected to welcome them with open arms?

In the next chapter, we shall start to look at the differences that often exist between expectation, reality and licence to operate (I didn't say mandate, because mandates often carry no weight). It is the first of many potential sources of frustration that require us to look not only at our own needs but also those of others.

With such a diverse range of archetypes, it's little wonder that SWP sometimes feels like a concept searching for its distinctive soul. I chose four, not because that's all there are, but because those are the main variants that I've observed over the years. But stereotypes have this habit of splitting into increasing numbers of smaller definitions, the more you look at them, a bit like looking at a test tube full of mercury; it looks solid enough until you tip it out onto a surface, where it becomes dozens of differently sized globules. So I think it's therefore legitimate to ask:

Is SWP even the most accurate description?

Hang on a minute. This is a book about SWP and I'm challenging its name? Well, it's a bit more complicated than you might think.

SWP is like sticking your finger into a large pond. The ripples fan out to almost every corner, with several of them rebounding back to you. There are a few HR disciplines, plus maybe a couple of non-HR ones, which could possibly argue that SWP is an extension of what they already do. The very fact that I have seen it positioned in Organizational Design, Capability, Talent Acquisition, People Analytics, Business Operations, Strategy and Risk suggests that it is at the very least suffering from some form of identity crisis.

I was asked recently to write an article for the *Organization Development Review*,[10] the topic of which was broadly the ways in which SWP helps to inform and direct organizational development. And yet, when I reviewed what the UK CIPD had to say about the role of an organizational developer[11] – maximising the value gained from the organization's resources, aligning to an organization's strategy, goals and core purpose – I could easily argue that the two roles are really one and the same. This overlap with organizational development raises questions about whether SWP is a distinct function or an extension of existing ones.

Does SWP serve as a catalyst for change, or is it a discipline in its own right? This is a whole subject of its own, as could be the contention I heard from Professor Nick Kemsley of The Henley Business School over a cup of tea that SWP as a function really exists only to bring about change in the way other functions operate and that, having brought that change about, it is no longer needed. Jaap Veldkamp of ABN AMRO refuses to use the term Strategic Workforce Planning at all – 'HR is strategic workforce management. That is the core thing HR should be besides all the operational stuff, right?' This is quite a soup, and you have to feel sympathy for others looking in wondering exactly what value (if any) comes out of this navel-gazing. Our next chapter brings this into focus.

We can see that SWP Practitioners come in all sorts of shapes and sizes. You will have encountered others. What they will have in common, though, is either the ability to address multiple situations and disciplines, or the need to acquire it. You have to be the business equivalent of a Werner Hinzel, the legendary one-person band who could apparently play 51 separate instruments.[12].

My final observation is this. Before Finony and I moved into our present home, we lived in six different houses over 16 years. We've now been in the same place for 25 years. There is something about where we live now that feels right for us, just as there is something about a life partner who we find, inexplicably, in a sea of billions of people and stay with forever. I'm struck by the number of SWP practitioners I've met who, after a succession of different roles, find themselves staying in this one, a vocational Hotel California. The dizzy combination of that big picture, the multitude of complex elements that converge and challenge them to emerge from the resultant fog with outcomes that can alter the course of businesses and individuals is addictive.

I didn't originally intend to conduct a forensic dissection of what an SWP practitioner is or does and we may find, as we progress, that my dissection is incomplete (which is likely: I was useless at biology). But the themes that we've considered here will run like a fast-flowing river through the following chapters. Your skills as a practitioner will help you as you navigate the many challenges, obstacles and hazards that disrupt its flow.

REFLECTIONS

- **You need to be a little bit of everything.** You're a detective, a conductor, a translator, organizational psychologist, a geek. Tumble dryer experience is not required, however.

- **Vague is good.** Partial information and shifting organizational winds don't just come with the territory: they are the territory. You need to be able to thrive in it.

- **You are a storyteller.** This can be so many different things to so many people; you have to make the complex seem simple through your narratives.

- **Frustration is a given.** Responsibility without authority is never great, but it is what it is. By the way, we don't always read the room well enough so some of that discontent can be self-inflicted.

- **You could never leave.** Whatever your background, this is a heady and addictive mix of big-picture strategy and forensic sleuthing. What's not to like?

Notes

1   Doyle, A C (1890) The Sign of the Four, https://americanliterature.com/author/sir-arthur-conan-doyle/book/the-sign-of-the-four/chapter-8-the-baker-street-irregulars (archived at https://perma.cc/TM78-VGSS)
2   Gibson, A (2020) *Agile Workforce Planning,* London: Kogan Page, citing Tripp, R (2013) Current practices. In Ward, D L and Tripp, R (eds.) *Positioned: Strategic workforce planning that gets the right person in the right job,* New York: AMACOM

3 Tuckman, B W (1965) Development sequence in small groups, *Psychological Bulletin*, 63, 384–99

4 Royal Air Force Museum (2020) How Radar Works. In History of the Battle of Britain [online exhibition] https://www.rafmuseum.org.uk/research/online-exhibitions/history-of-the-battle-of-britain/how-radar-works/ (archived at https://perma.cc/2U69-BWGM) Reproduced with the kind permission of the Royal Air Force Museum

5 Coakley, T (1992) *Command and Control for War and Peace*, DIANE Publishing

6 Moltke, H von (1900) Über Strategie, In *Militärische Werke, Vol. 2, Part 2*, Berlin: E.S. Mittler & Sohn, p. 291

7 Moltke, H von (1993) 'On Strategy'. In *Moltke on the Art of War: Selected writings*, translated by D.J. Hughes and H. Bell, Novato, CA: Presidio Press, p. 92

8 Secombe, H, Milligan, T and Sellers, P (1955) The Goon Show: 'The Jet-Propelled Penguin', Series 6, episode 4. First broadcast 2 March 1955, BBC Radio

9 Edwards, D (2025) LinkedIn poll: As a SWP Practitioner, to which level do you report? LinkedIn, https://www.linkedin.com/feed/update/urn:li:activity:7284626273136435200/?commentUrn=urn%3Ali%3Acomment%3A(ugcPost%3A7284626272087867394%2C7284897121802027009)&dashComment Urn=urn%3Ali%3Afsd_comment%3A(7284897121802027009%2Curn%3Ali%3AugcPost%3A7284626272087867394) (archived at https://perma.cc/R6ZG-2KSD)

10 Edwards, D (2025) Tweedledum and Tweedledee: SWP and organization development need each other, *Organization Development Review*, 57(1), pp. 31–34

11 Chartered Institute of Personnel and Development (2024) Organisational development factsheet, updated by Young, J, https://www.cipd.org/uk/knowledge/factsheets/organisational-development-factsheet/#what (archived at https://perma.cc/SCY7-YZTX)

12 Edwards, D (2023) Embed workforce planning the Werner Hirzel way, LinkedIn, https://www.linkedin.com/pulse/embed-workforce-planning-werner-hirzel-way-david-edwards/?trackingId=BGTOmAu%2FT4e6UZ3NOfJAeA%3D%3D (archived at https://perma.cc/NE9U-KTXX)

03

SWP is not a cure-all

How to limit leaders' wildest expectations of SWP

We modelled US retirements: around 40 per cent of the workforce gone in 10 years just through retirements. This excluded other attrition measures (voluntary or involuntary). A simple Excel scenario on replacement opportunities bent the cost curve by €30 million – and suddenly business leaders and planners cared.

DAVID SHONTZ, EX-NOKIA

Congratulations: you've navigated the complexities of what makes an SWP practitioner and you're now along for the ride (at least I hope so).

Now, if you look back at the 19th-century advertisements for miracle cures, you'll see a very similar testimonial on them all:

> Lady/General/The Revd. <insert grand-sounding name here> writes: 'I suffer from gout/rheumatism/boils/melancholy/eczema and after taking <insert miracle cure name here> within two weeks I was perfectly well again.'

Some people believe SWP is a bit like a 19th-century cure-all, the answer to every business problem. Others think it's a glorified spreadsheet, while others have never heard of it or want nothing to do with it. We're going to explore why that might be.

You would think this was basic stuff, but there remains a huge disparity of expectations about what SWP can do and, perhaps more importantly, what it can't.

Do you see what I see?

'I'm drinking from the fire hose,' one of my Irregulars (you know, those anonymous practitioners) said to me. 'There's a world of executive pain right now for which I seem to be the answer.' They seemed to be revelling in this nice problem to have, describing it as 'thrilling'. They are not alone. Several others described the same phenomenon, often with a mix of exhaustion and exhilaration.

My friend had gone through a few years of significant pain before becoming the one in demand with all the answers. Because I could empathize with that pain, I knew the executive attention they were now getting was based on having delivered outcomes that their audience valued. I felt good for them because, let's be honest, we all like a big, fat dose of recognition.

But contrast this with a job interview I had with an HR leader. We'd reached the end of the interview and I was invited to ask questions, so I asked the one I always asked, which was this: what's your biggest challenge right now?

My erstwhile boss sighed. 'The biggest challenge,' they said, 'is trying to convince my board that SWP isn't going to solve all their problems for them, because right now, they think it will.'

And then, somewhere else in this same solar system, you will find a band of executive leadership asteroids who have either yet to hear about SWP or who have heard about it and struggle to see how it's going to help them.

Surely not all these different viewpoints can be right. And yes, other viewpoints are also available.

Jaap Veldkamp of ABN AMRO was clear that his job was to ensure that the workforce was fit for (business) purpose. He actually went further. 'The **only** thing HR should do,' he said, is [make] sure we [the company's workforce] are fit for purpose.'

So why do these different perceptions co-exist, and are there limitations to each of them?

Well let's start with trying to baseline some of the things that SWP can do, because that might just begin to explain why people fall into these extremely divergent camps.

Where's the beef?

This phrase was adopted from a Wendy's Hamburgers TV advertisement in 1984 by the US Democratic presidential nominee Walter Mondale, who suggested the value of his opponents' policies was too small to see.[1] Alistair Cooke, from whose article I drew this information, paints a wonderfully vivid picture of political opportunism and TV advertising techniques: it's worth a read.

'Where's the Beef?' became shorthand for questioning whether something really delivers what it promises. So where's the beef in SWP?

Explaining this is not just arguably one of the more difficult aspects of the job. You're peering into the future, normally across a timeframe of two or more years. 'Some organizations rightly believe that you're not able to accurately predict the future,' says Ton van Dijk of Capgemini, 'but for that reason they say, "Well, it doesn't make any sense to start thinking about… what might come in the next three years. We don't even know what's going to happen in the next month, so let's not waste time looking into things that might not happen as well."'

So there's the conundrum. You're effectively trying to stop bad things from happening – in this case, not having a workforce that is fit for purpose. You're trying to lay down brand new railway track before any train passes over it. And when it does, neither the train nor its passengers and crew know that a crash has been avoided. There's no sign anywhere that says, 'We saved you from a crash here', so there's no real sense of relief, salvation or gratitude and the journey continues without incident.

But let's take the track analogy a step further. In 1836, the famous British engineer Isambard Kingdom Brunel began work on the Great Western Railway that would link the 116 miles between London and Bristol. He didn't start by saying he wanted to build a railway from London to Slough. Had he done so, he would soon have realized that Slough is not much of a destination on its own (sorry, Slough) and that it would be better to keep going to Bristol, where there's a port and a gateway to America. Of course, if you then have to re-hire the people you need to build more railway and you have to go back to the makers of steel for more track, you'll end up spending a lot more than you would have done had you planned to build the entire route to begin with. Brunel planned strategically – he knew what his end game was, why it was valuable and what it would therefore take to make it so.[2]

It is evidently sensible to plan ahead and ensure you have all of the right materials for the job ahead of time, especially for a project lasting, as this did, five years. There's seemingly nothing new in any of this. Except that this is not what we do when it comes to acquiring people. When it comes to workforce planning, too many organizations act like they're only building as far as Slough – then have to rethink when they realize they need to go further.

One of the true leaders in this business put it this way: 'Many of them [senior leaders] are short-term focused and are cynical as to the benefits of planning for the longer term and being proactive [about] medium- to longer-term talent interventions.' People are a commodity; you can pick them up whenever you want, there's a ready supply.

Not so fast.

The world of work has changed. Important sections of it now require clever people to do difficult, complicated stuff, using skills that can take years to learn and more years to perfect. We don't have so many of those anymore and, by the way, while the world's population might be growing at an astounding rate, there is no abundance of those skills.

So what happens when companies treat talent like a last-minute order from Amazon? Spoiler alert: it doesn't end well. Every business that fails to plan its workforce properly will eventually face one of these painful choices:

TABLE 3.1 Unpalatable choices

Choice	Result	Consequence	Reaction	Outcome
Pay more to lure people away from other employers.	You got people through the door quickly.	Your costs just went up, which means you either: • make less profit, or • you charge more for your goods and services.	Your Board isn't happy. Your shareholders aren't happy. Your customers aren't happy.	You're fired.
You pay an outside company for temporary staff at higher rates	You got the job done.	All of the above, plus: • Your employees aren't happy because they're not getting the interesting work and they start to leave. • None of the skills are in-house, so you're no further forward.	Your Board isn't happy. Your shareholders aren't happy. Your customers aren't happy.	You're fired.

(continued)

TABLE 3.1 (Continued)

Choice	Result	Consequence	Reaction	Outcome
You need to train existing people to do the work. Nine months later, they're ready.	You got the job done. You upskilled your people.	• Your competitors had thought ahead and are already delivering to the market. • Your customers are frustrated or even walking away.	Your Board isn't happy. Your shareholders aren't happy. Your customers aren't happy.	You're fired.
You hire whoever is available and hope you can make it work.	You get people through the door quickly.	• Your new hires struggle to meet expectations and turnover goes up. • Team morale dips as existing employees pick up the slack. • Productivity suffers. • You spend more on rehiring and retraining. • You miss your strategic goals.	Your Board isn't happy. Your shareholders aren't happy. Your customers aren't happy.	You're fired.
You get AI to do the job instead.	You're saving money and you're cutting edge.	• It's also a bleeding edge. Unplanned, it takes too long to make a difference. • You need to retrain staff, who feel threatened or disengaged. • Morale dips, costs increase.	Your Board isn't happy. Your shareholders aren't happy. Your customers aren't happy.	That's right: You're fired.

Jane Datta, former CHRO of NASA, pushed back a little on my use of the word 'unpalatable'. 'Are they ALWAYS unpalatable?' she asked. And of course she's right. In Chapter 11, we'll talk a lot more about optimized fulfilment, but the use of non-permanent labour is a wise, desirable lever to pull to keep an organization agile. As she puts it, 'If you know you need a skill for a limited time, or for surge, then it is kinder and more ethical to contract for it than to hire and then fire.' If taken knowingly, with foresight enabled by strategic planning, these are good decisions. But if it is a frantic last-minute fix, it reflects a failure to recognize – and mitigate – future workforce risks in time. Used correctly, SWP can be the mitigation.

Now, before any of you dismiss this as a frivolous statement of the obvious, ask yourselves this: do you **actually** know that none of this is happening in your organization? Are the foundations for your own dismissal already being laid, brick by relentless brick?

Workforce risk – hiding in plain sight

> '*I don't like strategic workforce planning as a term, because it isn't planning... it's more like scenario management; we like to re-frame it now as people-risk management.*' – Tobias Bartholome, Lufthansa

Do you know what forms of workforce risk are in your business right now?

Essentially, workforce risk is the danger that you won't have the people you need to do the work you need doing when you need it to be done. It can come in many forms, of which the following are just a couple of primary examples:

- **Ageing workforce.** Too much reliance on people who will retire before long, leaving no successors. How much future development is at risk, or even revenue?

- **Market shortage.** Do you know that you can get the people you want, when and where you want them? What's the reality of hiring lead times and cost? 'Your supply chain is at risk because the trucks aren't arriving,' says Kouros Behzad of Anaplan. 'The truck driver shortage is a workforce risk. Workforce risk translates directly into business risk.'

In Chapter 4 we'll be talking more about people analytics, which can help to spot some of the risks you need to think about. But, as another practitioner put it, 'People analytics produces dashboards but not the red flags; the SWP practitioner is placed to express the risk.'

In short, identifying risk and mitigating it is not just a nice option for the SWP practitioner; it is a defining objective.

Mining value

In Chapter 1, I gave an example of the kind of things that are possible if SWP is practised in the business – where it's possible to reskill and redeploy someone instead of letting them go – the principle being that, by planning further ahead, you have more time in which to bring about desired outcomes in a good way. What does good mean in this instance?

The obvious answer is 'better than the current mess' – where none of the nightmare scenarios in Table 3.1 materialize. In reality, though, it means something far more valuable; finding solutions to situations before they arise, rather than scrambling for last-minute fixes. You're creating time to address things more thoughtfully, a more scaled way, one which eliminates duplication of effort and reduces overhead, not people. There it is: there's the beef. Paul Habgood of Mercer puts it this way: 'The value of SWP is not the number. It's what you do when you've found the number.'

Now there's a lot to unpack there; we'll do that in Chapter 6, but let's dig deeper. Aside from a CEO getting nervous about getting fired – and, let's face it, that isn't happening every five minutes – why should anyone care about where this beef is? Let's recall my suggestion of what SWP does:

1 Identify the nature, scale and direction of workforce change needed to address existing workforce circumstances and to deliver the company's strategic objectives.

2 Give those making the workforce changes as much guidance as possible so they can optimize them.

What kind of 'existing workforce circumstances' might impel us towards doing something about them?

We gotta get out of this place

'There almost has to be like, an "I told you so". Like we said that this would happen if you did not take this particular direction... and so you're in the mess that you're in.' – Anonymous Practitioner

I sometimes make references to rather obscure people and things, but I'm guessing that pretty much everyone has heard of Mr Bean, he of the bendy face and body, the silent magnet for disaster and chaos wherever he goes.

The genius behind that extraordinary creation, Rowan Atkinson, began his career in the early 1980s, when he was known principally for comic monologues, often mocking establishment authority figures, which he would deliver with extraordinary vocal dexterity. Here's one he used to mock a particularly pompous politician; try saying it in one go and about twice as fast as you normally would, which is what Atkinson did:

'Where were we at first that we knew we had to leave in order to get to where we are now before we knew we'd got to where we want to be?'

Not easy, is it?

It's a mouthful, but it captures the challenge of workforce planning – figuring out where you were, where you are, and where you need to be. Let's look at three factors that drive the inception of SWP.

Crisis? What crisis?

> 'A sure-fire way to combat… resistance is to wrap everything in a risk wrapper – that's the burning-platform argument that works.' – Amit Mohindra (ex-Apple)

It's a curious thing that the Covid-19 pandemic of 2020–21, that long and bewildering period in which everything came to a halt, now feels like the distant past.

I remember going back in 2022 to a familiar haunt of mine, Bishopsgate in the City of London. Before the pandemic struck, Spitalfields – which is a sprawling complex of shops, bars, restaurants and market stalls nestled just behind Bishopsgate's broad concourse – was alive and pulsating, all of those enterprises feeding off the thousands of workers who would commute to the giant cathedrals of glass and steel that spoke of the power and wealth of the financial sector. Two years on, and the only reminders of many of those businesses were the faded logos on doors that had long since closed for the final time. The frailty of the familiar was brutally exposed.

When Covid hit, businesses panicked. With no clue how long the chaos would last, they slammed the brakes on spending. But here's the problem: workforce decisions made in crisis mode tend to expose what companies don't know about their own people.

Our company was pretty typical in having a large number of projects happening at any one time that were designed to introduce change into our systems, processes and so on. Because many of these projects were transient, we'd often engage non-permanent workers, some of which were supplied by third-party companies, to augment our own permanent employees.

Covid compelled us to stop several of those projects in order to preserve cash. But some of the projects we wanted to stop had permanent employees working on them, while some projects we couldn't stop had third-party staff working on them. Letting employees go was a last-resort measure, so we needed to move employees into projects we were keeping and curtail our third-party staff as quickly as possible.

Now at this point, you may be expecting me to go into excruciating detail about how we identified which people were working on which project, decided which people could be redeployed, decided which external staff should be let go, and so on. I don't want to do that, not because there isn't a story behind how we managed to achieve what we set out to do – reduce cost, redeploy and therefore save employees – but because that's not relevant to what it then led to, which was this: a realization that we had thousands of third-party staff working for us, people we knew little or nothing about, who had moved from one project to the next several times over, at great cost to our company and often at a time when permanent employees were being let go. To address that challenge, we would need to look at the situation more strategically and see how we might be able to reduce our reliance on that group of staff permanently.

As one of my colleagues put it: 'I've found it much easier when the organization is experiencing significant disruption and upheaval to win hearts and minds on the benefits of SWP compared to periods of perceived stability.' So there's a strong case for arguing that there's nothing like a good crisis to get SWP embraced. 'Do I think that executive pain is proving to be a valuable catalyst for making SWP a bit more mainstream?' asks Alan Susi. 'I think you're absolutely right. I think it gets to, like, "what's the imperative, what's the burning platform?"' I've long thought that this is the case, especially if, as in my example, there was also a strong financial imperative.

If you'd asked me a year or so ago whether I felt that there always had to be a financial angle for SWP to have even a chance of being adopted, I would have given you an emphatic 'yes'. Now, I think it matters but not as much as strategic risk, the possibility that aspects of the workforce could derail strategy execution; perhaps it's both.

Is there a solution?

> *'We don't illustrate the kind of value and we don't talk, I think, in terms of risk and opportunity.'* – Anonymous Irregular

'We're doomed.' This catchphrase of a UK TV comedy character was always uttered when situations of varying degrees of risk presented themselves. Our attitude to risk is hopefully a bit more nuanced than that, but workforce risk seems to be an under-researched subject. Ask a friendly local Generative Artificial Intelligence (GenAI) chatbot to list any works that even reference the subject, and you'll find the list is painfully small.

I find this odd. If the cost of workforce is generally accepted as being between 50 and 70 per cent of the cost of running a business, you'd think that workforce risks should be pretty high up anyone's agenda, wouldn't you? Yet here's a survey that suggests that 'Most organizations have neither a clear, holistic definition of workforce risk nor widespread knowledge and expertise about the topic.'[3] The same survey also suggests that most respondents 'focus on reacting to the workforce risks that threaten short-term business objectives at the expense of strategically planning for tomorrow's challenges.' We should take this much more seriously than perhaps we do, and there are signs that we are beginning to see SWP becoming part of the response. 'The biggest part of our transformation under our new CEO,' said a world-leading engineering SWP practitioner, 'was the fact that we had identified internally that we had a technical skills crisis looming.'

The thing I like about this last quote is just how much it actually tells you in a few short words. So why does this work so well?

- **This is a transformation.** It's not just a tweak to what we already do – we know we need to do something radically different and better.
- **The CEO is behind this.** The risk to the organization has been recognized at the very top and there will be drive and sponsorship to deliver the change deemed necessary.

- **There is an evidence base.** The organization has amassed data about its workforce that it has not just explored, it has revealed knowledge about itself that has meaning.

- **There is an understanding of what the future needs to look like.** It's not explicit, but there is clearly a strategic endpoint to which the organization aspires.

- **The risk has been defined and is specific.** There's no generalized concern here. The organization knows that this is a problem with a part of its future.

- **There is a clear understanding of strategic importance.** This part of the workforce is not just critical to the organization's future, it is known to be critical.

- **There is a tangible relationship between a desired workforce outcome and a business outcome.** We're not just concerned for the sake of the workforce; there is a clear business imperative.

- **There is a sense of quantity, urgency and consequence.** The organization may not know exactly how bad things could be, but it's already got a decent idea.

These aren't just themes of this book (all of which we will delve into further), or even just themes for SWP in general. They are the difference between organizations that thrive and those that fall behind. In the next chapter, we're going to look more closely at what those risks are and how to measure them.

I want what they're having

If, as I have, you watch tennis matches between the greatest players of the game, you can't help but notice the fire that burns within them; how a massive point won can cause its winner to erupt in visceral fist pumps and primaeval roars. I was a big fan of the British player Andy Murray, and if you look at photographs of him mid-yell, there is this near-chasm between his upper jaw and his lower one: his passion is undeniable and tangible. Contrast this with other players you might see who shake a fist at the end of a rally and look as if they are doing so because someone's told them it would be a jolly good idea. There's a received wisdom that fist-pumping is good for you but you can see that some players are doing so because they believe they should, not because they feel it.

You do come across some organizations that appear to be implementing SWP because they believe they should, but whose reasons for doing so threaten its successful launch. A few examples:

- We need to implement SWP because Audit have told us we should.
- We purchased a new HRMS and the vendors gave us their workforce planning module for free, so we're going to implement that as well.
- I've seen these great articles on LinkedIn about what SWP could do for our business, so let's establish a framework and start making some improvements.

There's nothing intrinsically wrong with any of these, provided they're tied to some form of business situation or risk that SWP can help to alleviate. Otherwise, you're simply providing a solution that's in search of a problem; we know how that ends.

REFLECTION

We're revealing circumstances where SWP might be able to help organizations to deal with situations before they become extremely difficult to manage. Some important questions emerge:

- **For the CEO:** Do you know which current workforce circumstances pose a potential risk to the company's future and, by extension, yours?
- **For the CFO:** Have you considered the financial consequences of those current workforce circumstances?
- **For Strategy:** To what extent do those circumstances require any rethink of company strategy?
- **For the CHRO:** Have you set out these circumstances to the CEO? Did you know about them?
- **For the SWP Practitioner:** Do you know about these circumstances? Are you already thinking about how they could be resolved, and by whom?

Now it may feel as if it's taking time to get to the specifics. Einstein reputedly said, 'If I were given one hour to save the planet, I would spend 59 minutes defining the problem and one minute resolving it.'[4] SWP doesn't save the planet – and it won't cure gout – but it's worth spending time on the problem before moving to implement it as a solution. It may sound dramatic, but it could be the difference between your leading your sector in the future and your still being even a part of it.

Notes

1   Cooke, A (1984) Where's the beef? BBC, https://www.bbc.co.uk/programmes/articles/432ky7cY5ZDC9hJpkpcdsmZ/wheres-the-beef (archived at https://perma.cc/PDQ6-32EY)

2   Dunn, T (2020) The Architecture the Railways Built – Great Western Railway, Network Rail, https://www.networkrail.co.uk/stories/the-architecture-the-railways-built-great-western-railway/#:~:text=This%20116%2Dmile%20route%20from,consuming%20than%20he%20had%20estimated (archived at https://perma.cc/4ETT-GJBD).

3   Fuller, J B, Griffiths, M, Janho, R, Carey, M S, Calagna, O K, Jones, R, Cantrell, S, Shaw, Z and Fackler, G (2023) Workforce risk management solutions, Deloitte Insights, https://www2.deloitte.com/us/en/insights/topics/talent/workforce-risk-management-solutions.html (archived at https://perma.cc/XHL2-J6MK)

4   Spradlin, D. (2012). *Are you solving the right problem?* Harvard Business Review, September. Available at: https://hbr.org/2012/09/are-you-solving-the-right-problem (archived at https://perma.cc/8GAD-7SXA) [Accessed 14 Jan. 2025].

PART TWO

How to practise it

04

The truth is out there – and it's hidden in plain sight

So the best thing is to provide some examples where you have seen significant… issues in your organization that you could have avoided if you [had] some proper planning.

TON VAN DIJK, CAPGEMINI

Wot we got, not a lot

On 13 December 1975, I went to see the band Supertramp live. It was my very first concert and I went on my own. Aged just 15, I didn't know how the whole concert thing worked, so when they finished their set and everyone was stamping and cheering for ages, I thought it was time to leave. So I left my seat, went outside and called my Mum from a payphone so she could come and pick me up. On hanging up, I could hear, through the still of that cold December evening, the band playing their most well-known song as an encore. I didn't know that such things happened – you could say that I didn't know what good looked like – and no one was there to tell me that if I left when I did, I wouldn't get full value for my ticket. Just as I didn't realize I was missing the best part of the concert, organizations often fail to recognize workforce risks until it's too late, by which time, the opportunity to fix them has already passed.

A reminder of the first of the two things that SWP seeks to do: **identify the nature, scale and direction of workforce change needed to address existing workforce risks and deliver the company's strategic objectives.**

We start this chapter by looking at how we know whether we have workforce risks, because a sure foundation for SWP is having that evidence and being able to interpret it. And the fact is that many organizations don't know the workforce risks in their business, as we saw from the Deloitte survey in Chapter 3.

You'll be relieved to know that I'm not going to explore the intricacies of people analytics and how to build a successful people analytics platform. That job has been done supremely well by others, particularly Jonathan Ferrar and David Green in their seminal comprehensive work, *Excellence in People Analytics.*[1]

In the SWP context, people analytics are a way of telling you when your workforce situation is currently sub-optimal; SWP is reliant on those analytics to drive actions. They also help to identify future potential for problems to develop, which is critical in determining the longer-term fitness of the workforce for business purposes. I say 'in the SWP context' because people analytics is capable of so much more than just helping out SWP.

That's not to say that SWP isn't of value to the People Analytics profession; a 2025 survey of 348 companies[2] suggests there is 'a long way to go before business executives realize the full value of their investment in people analytics'. The dependency is therefore mutual: people analytics functions need SWP to address the issues they reveal, and you can't plan to solve things you know nothing about. Without that solid platform, SWP is just an exercise in guesswork. My own experience showed me just how messy things could get. It occurred before we had data in the quantity and accessibility we have now, but it's nevertheless worth dwelling on how my moment came about.

I saw something nasty in the woodshed – discovering uncomfortable truths

So said the magnificently named Aunt Ada Doom in Stella Gibbons' 1932 book, *Cold Comfort Farm.*[3] I was nowhere near a woodshed, but I did uncover something unsettling that had been hiding in plain sight, which exemplifies the value of people analytics: it either corroborates your existing suspicions or it throws up something unexpected and revelatory.

I'd just recently concluded an overhaul of third-party suppliers of workers in our company's investment projects. These workers were drawn down from those suppliers as and when we needed to top up our existing staff: we called them Resource Augmentation Workers and we'll return to these when I discuss the extended workforce in Chapter 14.

Because I'd acquired a reputation for understanding workforce data, my boss asked me to identify something a bit unusual. There was this belief that some of our investment projects were more efficiently managed than others; that some had a greater proportion of managers and administrators – grouped under the rather harsh banner of 'non-producers' – than others. The precise definition of 'producers' and 'non-producers' was itself a warzone, with different teams arguing over which roles truly created value versus which were seen as overhead. Just listing them here could be triggering for some.

But at stake wasn't just a theoretical debate about definitions – it was about huge amounts of project cost and whether our organization was quietly bleeding money in the name of 'best practices' or because some project managers liked to have things organized just to suit them.

At first, I thought this would be a relatively straightforward data exercise. I was wrong. What I uncovered would not only challenge our assumptions – it would expose just how little we truly understood about our own workforce.

You only have to answer two questions:

a What does each member of staff do?

b Which project are they working on?

Now you'd think that large organizations have fantastic systems, wonderful records and answers to hand at the press of a button. At the beginning of my career, my then-CFO said he wanted a system that would give him the answer at the press of a button. Forty years later, we're still waiting for the button. Yes, companies often make delightful presentations at conferences where they wax lyrical about how well they manage their systems and data but, as Paul Habgood of Mercer says, 'I fear a lot of them are the swan floating across the lake. Where, from way out looking from the shore, it looks wow – that's serene and beautiful. Yet underneath, there's a massive, frantic paddling of feet and legs and all sorts of things going on, which hides the true picture.'

And so it was that when I received a list of all staff we had in our HR management system, I discovered that we didn't actually know what everyone did at all. A simple scan of all 150,000 records showed large numbers of people who didn't have a role entered against them. Well over 10,000. I mean, I expected to find the odd gap here and there. I didn't expect to discover we were essentially blind to about 10,000 employees.

So what do you do? Well, you look at other pieces of data that might give you a clue as to who they are, for example:

- **What's their job title?** These throw off an abundance of clues as to what someone self-declares themselves to be (although I've always been entertained by the number of people who promote themselves through their job title: programme manager becomes senior programme manager, senior programme manager becomes programme director and so on).

- **Who is their line manager and what do they do?** By looking at people with the same line manager, you can infer what someone without a role might also be doing.

- **What is their cost centre?** This can often tell you something about what they do by reference to their colleagues.

You get the idea. But I also knew – and again, I'll return to this in Chapter 14 – that if I was to arrive at anything even vaguely close to a reliable answer, I would need to include those resource augmentation workers. I knew this, because I knew that they represented 30 per cent of the people working on projects, and I would also need to include our contractors, who had yet another system of their own. And I would have to do all these same inferential things on each of their systems too.

So, to establish just what somebody did, I had to do multiple sweeps across three separate sets of data, none of which were complete or consistent with the other. This was all before I could say with any certainty what all of these people – about 17,000 of them – were working on.

Yes, *about* 17,000. Whenever I was asked how many people we had working on projects, I'd usually say 'somewhere between 16,000 and 18,000', not because I was feeling especially flippant (fun as that might be) but because I genuinely couldn't be sure. Finding out what they were working on turned out to be altogether worse.

I started by looking at the project data in our Enterprise Portfolio Management (EPM) system. There you will find a list of projects, their umbrella programmes and the programmes' overriding portfolios. You would also find the names of everyone who was expected to be working on them. Fabulous – run the list of names, group them by projects and you're done, right?

Wrong.

At best, this system told me half the story, because there were a huge number of people known to be working on projects whose names didn't appear. Finding out what the rest of them did required me to go into not one, not two, not even three, but five separate sources of timesheet information where project time could be found – connecting people IDs from one system to the other, connecting project codes to project titles (and discovering that the same ID would have different descriptions in different systems). Huge holes remained.

It took me weeks and what did I have at the end of it all? Well, I had a dataset that had been connected and linked together from roughly 10 separate systems, using a range of different techniques ranging from the reliable to the rather questionable. It was still incomplete and any conclusions I might draw seemed – as they were indeed described to me when I presented them – highly speculative and unreliable. Moreover, I was completely unable to offer any evidence that projects with more non-producers were inherently less efficient or less well-run. Finally, by having to draw conclusions from something I knew to be fallible at best, I had pretty much dried up any well of goodwill I might have accumulated over time. Weeks of work and no clear picture. It didn't do my end-of-year performance rating a lot of good either.

The lessons for me were stark:

- **Certainty and precision in people data is a mirage.** Data lakes are the result of multiple tributaries, some very large, some very small. Sometimes they dry up and sometimes the lake gets polluted by sewage.

- **CEOs don't have a secret stash of perfect data.** They sail on the same sludge of imperfection as the rest of us; the only difference between them and us is that the decisions they make based on this sludge have real consequences.

- **Good enough is good enough.** Presenting something as thorough simply because it took you ages is a myth. Ton van Dijk of Capgemini thinks 'it's better to be approximately right than to be precisely wrong'. If the data won't support a good enough outcome, don't offer one.

- **Get comfortable with vague.** If you want perfection in workforce planning, then you're in the wrong job. It's not about perfection – you have to make decisions in uncertainty, with just enough clarity in hand to provide relevant advice.

- **'Be curious'.** So said one of my colleagues in this space – sometimes you'll come across something that demands a closer look. This was to provide a silver lining to the cloud this exercise had cast over me.

A former colleague puts it like this:

> '*So many companies are on shifting sands trying to predict the future, which in my experience results in garbage in, garbage out... You have to start with a bedrock of trusted information. Even if some of it isn't right, at least admit that it's not right and agree to fix it. But if you don't even know what headcount means in your organization, what business have you got trying to plan the future?*' – Daniel Mason

While doing this work, I noticed the large number of records for people who had left the company in the previous five years. I noticed the roles they held (where that was clear) and it got me wondering how many of these leavers had not left voluntarily. There were a lot, which then made me wonder how many people had joined our company over the same period, either as permanent or non-permanent staff.

I dug deeper, and I filtered and narrowed the population down until I was able to say, with enough clarity to feel safe, that we had exited 900 people over a two-year period while hiring 900 non-permanent staff into the same roles, at the same times and in the same cities. Moreover, over 200 of those non-permanent staff were still in the company two years later.

And with that, my SWP journey had begun.

What are we looking at here?

At the time, I wasn't working in an HR function (I only entered HR for the first time in the 43rd year of my working life). So what was I supposed to make of what I'd found? I first looked at it from my own prior experience of trying to help people who were at risk of losing their job find something else. Remember what I said in Chapter 1: the Moment of Likelihood when it became clear that someone might lose their job came late and the Window of Opportunity that opened up before a Point of Exit was a very slender one. If, in a different part of the company, someone was planning to recruit somebody to do similar work to that being done by somebody about to lose their job, that window had the potential to open up, substantially.

For an individual in this situation, that potential was of enormous personal value, and I felt that, deeply – the sense of waste when someone leaves and it turns out that they didn't have to. The *Sliding Doors* moment that means the ending, which could have been a happy one, takes a different turn.

This may sound a little callous, but companies don't typically operate to serve the needs of individuals; if they did, they would get unmanageably lost in thousands of individual life stories that would make it virtually impossible to run them effectively. There has to be a macro implication as well; SWP requires you to think at that level, not to the exclusion of the effect on people (because if you lose sight of the person at the receiving end of what you do then you risk losing your own moral compass), but because you have no choice but to do so. You work for a business, and you have to see these situations as either an opportunity or a threat to the business.

There were three angles that I took with this:

1 This was costing us money, and not just small amounts. In the UK, it is estimated that letting one person go and hiring somebody else (as opposed to retraining them to do that job instead) can cost a business £49,000 per person.[4]

2 I could have said we were losing lots of people with good skills and chose to present it as a threat. We were increasingly reliant on a temporary workforce that could disappear at short notice, taking with it intellectual property that we should have retained in-house, threatening our growth and sustainability as a company.

3 Internally and externally, it wasn't a good look.

Just in case anyone needs reminding, as many as 900 people may have lost their jobs needlessly. Nine hundred families pitched into uncertainty; 900 loyalties lost. I can't honestly say that this interpretation came to me more naturally because I wasn't an HR Careerist; but whichever route you've taken to becoming an SWP Practitioner, two things must always be paramount:

1 Always look at the big picture.

2 Always consider the effects on the business and on the people.

If you're a true SWP Practitioner, you occupy a very privileged position in that you get to see the full company landscape. Imagine that each time a part of a business presents you with a set of data or a plan: they will have laboured over that for some time, taking care to check it over before sending it to you. It will be their own masterpiece. Each part of the company goes diligently about its business, creating its own individual Canaletto. But when you put these masterpieces together, you get to see the *Mona Lisa* and *only you can see it*. Something different appears that is more than the sum of its parts and that's the view that you have to manage for the company; it's your task to interpret that view and bring it to life for your leadership, showing them what they might not be able to see for themselves. As a consultant friend puts it:

> 'In a federated environment, you can't just have one universal plan. You do partial planning per unit, then bring it all together – yet you must also see how the enterprise benefits, like re-skilling from one surplus to another unit's shortage.'

A prospect looking to buy people analytics software for their business said to me once: 'I want this stuff to matter to our CEO: I want them to be lying awake at night worrying about things in this space that they don't even think about.' They knew how workforce blind spots can cost businesses millions and they knew they had them. But there are multiple potential risks, so what should an SWP Practitioner be looking for? What metrics should be of particular importance?

Measure for measure – measuring what matters

The glib answer is 'anything that poses a risk to the business', but you could spend the rest of your working life stacking those up. In any case, looking at metrics of value to SWP in any kind of abstract way runs a substantial risk of irrelevance. Relevance requires meaningful connections to be made between adverse metrics, their impact on the business and their consequent impact on its customers.

It's also important to recognize that what central leaders might see as a company-wide challenge is frequently not so. 'Why am I being pressured to increase my early careers intake?' someone asked me a while back. 'I don't have an early careers problem, and I don't have an ageing workforce [I didn't work for them], so why am I being given this grief?' Part of the SWP Practitioner's toolkit needs to include a degree of spatial awareness of not just the sum of parts, but also of the parts themselves. If workforce metrics don't have a clear link to business risk, they won't be taken seriously. These examples highlight where SWP Practitioners should focus their attention.

TABLE 4.1 The effect of adverse metrics on the business, its customers and its cost base

Issue	Effect on the business	Effect on customers & competitiveness	Measurable costs	Likely additional costs
Skill shortages	Reduced productivity, inability to deliver	Delayed innovation & service	Hiring cycle, salary inflation	External staff costs Revenue loss
High turnover rates	Operational disruption	Service disruption	Recruitment, training, onboarding	Productivity
Low staff engagement scores	Poor performance & customer service	Dissatisfaction & reputational damage		Productivity, turnover
Lengthy time to hire	Late delivery	Capacity constraints, delivery delays	Project penalties, overtime	External staff marginal cost
Prolonged onboarding	Delayed productivity boost	Slower market response		Productivity, benefit loss
Aging workforce	Leadership & succession gaps	Knowledge loss	Younger staff attrition	Health insurance, succession gaps
Piecemeal hiring	Inefficiency, high unit costs	Price increases	Sourcing overhead	
Low early career staff retention	Talent drain, wasted spend, future leadership gaps	Declining capability	Turnover, retraining	Team disruption, succession gaps
Use and retention of external staff	Increased dependency and knowledge flight risk	Core capability erosion	Marginal unit cost	Permanent staff opportunity cost
Ineffective internal mobility/ redeployment	Wasted resource, huge costs	Operational inefficiencies	Severance, rehiring	Additional attrition

(continued)

TABLE 4.1 (Continued)

Issue	Effect on the business	Effect on customers & competitiveness	Measurable costs	Likely additional costs
Limited diversity & inclusivity	Reduced creativity & innovation, idea blindspots	Reputational damage, regulatory breach, reduced market reach	Legal/ compliance	Innovation opportunity cost
Rollercoaster funding	High overhead, delayed delivery, regretted redundancies	Delivery delays, customer dissatisfaction	Severance, marginal external staff cost	Process overhead, productivity loss
High-cost location ratio	Higher costs, lower output	High prices	Marginal unit cost	N/A

Now I have several really good friends in this field, and I can almost hear the blood pressure of some of them reaching dangerous levels. This is because they will argue that I'm looking at the wrong thing entirely – what we call Supply, the workforce that you currently have. I make no apologies for explaining what it is; we throw terms around as if everyone is supposed to know what they mean. In one organization, I was mystified whenever people mentioned the KSOR team (pronounced Kay-sore). It was only after being there for two years that I learned that it stood for Keep the Show on the Road.

Yes, of course it is essential to know what future needs arise from changing market conditions, geopolitical shifts, business strategy changes and so on – your Demand. But problems on the Supply side create their own Demand that is no less important than future needs, mainly because you will need to do something about them in the future if you're to remain competitive or even exist. We'll get to Demand soon enough.

There's something else that needs to be called out here, although you might say that it's obvious (acknowledging the obvious and actually doing something about it can be two entirely separate things). We're not just looking at headcount here. Yes, pretty much all of the measures have some form of numerical basis, but that's just our way of trying to rationalize things that are more ethereal than that. Our sphere of interest strays inevitably into areas that others might consider their sole preserve: how people are hired, how projects are funded, how workers are organized, rewarded, nurtured. If these and so many other factors are awry, then they have to be planned back to an optimal shape. SWP is about a lot more than just headcount and cost.

That said, some workforce risks impact the entire business, while others are concentrated in critical workforce segments. Understanding this distinction is key to focusing your efforts on those areas facing the most business impact.

Let's get critical – which parts of the workforce could you not do without?

If 'it is the primary role of the CEO to define big-picture threats',[5] then people analytics, as interpreted through an SWP lens, is one way to help to identify them. The thing is that the threat doesn't always loom large in the picture and here's where the SWP Practitioner comes in. You're the crucial connective tissue between what analytics are saying and what the future might need to be; more importantly, you're in the position where you know – or you should know – what plays a critical part in that future.

Let's take an example that's current. There's much talk about the ageing workforce and the notion that it's not a good thing. Is that a universal truth, or does it need context?

There are many reasons why there is a growing number of people over 55 in the workforce – projected, in developing countries, to grow by 40 per cent in the 10 years to 2030.[6] People are living longer, healthier lives and have an interest in working that may have waned by now in previous generations; that work is also likely to be less physical and wearing than it once was. Governments are raising statutory retirement ages – over half of OECD countries have done so[7] – requiring people to stay at work for longer than they had planned, and the financial crisis of 2008 may have contributed to a loss of pension value that needs to be recouped by additional years of work.[8] These ideas and more are explored elsewhere more thoroughly by Gratton and Scott,[9] although you're more than welcome to ask me, since I'm in that age group.

While not necessarily being a problem in general, a concentration of this group in key parts of the business very much could be and not just because of the risk that they might all suddenly decide that they've had enough and want to retire.

Organizations for whom intellectual property rights (IPR) represent a sizeable chunk of revenue have built that stream up through the thousands of patents that they've been able to file arising from the innovative genius of their research and development (R&D) departments. If, as in a situation I encountered a while ago, 35 per cent of that department's leaders – 2,500 such people – are over 55, then the next generation of leaders needs to be found quickly before these people leave.

Adaptability and adoptability (fluid intelligence) decline gradually as we age, just as accumulated knowledge (crystallized intelligence) grows,[10] while more recent studies point to a gradual change in the way we older people respond to changing workplace demands and new technologies.[11] I think this matters, because while I use AI in my day-to-day work, my 10-year-old granddaughter already probably knows more about *how* to use AI than I do. Having older people running R&D may risk it becoming less innovative than it could be.

Figure 4.1 is a nice example of workforce segmentation, where you split the workforce into four distinct groups.

Conventional wisdom is that your planning should major on the critical workforce.

FIGURE 4.1 Prioritizing workforce segments

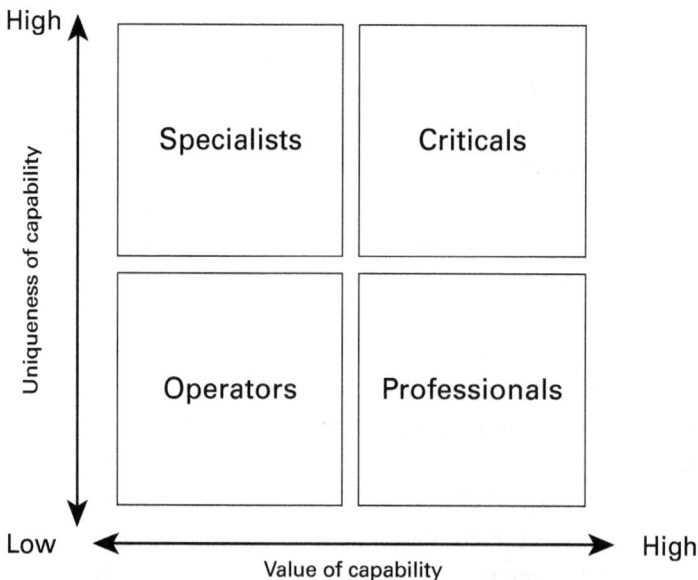

SOURCE Adapted from Lepak and Snell (1999), reproduced in Gibson (2021, p. 89)[12, 13]

IT'S NOT....

A few years ago I worked with a company involved in space travel. Their SWP Practitioner – new to the role – wanted to know how to categorize their interns for planning purposes. This was taking up a lot of time and internal effort. 'So, you want to know how to plan your interns, yes?' I asked. 'You're a rocket company right?' My practitioner friend looked at me as though I'd lost my senses. 'You know we are,' they said. 'Well,' I said, 'I wouldn't bother. Your rocket engineers are your critical people, so I'd focus on them.'

For once, you could say that it really <u>was</u> rocket science.

Mark Jackson of Nationwide Building Society doubles down on this: 'I refuse to do "SWP across the entire enterprise",' he says. 'Once you reach a certain level of abstraction, you lose everyone. We focus only on mission-critical pockets.' I understand that but I'd suggest that criticality can sometimes acquire different criteria. For example, a planned reduction in the workforce could result in a significant lowering of morale and productivity[14] – the SWP Practitioner should recognize the propensity for criticality to move around the organization and continually evaluate where it currently sits. And that leads me to conclude that the conventional segmentation diagram needs a bit of a revamp (Figure 4.2).

FIGURE 4.2 Workforce segments – the reality

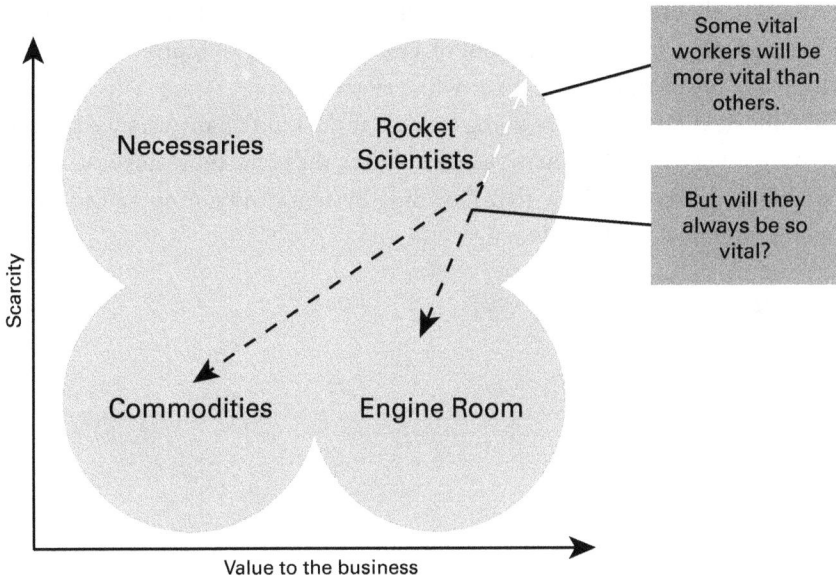

I call it the reality, because that's what it is. Nothing else remains static and segmentation is no different.

Layer cake – mixing insights yields nuggets of value

This is one of the centrepieces of the SWP Practitioner's craft – layering one piece of information over another in order to isolate the insightful nugget that brings a situation into sharp relief. How might any of the metrics in Table 4.1 impact your organizations to deliver on the programmes it wants to execute, on the strategy it wants to bring about?

If you look back at the Dowding System in Chapter 2, you can again see how the practitioner occupies a pivotal role in consuming a range of different signs and data which, when added to their understanding of the required composition of the future workforce, enables them to produce a filtered and focused view of the risks that need to be addressed most urgently and convey them to their leadership. This is an extremely broad view, taking in awareness not just of people factors, but also of those relating to strategy, production, delivery and finance; it's a view that many people in your organization may carry in part in their heads or which they may talk about in broad terms. But the core responsibility of their role is to focus on elements of that view. The SWP Practitioner's responsibility is to see its entirety, a responsibility virtually unique outside of the very highest echelons of leadership. It's part of the thrill and a profound part of the challenge.

Back to that revelation of mine about redundancies and contractors. I felt I had enough to put myself in front of a member of our Executive Committee and make my case. But a case for what, exactly?

In the next chapter we're going to look at the kind of answers we need to provide for some of the situations we uncover, the value those answers might be able to realize and how that Dowding System can be re-imagined as an operating model for SWP Practice.

REFLECTIONS

- **Data and analytics are your friends.** They are the key to showcasing your expertise.
- **Data is imperfect.** Get used to it.
- **Dig deep and then dig deeper.** Find the nuggets of real value.
- **There are consequences for the business.** Make sure you know how to present the risk posed by a workforce situation to business success and customer satisfaction.
- **Data are not numbers.** They are people. We forget this at our peril.

Notes

1   Ferrar, J and Green, D (2021) *Excellence in People Analytics,* London: Kogan Page

2   Ferrar, J, Verghese, N and Chakrabarti, M (2025) *Harnessing Data for Growth: The impact of people analytics*, London. Insight222 Ltd

3   Gibbons, S (2006) *Cold Comfort Farm,* London: Penguin Books

4   Financial Services Skills Commission (2022) Reskilling: A business case for financial services organisations, https://financialservicesskills.org/wp-content/uploads/2022/01/Reskilling-A-business-case-FINAL-Jan-2022.pdf (archived at https://perma.cc/S2MZ-B422)

5   Reimer, D and Bryant, A (2024) The X-factor in strategic workforce planning. In: M Sokol and B Tarulli, (eds) *Strategic Workforce Planning*, New York: Oxford University Press, p. 270

6   Harasty, C, Ostermeier and M (2020) Population ageing: Alternative measures of dependency and implications for the future of work, ILO Working Paper 5 (Geneva, ILO)

7   OECD (2023) Pensions at a Glance 2023: OECD and G20 Indicators, OECD Publishing, Paris, https://doi.org/10.1787/678055dd-en (archived at https://perma.cc/8BXL-QMUP)

8   Munnell, A H and Rutledge, M S (2013) The Effects of the Great Recession on the retirement security of older workers, *The Annals of the American Academy of Political and Social Science*, 650(1), pp. 124–42

9   Gratton, L and Scott, A (2016) *The 100-Year Life: Living and working in an age of longevity*, London: Bloomsbury Business

10 Horn, J L and Cattell, R B (1967) Age differences in fluid and crystallized intelligence, *Acta Psychologica*, 26, pp. 1–23

11 Czaja, S J and Sharit, J (2013) Aging and work: issues and implications in a changing landscape, *The Journals of Gerontology: Series B, Psychological Sciences and Social Sciences*, 68(4), pp.535–41

12 Gibson, A (2021) *Agile Workforce Planning: How to align people with organizational strategy for improved performance*, London: Kogan Page,

13 Lepak, D P and Snell, S A (1999) The human resource architecture: Toward a theory of human capital allocation and development, *Academy of Management Review*, 24(1), pp. 31–48

14 Datta, D K, Guthrie, J P, Basuil, D and Pandey, A (2010) Causes and effects of employee downsizing: A review and synthesis, *Journal of Management*, 36(1), pp. 281–348

05

Emotively captivating

The necessity of vision and coherence

In Chapter 4, we explored how workforce risks often remain hidden in plain sight. This chapter looks at defining an SWP vision that shows how risks can be both identified and acted upon.

I can see clearly now

I am from England, which you may have noticed, and I fit many of the perceived caricatures of Englishmen (which I realized one morning on the New Haven line in Connecticut, when I was the only one not wearing a grey suit, starched white shirt and red tie).

Aside from a slightly maverick dress sense, part of my Englishness is a love of cricket, although the less said about my playing record the better. Someone who does have a record or two is Ebony Rainford-Brent (or, to give her wonderfully full name, Ebony-Jewel Cora-Lee Rosamond Camellia Rainford-Brent). She was the first black woman to play cricket for England at full international level, was a World Cup winner in 2009, the first woman to be Director of cricket for a Championship side, is a non-executive director of the England and Wales Cricket Board[1] and is now a motivational speaker. That's how she comes to be in this book, because she said something rather profound back in 2022 that deserves repeating.

In an interview with *The Cricketer* magazine, she said this:

> Take someone like Martin Luther King, who said 'I have a dream.' If he'd said, 'I have a plan', no one would have got on the train. It's corporate. But he emotively captivated.[2]

Now I'm not suggesting that you should all now start Strategic Workforce Dreaming, but as a guide to painting the picture of what SWP might enable, her quote is as good as it gets. You might reasonably ask how SWP can ever be *that* emotively captivating, but I shall do my utmost to persuade you.

So what's the dream about? Let's bring together the themes that will have been apparent so far:

- existing workforce circumstances that may pose risks to the organization's future;
- existing workforce circumstances that incur unnecessary cost or which are inherently inefficient;
- ensuring that the workforce is fit for its future purpose as determined by the organization's strategy.

There are at least a couple of others that we haven't really explored so far, but which can't be excluded from the consideration of an overarching vision. But I don't want to over-complicate things just yet by throwing everything into the mix. For now, let's just focus on these three items and turn these into outcomes:

TABLE 5.1 SWP outcomes

Theme	Desired Outcome(s)
Existing workforce circumstances that may pose risks to the organization's future.	We know what the critical workforce risks are, we continually evaluate them and we have plans in place to mitigate them.
Existing workforce circumstances that incur unnecessary cost or which are inherently inefficient.	We have optimized our fulfilment channels and our processes to eliminate unnecessary attrition and spend.
Ensuring that the workforce is fit for its future purpose as determined by the organization's strategy.	Our workforce knowledge, strategy and fulfilment are fully oriented to delivering the strategy of the business.

Let's break each of these down into the elements that can form a coherent vision of what good might look like.

1. We know what the critical workforce risks are, we continually evaluate them and we have plans in place to mitigate them

WHAT DOES IT MEAN TO 'KNOW' YOUR WORKFORCE RISKS?

Spotting risk isn't just about data. Many organizations collect data on workforce trends, and there are often huge swathes of analytics across these data that produce more charts and tables than you can eat. If you can't spot the table that should cause alarm, you will still be blindsided by sudden talent shortages or attrition spikes. These insights have to be translated into a clear business narrative.

For example, imagine a technology firm heavily reliant on a small pool of specialist engineers. They have data showing that 20 per cent of this talent pool is at retirement age, yet no structured plan exists to transfer knowledge or recruit replacements. This is a workforce risk hiding in plain sight. Would your current analytics set-up bring this to your attention?

SO, WHAT DOES KNOWING OUR RISKS REALLY MEAN?

- **Access and awareness.** We have real-time visibility into workforce data and analytics across people and business domains.

- **Strategic context.** The practitioner aligns workforce insights with broader business strategy and market trends, using both data and instinct to spot emerging issues.

- **Early detection.** We don't just track trends. We isolate leading indicators that may signal future workforce challenges, such as those we considered in Chapter 4.

- **Clear communication.** We translate risk into business terms, ensuring leadership understands both potential impact and probability.

Workforce risks may emerge from multiple different situations. Knowing them ahead of time before they disrupt your business sets you apart and elevates your personal value.

You may feel that this is a somewhat pedantic approach to crafting a vision, but too often I come across leaders who, within a nanosecond of hearing a wonderful vision then want to know how you're going to do it. This doesn't give them all of the how, but it does at least show that you've thought about it. So....

HOW DO WE ENSURE WORKFORCE RISKS DON'T TAKE US UNAWARES?

Just as business conditions change, so do workforce risks evolve. It follows that evaluating them isn't a one-time exercise but an ongoing and adaptive one.

For example, a pharmaceutical company identifies a potential workforce risk: a high number of senior R&D scientists approaching retirement. The initial solution? A talent pipeline campaign focused on mid-career hires. But three months later, a new risk emerges: rising competition for biotech talent from the technology sector. Suddenly, the mitigation plan needs adjusting to focus on retention and internal development.

So what does continual evaluation involve?

- **Regular risk audits.** We don't just review risks annually; we monitor them through continuous governance checks and analytics and test our own risk appetite regularly.

- **Scenario planning.** If we have the capacity, we use workforce modelling and we overlay that with business context to predict how new risks may emerge or existing ones may shift.

- **Dynamic criteria.** We recognize that what's critical today may not be critical tomorrow, so we challenge our assumptions frequently.

Workforce risks are not static. They require continuous scanning, stress-testing and adjustment to remain relevant and actionable.

Remember that this is the vision we strive for; it's not necessarily one that we can achieve, or at least not all at once.

MITIGATING WORKFORCE RISK ISN'T JUST ABOUT HAVING A PLAN

Many organizations identify risks but fail to follow through because mitigation stalls at the planning stage. The difference is execution.

What does effective mitigation require?

- **A clear end goal.** We don't just react to risks when they happen; we know what good ought to look like. I say 'ought' because we can't be certain about much in life, so be realistic. If everything that politicians told us turned out to be correct, then we probably wouldn't have politicians.

- **Feasibility checks.** We test our mitigation strategies for viability, cost-effectiveness and for potential unintended consequence, the most important of which is whether people – actual people, our product, remember – will go along with it. An approach that is purely scientific is unlikely to ever escape the laboratory and survive.

- **Actions.** A mitigation plan isn't a document; it's a series of coordinated actions with accountability, ownership and tracking mechanisms.

These are the building blocks that enable the articulation of at least a part of the vision, one which will eventually lead us to creating an operating model that can make it real. In Chapter 2, I explored how The Dowding System mirrors the role of an SWP Practitioner. Now, let's put that concept to the test with a re-imagining for SWP.

You'll recognize the broad shape of the Chapter 2 model, although I've thrown in a few pieces of jargon and they need to be explained before I go much further. The jargon is mostly shorthand for describing perfectly sensible ideas in a single word instead of several, so let's clarify:

- **PESTLE Analysis:** Stands for Political, Economic, Social, Technological, Legal and Environmental. It's an acronym used to describe the kind of external scan you'd conduct on the external workforce world, along with Workforce Trends and Market Insight. A hypothetical workforce PESTLE analysis could be like this:

  o **P:** A change of government will result in greater employment rights, limiting the ability of employers to exit staff at will.

  o **E:** A prolonged period of inflation has resulted in significant wage increases.

  o **S:** Generation Z employees are increasingly reluctant to commute to an office, altering the view of talent as necessarily regional in nature.

  o **T:** The rapid spread of Agentic AI is reducing the need for clerical labour in administrative and back-office functions.

  o **L:** Recent judgements make it possible for older people to continue working without being forced to retire.

  o **E:** The growth in renewable energies is creating shortages in wind turbine mechanic skills.

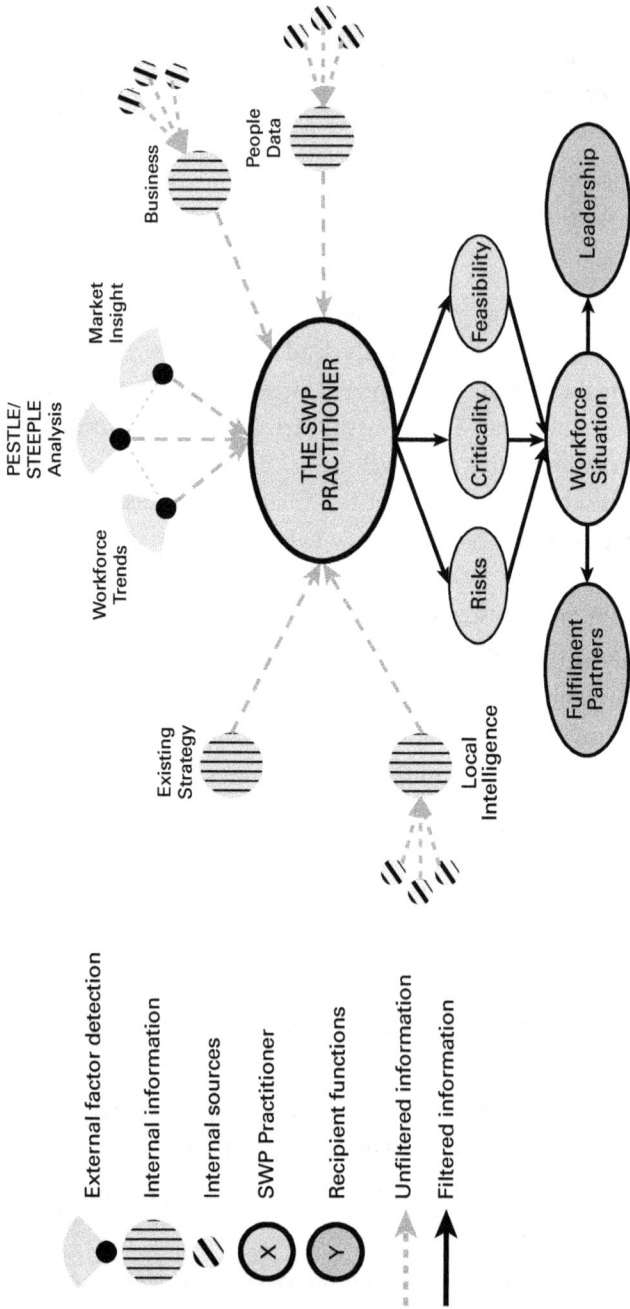

FIGURE 5.1 Dowding Re-imagined part 1

- **STEEPLE Analysis:** Same as PESTLE but with an extra E for Ethical. A good example is the drive to bring about equitable hiring and career progression. These items, sometimes grouped together under the term 'Environmental Scanning',[3] don't exist in isolation, however. The widespread rollback of DEI (Diversity, Equity and Inclusion) initiatives in the United States in 2025 is a clear example of how political decisions can have significant ethical implications.

- **Market Insight:** There's nothing terribly new about trying to find out what the market is like for hiring particular types of people in particular geographies, for particular industry sectors. But we now have technology that can enable enquiries of incredible sophistication. It won't yet tell you how much it will cost to hire an Ipswich-based opera singer to recite the whole of Wagner's *Ring Cycle* outside your annoying neighbour's house; but it will, one day. We'll talk about technology much more in Chapter 15, but the broader point is this: workforce insight tools no longer just tell us what the market looks like; they help us assess the feasibility of talent strategies. The ability to predict hiring bottlenecks or skill shortages is now a tangible input into risk-based workforce planning.

- **Workforce Trends:** So far in this book I think I've managed to avoid the S-word, but there comes a time and a place for everything. While I'll explore the current Skills obsession in Chapter 14, it's already shaping how organizations assess workforce risk and opportunity. Skills don't represent the only principal workforce trend, but with so much attention on them now, it would be unwise to ignore them as part of your overall understanding of workforce circumstances.

- **Workforce Situation:** This is where it all comes together. At this stage, you're making an assessment and providing that to relevant parties, either directly or indirectly, depending on your place in the leadership chain. Regardless of level, your product is your judgment.

- **Leadership:** We'll talk a lot more about who you talk to and what you tell them in Chapter 12 but for now we can just assume that you're telling somebody something. After all the work that will have brought you this far, it would be a shame to keep it all to yourself.

- **Fulfilment Partners:** Let's get something straight before we go any further: the value in SWP doesn't come from SWP at all. Unless you are going to hire the people yourself, train them yourself, move them around yourself, you are going to need others to do those things for you. And it's how they act that matters most of all. A consulting partner says: 'Ultimately, it's not just the plan that matters, it's whether we actually do something with it. SWP is worthless if it sits in a drawer and everyone carries on as before.' Now we'll see what this means shortly, but for now, let's just concentrate on who these partners are. They're anyone who has anything to do with the hiring, retention, procurement, pricing, nurturing and stewardship of the workforce.

You'll be noticing how this is already looking a lot like a vision of an ecosystem of some scale. We're now going to build out the vision a bit further by taking the second of those themes and breaking that down.

2. We have optimized our fulfilment channels and our processes to eliminate unnecessary attrition and spend

---

WHAT'S A FULFILMENT CHANNEL, LET ALONE AN OPTIMIZED ONE?

A fulfilment channel is any route through which people get hired, retained, retrained, redeployed, promoted and, yes, exited. This will include, but by no means be limited to Talent Acquisition, Learning & Development, Internal Mobility, Total Reward, Real Estate and Supply Chain (aka Sourcing, Procurement or Vendor Management). You could have any number of additional channels to those operated by the mainstream Fulfilment Partners, while the partners may themselves have a variety of external relationships that essentially do similar things. In-house recruitment may be augmented by Recruitment Process Outsourcing (RPO) for certain roles or locations; you may use a range of specialist resource providers to meet specific needs.

As an example, Code First Girls is a UK company that trains women to become software developers with the express aim of increasing female representation in the software engineering sector.

Optimizing the channels means streamlining their number, their scope, their terms, pricing and approach to bring about reduced cost and increased speed of delivery. The additional time that SWP gives you – that earlier Moment of Likelihood that I illustrated in Chapter 1 – makes this possible. This is a fundamental origin of value that is attributable to SWP.

So:

- **We know what all the channels are.** There will be many more than you think, and many that will be operated locally.
- **We've made them better.** If you just keep doing the same old things, you'll get the same old result.

We have lots of fulfilment channels, many more than will be first apparent. To manage all of these and to ensure that anyone using them does so in a responsible way, we like to create a range of processes designed to oversee behaviours and limit excess, mimicking our desire to keep control of things. I don't need to give you any scientific analysis of the utter miasma of process that this desire engenders.

WHAT DOES OPTIMIZING OUR PROCESSES LOOK LIKE?

Every fulfilment channel will have its baggage train of processes – requisitions, approval chains, purchase orders, internal redeployment, reskilling, pre-employment screening, financial and headcount controls to name a few:

- We have streamlined every fulfilment-related process to reduce unnecessary steps and embed behaviours that drive more beneficial hiring decisions.

Optimizing also means levelling.

'... to eliminate unnecessary attrition and spend' means:

- We have identified avoidable instances of staff attrition, whether through redundancy (aka Reductions in Force) or resignation, of unnecessary or inflated cost and overhead, and of lost business value (much more about this shortly).
- We have systematically taken steps to avoid those instances.

There is an awful lot more about this in Chapters 6 and 11.

Let's add then to the diagram that we started earlier in this chapter.

Now I'm not asking you to play Spot the Difference here; I've simply added the various Fulfilment Partners and, importantly, the practitioner's advice or direction.

Why do I say Advice or Direction? Well I don't want to spoil it for you, but the fact is that there is no one-size-fits-all when it comes to the authority

FIGURE 5.2 Dowding Re-imagined part 2

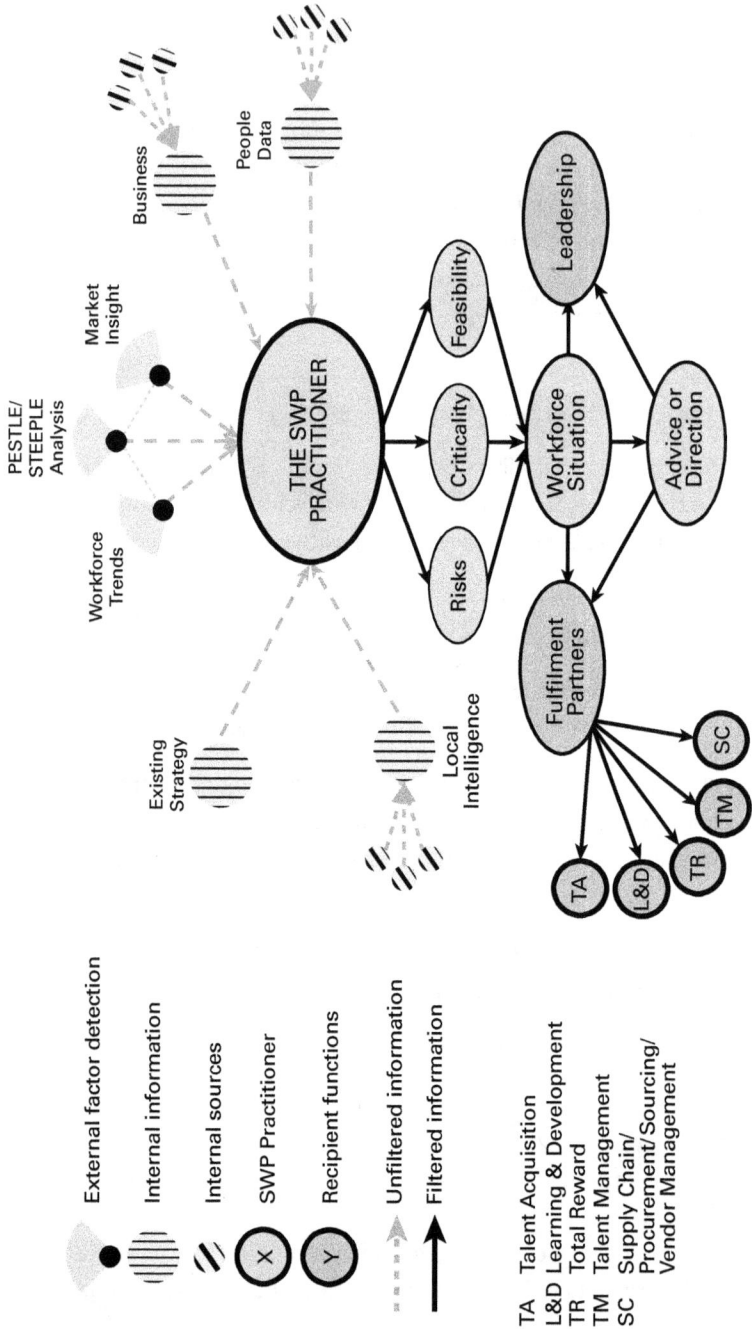

External factor detection

Internal information

Internal sources

SWP Practitioner

Recipient functions

Unfiltered information

Filtered information

TA   Talent Acquisition
L&D   Learning & Development
TR   Total Reward
TM   Talent Management
SC   Supply Chain/
      Procurement/Sourcing/
      Vendor Management

Business

People Data

Market Insight

PESTLE/STEEPLE Analysis

Workforce Trends

THE SWP PRACTITIONER

Feasibility

Criticality

Risks

Existing Strategy

Local Intelligence

Workforce Situation

Leadership

Advice or Direction

Fulfilment Partners

TA

L&D

TR

TM

SC

of the SWP Practitioner. I'm not aware of any example where the practitioner is in charge of one or more Fulfilment Partners, able to order them to take actions x, y or z; there are some that act without questioning the practitioner's judgement because it has been shown to be persuasive. Most of these partners, however, will take their practitioner's advice and then decide what to do with that advice **in their own teams.**

Why the bold type? Because if this is a vision, then we have to ask ourselves if acting in silos is the best way to build a workforce. That brings us neatly to the third statement in this trilogy.

3. Our workforce knowledge, strategy and fulfilment is fully oriented to delivering the strategy of the business

- We have assessed the emerging strategy of the business against the current workforce construct and we have determined the nature and degree of change to that workforce that is needed to make strategy execution possible.

- We have considered the workforce changes needed to execute the strategy and we have highlighted the risks to that execution.

- Our workforce fulfilment processes are optimized not simply around achieving efficiency and value but around meeting the most critical business need.

Let's complete the model in Figure 5.3:

Despite appearances, there are just three sets of changes, both on the left-hand side of this diagram.

The first covers strategy. In this now fully built vision, we can see how strategy, drawing on its own distinct sources as it evolves, both informs the SWP Practitioner and is informed by them. Professor Nick Kemsley of the Henley Business School is clear: 'What we badge as SWP,' he says, '… is in reality simply the third dimension of how good organizations should be running Integrated Business Planning.'[4]

His article contains so many good observations that it makes no sense to repeat them here, although we'll probably return to some of them when we look at SWP ownership in Chapter 16.

The second addition is, of course, Finance. I know you're all itching to talk about that subject. At the 2024 London SWP Conference, there were queues of people trying to get into a session about forging closer links with them, so it's clearly something that matters. We'll get there in Chapters 6 and 8. For now, it's important to understand that no consideration of the

FIGURE 5.3 Dowding Re-imagined part 3

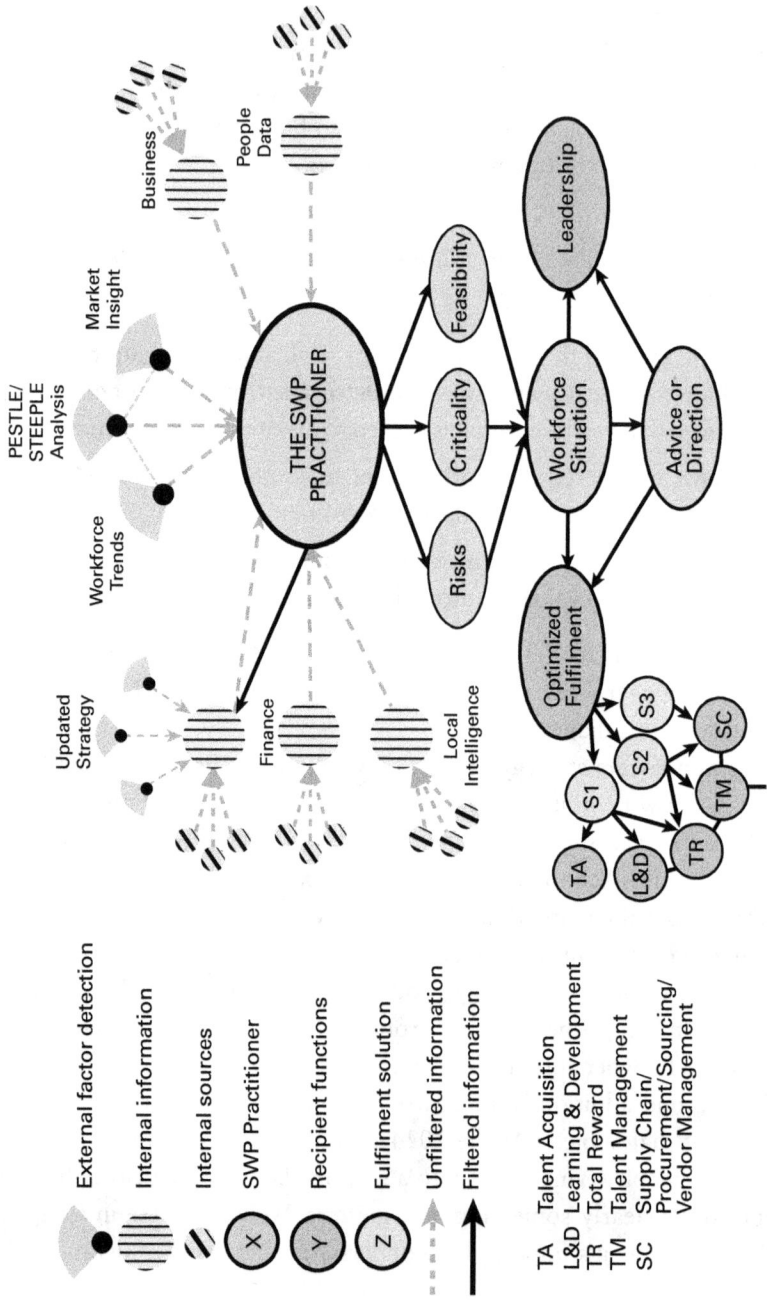

External factor detection

Internal information

Internal sources

SWP Practitioner

Recipient functions

Fulfilment solution

Unfiltered information

Filtered information

TA   Talent Acquisition
L&D Learning & Development
TR   Total Reward
TM   Talent Management
SC   Supply Chain/
     Procurement/Sourcing/
     Vendor Management

overall workforce situation can be complete without knowing the current financial state and its future direction.

From a vision perspective, the key thing is that the SWP Practitioner is interacting fully and constantly with both business sources and the company's strategy development and ensures that those strategic needs find their way to the people who will need to meet them. Which brings us to the third change.

The bottom left of this diagram now looks like a complicated bunch of grapes. Well, it is complicated. You'll notice that I now reference Optimized Fulfilment instead of Fulfilment Partners and that the first output from Optimized Fulfilment is a series of Solutions which then involve various combinations of Fulfilment Partners. So what's going on here?

There are three layers of optimization taking place:

1 Each fulfilment channel is making its process as efficient as it possibly can to aid the business.

2 Each fulfilment channel is then maximizing the value from having the longer-term view that SWP can give you of likely workforce changes.

3 Those fulfilment channels are then combining their respective capabilities to forge outcomes that maximize value to the business in the execution of its strategy.

COMBINING FULFILMENT CHANNELS

A global retailer anticipates a seasonal labour shortage due to tightened immigration laws. Instead of waiting for hiring shortfalls to materialize, they pre-emptively:

• expand their contingent workforce agreements

• fast-track cross-training programmes to redeploy employees internally

• partner with universities for short-term hiring solutions

It's not a case of doing one thing or another; it's about the combination that delivers on speed, quality and cost. The result? When peak season arrives, they are prepared and not reactive.

I've been holding off this for a while now, but now we really must talk about B's.

B's around a honeypot – not just build, buy or borrow

'SWP enables CoEs across HR to work together to go, "OK, we got skills gaps to close. We've now got multiple levers to close those skills gaps. How hard are we going to pull each one?"' – Anonymous Consultancy Partner

There's a kind of cycle in business and life that probably has a lot of research and science behind it. I haven't read that science, but I know it to be true. But unscientifically, it is how we progress from finding an activity extremely challenging and time-consuming the first time we do it to the point where we refer to it with a shorthand phrase that encompasses all of its complexity. The more experienced we come, the more encompassing the shorthand becomes (of course, there is thinking behind this, involving a concept described as perceptual chunking[5]). I think something attains that status when a shorthand is used in a meeting and everyone hearing it nods sagely either because they know what it means or because they don't know what it means but don't want to appear stupid by admitting it.

The phrase 'Build, Buy, Borrow' is one of these. It's shorthand for the myriad ways in which organizations address workforce gaps. This was somewhat codified by Dave Ulrich in 1998[6] into five categories:

- **Build** – train or develop internal talent (sometimes referred to now as upskilling)
- **Buy** – hire employees from the external market
- **Borrow** – use the extended workforce of contractors or third-party staff
- **Bounce** – terminate staff
- **Bind** – retain staff

We then have a clutch of B's that have emerged since then, some of which are in common use, while others are becoming more mainstream:

- **Bound** – moving talent around or upward within the organization.[7]
- **Boost** – accelerating the development and advancement of high-potential staff.
- **Bridge** – a variation on Bound, in the sense that internal mobility is a likely outcome, or a more radical reinvention of someone from an obsolete role into an option for new, emerging ones. This involves reskilling

somebody, such as training bank branch staff to become software engineers as digitization reduces the need for physical presence on the high street.

- **Bot** – the newest kid on the block. Integrating bots (robots) into the workforce.[8] More recently this has come to encompass the use of artificial intelligence as a replacement for routine and repetitive transaction tasks.

Phew. There's a lot of these terms and they serve to highlight just how complex the business of addressing workforce needs can be.

I'm afraid I'm going to make it more complicated…

Mary Young's excellent article (already referred to) from 2015 – yes, 2015 – highlighted a bunch of activities that fell into what she called None of the Above and which I believe we can group into a new B Activity:

Bend

Instead of trying to find ever-more exotic ways of filling existing positions in the existing shape of the business, change the shape of the business. That can come through all manner of approaches, all of which are already established:

- **Business process redesign** – changing what we do or how we do it.
- **Organization redesign** – rearranging the organization to address new challenges, often referred to as restructuring.
- **Job or work redesign** – breaking the tasks down for a job or a collection of jobs and reconstituting them into a different set of jobs.
- **Demographic and diversity shaping** – Contrary to what you might immediately think, I don't see this as positive discrimination, which can be something of a pejorative. I've already offered an ageing workforce example in Chapter 4, so doing something about it is a natural sequitur. Diversity shaping is a commercial imperative as well as a moral one. A diverse customer base that isn't served or understood by a correspondingly diverse business is unlikely to have its needs met.

In the next chapter, we're going to look at how these things not just flow from SWP but can also realize tangible value.

As I've said, these are not either/or choices. It is the act of blending them and the magic happens through the way in which they are blended.

Where's the emotional captivation?

I know – a series of diagrams, process descriptions and workforce activities is about as emotively captivating as a dirty puddle. This morning, Finony and I took Dylan on his latest walk. The sun was out and I noticed the very first buds of a hawthorn bush opening, with leaves that were lime-green in colour, a freshness that fades as the summer sun darkens them. They herald the beginning of spring, with all the feelings of renewal and thrilling anticipation of long, warm days to come. You'd need a heart of stone not to be captivated by that.

There is nothing I could say about SWP that is remotely as engaging. But context is everything.

Chapters 9 and 12 will look more closely at the personal as well as organizational factors that can impede SWP's introduction, but it's enough for now to say that organizations are frequently dysfunctional. Of course there will be other reasons besides dysfunction for last-minute hiring or layoffs. But the idea that a selfless and collegiate sharing of information between all concerned functions and teams, which results in an equally selfless and collegiate determination of responses that are planned out in advance leads not only to more efficient and effective resourcing but can also lead to fewer demoralizing shocks for a company's people and a positive impact on their careers and loyalty is for the birds.

That's more than just a pity. An organization functioning that well will not only be more productive and cost-efficient, but it will also be recognized as a global leader in doing things well. And when employees see the organization planning proactively for their future in a way that is tangibly beneficial, they will not only gain confidence in their own career paths, but they will increasingly trust leadership's foresight. I can get captivated by that and I believe most of you can as well.

And yet there's the prize, folks. An organization where the teams all pull together in the name of delivering the workforce it needs and where, in so doing, *everybody wins*. Now I could have made this chapter a lot shorter by saying that at the beginning. However, the first response you'll get from a senior leader if you put that to them will be a sceptical 'Oh really? I'd love to hear how you propose to make that happen.' Their second response is likely to demand an explanation of the results you expect from doing it. And for you to do that, you need to become friends with benefits. And to find out how to do that, you'll need to turn this page.

REFLECTIONS

- **Vision yes, plan no.** You won't inspire anyone without an idea of how better might look. Only then can you start talking about how you'll bring it to life.
- **Visualize your framework.** It doesn't have to be Dowding Re-imagined: whatever visual works for you will do, so long as it shows how you'll take information in and then filter it out.
- **Three main themes.** Minimize existing risk, reduce inefficiency and align with business strategy.
- **New B on the block.** Bending the organization is a valid response to a workforce plan.
- **Emotional captives.** Doing the right thing for your both business and your people is possible. Your people will thank you for it, and your shareholders will too.

Notes

1   BBC Sport (2023) Ebony Rainford-Brent: England World Cup winner joins ECB as a non-executive director, BBC Sport, https://www.bbc.co.uk/sport/cricket/65531257 (archived at https://perma.cc/H5P9-RHLU)
2   The Cricketer (2022) Ebony Rainford-Brent: Cricket vehicle helping people from different backgrounds, https://www.thecricketer.com/Topics/kia-oval/ebony_rainford-brent_cricket_vehicle_helping_people_different_backgrounds.html (archived at https://perma.cc/4KP3-V8YB)
3   Gibson, A (2020) *Agile Workforce Planning*, London: Kogan Page
4   Kemsley, N (2019) SWP: Another HR process or just part of how good businesses plan? LinkedIn, https://www.linkedin.com/pulse/swp-another-hr-process-just-part-how-good-businesses-plan-kemsley/ (archived at https://perma.cc/U92B-DV3H)
5   Chase, W G and Simon, H A (1973) Perception in chess, *Cognitive Psychology*, 4(1), pp. 55–81
6   Young, M B (2015). Buy, build, borrow, or none of the above? New options for closing global talent gaps, *The Conference Board*, Research Report R-1572-15-RR https://www.cewd.org/documents/BuyBuildBorrow-ConferenceBoard.pdf (archived at https://perma.cc/PM6V-GK3X)

7 Ulrich, D, Brockbank, W, Johnson, D, Sandholtz, K and Younger, J (2009) The Six 'Bs' Overview, Tool 5.1, *HR Transformation: Building Human Resources from the Outside In*, The RBL Group, https://hrtransformationbook.s3.amazonaws.com/Documents/5.1%206Bs.pdf (archived at https://perma.cc/T8DS-AN33)

8 airSlate Team (2019) Humans and bots: The new blended workforce, airSlate Blog, 4 January, https://www.airslate.com/blog/humans-and-bots-the-new-blended-workforce (archived at https://perma.cc/NVR9-PXRG)

06

Making friends with finance and benefits

When we first tried to roll out SWP, Finance pushed back. To them, HR was just asking for 'more planning'. Their response was, 'We already have our forecasting – why add more layers?' Unless you clearly connect SWP to tangible cost savings or margin improvements, you won't get their buy-in.

JEFF MULLEN

In this chapter, we'll explore *why* Finance often resists SWP, *how* to frame SWP in financial terms that resonate and the practical steps you can take to secure their buy-in.

The first substantive part of my career was as an accountant; it was a far from distinguished one. My most memorable accounting achievement was holding a 10-minute conversation with my then-CFO before he burst out laughing and suggested I should look down. In the darkness of the morning at home, I'd managed to put a black shoe on my left foot and a brown shoe on my right one. That's how memorable my accounting career was.

Nevertheless, I've had a lifelong affinity for numbers and for spreadsheets (when they eventually came along) and the knowledge I acquired in those early years stood me in good stead when, many years later, I found myself facing a Finance function deeply sceptical about the idea of implementing workforce planning.

In Chapter 3, I described the realization in a former company that we had a huge number of non-permanent staff that we knew little about and that we needed to see how we might reduce our reliance on that staff type. I also said that I was no longer sure that there always has to be a financial angle to get SWP adopted.

Yet it was exactly that angle that landed me the opportunity to put into practice everything that I had begun to believe was possible. Without it, I might have continued to wander around managerial corridors like a vagabond prophet, clutching a tattered vision that would grab someone's attention right up until the moment my meeting with them ended.

It came because of the work I set out in Chapter 3 which, in turn, prompted analysis of the cost of this external – also called extended by some – workforce. I'll stick with external, not least since Josh Bersin[1] and Gartner[2] both describe the extended workforce as including the whole workforce – internal and external.

Oranges are not the only fruit – there's more than one kind of worker

Now, I didn't originally intend to dive into the murky waters of external workforce definitions until Chapter 14 but you'll have to indulge me now because it's integral to this section. I've been involved in entire projects whose sole purpose is to arrive at a set of definitive, comprehensive definitions for all of the different types of worker under the sun, so don't expect me to be able to do the same in a couple of paragraphs. Let's deal with some of the relatively simple ones first.

THE RELATIVELY SIMPLE ONES

Employees. Anyone directly employed by the company. Includes full-time, part-time, students, graduate entrants, interns, people on secondment, working as expatriates, on a fixed-term contract. That's rather a lot of different types of employee and they're not all the same.

Contractors. Anyone who is not an employee who operates either as a freelance contractor or is supplied through an agency or an umbrella employer for what is usually a fixed but extendable term. They're not subject to a Statement of Work with specific deliverables. They may have specific expertise or may have been engaged to augment the existing workforce to deal with short-term employee capacity challenges.

Like I said, simple.

Now it doesn't help that the word 'contingent' is sometimes used to describe contractors, because it's also sometimes used to describe contractors and the group that I'm about to dip into. There are many aspects of the people business that are, to say the very least, complex but few can match the bewildering complexity of the terms used to describe different types of worker.

I could incite unrest simply by calling this next group Third-Party Workers. 'They're Managed Service', some will say; 'No, they're Statement of Work', say others. But I'll persist: the one thing that unites this group is that it is a Third Party that employs these workers and supplies them to somebody else. I won't reply to any letters of complaint.

What most people will agree on, however, is that this group of workers will rarely be treated or seen as part of the company's headcount. They will usually be managed through Supply Chain as a non-headcount expense, rather than through HR. You're going to have to reach Chapter 14 for more thoughts about that.

THIRD-PARTY WORKERS

Advisory/consultants. Typically supplied by large or boutique consultancy firms to advise senior leaders. Can be very expensive ways to create a PowerPoint deck.

Business process outsourcing (BPO) or managed service. There will be outrage somewhere at my grouping these together, but for me the literal interpretation is that these workers do something which, for a variety of reasons, the company prefers not to do itself. Catering, security, IT product support – a range of roles that are not part of the company's essence.

Resource augmentation. Again, a bit controversial because a lot of people might describe these as Statement of Work staff, because much of what they do is covered by such a statement ('the staff will deliver x by the end of y for amount z'). But advisory staff do that too, even if it's just a very expensive PowerPoint presentation. The distinction is that these are roles also performed by the company's own employees, hence the naming I've given them. These staff are frequently co-located with employees and may even report to an employee line manager.

This is not an exhaustive list. The appearance of gig workers – internal and external – alongside companies supplying purpose-oriented labour (graduate entrants, career changers, diverse cohorts) has served only to complicate the landscape further. But these definitions will suffice for now.

Digging for gold

Having established that we had an awful lot of these third-party staff, our leadership determined that we needed to reduce our spend on them, a spend which at the time was a few degrees north of astronomical. How to do that? And how would SWP be the catalyst for doing so? Well it's another great example of layering different indicators to arrive at an answer which, in this important case, had to be something that could be monetized. Any project whose sole *raison d'être* is to save money always has multiple parties poring over the forecasts, first challenging them then demanding updates every five minutes. Outcomes for people must take second place to the need for hard cash ones, even though it's often people outcomes that companies like to publicize.

Now in case you're wondering how important it is to lay this out in the detail that I am, here's an observation from another practitioner:

> 'Finance was not just going to sign off. They're the pivotal point – they approve the budgets. If they see SWP as intangible or "HR telling us we have to do new tasks", they won't do it. They needed to see exactly how it improves margin. Then they gave us the green light.' Dibyendu Sharma, Unisys

I've got 10 more quotes from people that are more or less identical. Like it or not, showing benefit is quintessential to securing Finance department buy-in. You need to be as forensic as them and you need to be as numerate as they are.

REAL-WORLD EXAMPLE
Shaping the opportunity

1 Narrowing the target population didn't take long. The only realistic third-party group that we could go after would be Resource Augmentation workers. Why?

○ Because BPO services were locked-in contracts and in any case the alternative would be to take on those services ourselves, which made no sense whatsoever.

○ Advisory services, while expensive, were always in demand at executive level because of the credibility they gave to executive decisions. They weren't going to budge.

2   Our data told us that most resource augmentation workers were working on our investment portfolio, and when you added them to the headcount, external staff made up over 45 per cent of the portfolio workforce of 13,000. This was not just a cost issue, it was a significant business risk too.

WAIT A MINUTE...

Non-permanent staff are not inherently a business risk. In many situations, they're ideal for mitigating the risk of employed workforce surpluses. It's all about the mix. A business that lacks the ability to flex in times of growth and contraction is every bit as exposed as one where that ability greatly exceeds any likely need.

---

3   When you looked at these 6,000 or so people, six things emerged:

○ The average number of Full Time Equivalents (FTE) per Statement of Work was 1.5. Yep, 1.5. This meant that the SoW processing overhead for Supply Chain was huge and that unit cost of labour was high because there was no discount for volume.

○ These SoWs were being raised by individual hiring managers according to their need, but they were being raised this way so that the total cost fell below the limit of their own signing approval. The controls that were meant to limit managerial excess were simply enabling something worse.

○ The same people were being procured on a rolling basis. No sooner had they delivered one thing than they were delivering something else. There was nothing temporary about many of these staff at all.

○ A further perception was that the majority of these SoW staff were working on a fixed price basis, i.e. that the price for delivering the work would not fluctuate regardless of any delays in its delivery. Companies see this as a good way to do things, because it places all of the risk onto the supplier, who will only profit by delivering either on time or earlier (which is why this is sometimes called Risk and Reward). Unfortunately, most of them were no such thing. People were entering timesheets, some managers would sign them off without so much as a glance, and their supplier company would just be paid for the hours worked.

o The same or similar roles were being supplied both to onshore and offshore locations, onshore being five or six times more expensive.

o Just to make things that bit more entertaining, we had multiple suppliers providing us with the same roles. Our business analysts came from 48 separate companies.

4 These data points gave us:

o a target population

o a target area of the business

o a set of operational circumstances that just felt wrong but which, more importantly, could be quantified.

So that's what was happening. But why was it happening? And before anyone asks what on earth this has to do with SWP, the answer is absolutely everything. If, as I have already said, the value of SWP isn't in SWP itself but in what is done with it, then what gets done with it is *absolutely* your business.

UNDERSTANDING WHY

One of the dubious joys of SWP is that almost any conversation about a fairly narrow topic can rapidly mushroom into an unimaginably vast and unmanageable conversation. Similarly, diagnosing causes can quite quickly expand to something very wide-ranging that you can do nothing about personally ('You know, the problem is that no one ever gets fired for screwing things up'). My point is that for every cause I might list, you'll probably have another three or four. Never say that SWP isn't the gift that keeps on giving:

1 **It was easier for managers to hire these staff than to hire employees.**
Well of course it was. As in most organizations, budgets are based on an assumed cost per employee, which therefore determines how much headcount we can afford. This directly causes the dreaded headcount limit. Hiring any extra employee can sometimes feel as though you've committed some sort of unspoken crime. Compare this with hiring a third-party worker; it's not treated as headcount, just as another purchase. And guess what?

Because it takes a long time to hire people, you're underspending on your headcount budget, so you can afford to buy these people instead.

2 **Late-onset budget settlement.** I've often wondered why, in December, we talk about next year as though it is another country when it's just a few weeks away. Much of this is driven by the financial cycle and a tendency to settle budgets on an annual basis, frequently finalizing them only after the new year has just begun. So if your project does need more people in the new year and you can't hire them until the budget (and headcount) has been approved, the chances are that you're unlikely to be able to hire those staff until April or worse. So if your project is to land successfully, you need to call in resources more quickly from outside. And how can you afford that? See Item 1.

3 **Enabling governance.** We all believe in rules, right? And we all pay our taxes, don't we? And we never look to minimize our tax bill by working those rules to their limits, do we... You get my point. If there's a rule that you don't have to get anyone else's approval to raise a purchase order for under a certain amount and you have the spare budget (see 1 and 2), that's what you'll do. And if that limit covers the cost of about one FTE, that's how you'll end up with that average.

4 **We don't have the skills in-house.** The value proposition of third-party suppliers rests substantially on the premise that they can get you the skills that you haven't got. Learning and Development (L&D) budgets are rarely high and are frequently one of the first targets in cost-cutting cycles, which just reinforces the belief that we don't have the people with the right capabilities. Without them we won't deliver on time and...

5 **We get rewarded for delivery, not for developing our people.** We'll explore manager motivation in Chapter 9, but for now it suffices to say that managers, especially those at the more junior levels, have to deliver stuff. The reward for ensuring that the company will have plenty of up-and-coming managers and experts of the future is...well, it's not very much. This also explains why...

6 **... Managers insist on owning the whole hiring process, and you can't blame them.** If you know that your future gainful employment hinges on delivery and that successful delivery hinges on hiring the right people, you're not going to entrust that to anyone else except in the early stages. Then you're so busy trying to deliver that you have no time for reviewing candidates, so you hire third-party staff. You'll get to know which people are keepers, which suppliers understand you and you'll keep going back to

> them. Never mind if Supply Chain say their rate is above the norm, because all you'll do is pick up the phone to your boss who will tell Supply Chain where to go because this delivery is essential and (they don't tell them this bit) they're also rewarded for delivery...
>
> So... we've set things up in such a way as to make these things almost inevitable.

Do Finance ask for this information up front? Probably not, but you're the new kid on the block. Finance has been around for centuries, so why should they pay attention to you? You've got to establish your credibility. Remember your maths examinations? It's not enough to just write down the answer; you have to show how you got there.

That's why this stuff can be so much fun (yes, I should get out more). You're taking in the whole flow, because you know that only by understanding it can you both diagnose the problem and identify solutions. But your operational credentials are not enough; now you need to establish your financial credentials too.

An open and shut case

Now you may think that it's one thing to offer a solution with all manner of cost savings and that it's quite another to implement it. You're completely right, of course. There's many a great idea that gets approved that founders in its execution: just ask any moviemaker. We'll be looking at that challenge soon enough in this book. For now, we'll focus on what will get you through to experience that Nirvana: the business case.

Just before we go any further, you can also be forgiven for wondering where the people went. You know, those people who do the work, whose livelihoods and families provide them with reason to come to work in the first place, with all their aspirations and ambitions for the future. They aren't forgotten but, whether we like it or not, the benefits that can accrue to them will count for nothing unless you can show financial value. Does that make this a cynical exercise? No, it makes it a realistic one, and one that is a call to arms for any HR professional. You work for a business. The business exists to make money – that's the capitalist system. To be a successful HR professional, you need first to be a business professional.

REAL-WORLD EXAMPLE
Jeff Mullen – integrating SWP with finance[3]

Context and challenge

Jeff has worked in both Finance and HR/SWP, seeing first-hand how Finance often views SWP as 'HR overhead' unless it's reframed in financial terms.

In multiple companies (social media, finance, defence), the cultural stance on growth vs. short-term results heavily impacted whether longer-horizon SWP was feasible.

Approach

- **Listen and solve:** He emphasizes approaching Finance with 'What are your day-to-day pains?' then showing how SWP can resolve those pains.
- **Speak finance:** Building a benefit case that ties to margin, cost forecasts or stable revenue projection is essential: 'people-friendly reasons alone don't cut it.'
- **Top-level sponsorship:** Jeff urges, 'CEO needs to sponsor SWP', or at least CFO buy-in is needed to ensure it's not seen as 'just HR tasks'.
- **Cultural constraints:** Lockheed's rigid quarterly mindset differs from LinkedIn's freedom under Microsoft. That difference shapes how strategic or short-term SWP can be.

Outcomes

- **Quarterly relief:** Where Finance accepted SWP insights (e.g. attrition forecasting), the frantic short-term scramble lessened.
- **Missed opportunities:** In more conservative environments, short-term constraints limited the scope. 'Directionally correct' logic wasn't acceptable.
- **Lessons:** If a CFO or CEO truly invests in longer horizons, SWP can thrive. If not, it stays in the short-term rut.

Key takeaways

1 **Speak finance:** Without a financial argument, SWP is often dismissed by FP&A.

2 **Start at the top:** CFO/CEO sponsorship is crucial for real traction.

3 **Know your culture:** High quarterly pressure? SWP likely remains short-term. Freed from short-term obsession? You can do real strategic planning.

Building the Business Case

While I agree wholeheartedly with Jeff, getting that CFO sponsorship isn't just a case of wandering into their office and wandering out again with the promise of unwavering support. Not only will your wandering out be rapid and forceful, it's also not your job. You want Finance to convince the CFO? You do that by enlisting their help to build the business case with you.

So, let's take the issues we identified earlier and describe a counterpoint for each of them.

TABLE 6.1 Responding to the issues

Issue	Doing something about it
Low average FTE per SoW	Raise the average by combining SoWs into larger groups.
Avoiding approval chains	Reset the people spend threshold to zero or something less enabling.
Rolling repeats	Set the engagement term for no longer than it takes to get an employee operational with the same skill set. Don't allow extensions.
Fixed price/time & materials	Treat all T&M staff as headcount, just like you would contractors.
Onshore or offshore	Make it hellishly difficult to engage staff onshore when the same role is available offshore.
Multiple suppliers	Rationalize supplier numbers: maximum of five.
Too hard to hire employees	Flip it around. Make it easier to hire employees (within limits).
Late budget setting	Set the one-year budget but add at least two more years to it for direction. If yours is an established business, by how much is it going to vary over those two years?
Enabling governance	Set the governance to work for your hiring managers, not against them. Reshape it from its current preventative focus.
In-house skills	Why are we surrounded now by the importance of building skills-based organizations? Because we're waking up to the fact that if we don't, we might founder.
Manager incentive	Make doing these things part of the incentive package. This isn't just bolting some behavioural objectives onto the existing delivery-first agenda. It means making things like stewardship a fundamental responsibility of management.
Sole ownership	Take scaled control of commodity hires so that managers can spend more time doing what they were hired to do.
Excessive quantum	Too many third-party staff? Train employees to take these roles on, especially if those employees are in roles that are phasing out.

What enables these things will be that Moment of Likelihood from Chapter 1 again. The overwhelming majority of actions you can take differently stem from having that longer runway; put another way, SWP creates a different pathway for hiring managers to follow. Now, it will be immediately apparent that some of these actions will be harder to implement than others. That's fine: it just gives you a nicely phased approach to delivering a growing pile of benefits. Let's now consider those items, line by line (Table 6.2).

TABLE 6.2 Actions and benefits

Doing something about it	Mechanism	Effect	Benefit Metrics	Difficulty/Speed
Raise average by combining SoWs into larger groups.	Rationalize supplier numbers (see below).	Reduced process overhead.	Procurement process overhead.	Medium. Adopting a longer-term mindset to requesting RA staff is not easy. But the overhead argument is a strong one.
Reset the people spend approval threshold to zero or something less enabling.	Alter standing governance rules for staff procurement.	Reduced number and frequency of RA Statements of Work.	Lower process overhead. Lower cost of RA staff.	Low. People won't like losing control, but it will act as a disincentive.
Set the engagement term for no longer than it takes to get an employee operational with the same skill set.	Alter governance for SoW approval.	Reduced repeat SoWs and process overhead. Increased internal capability levels, reducing need for RA staff.	Procurement process overhead. Lower total cost of labour.	High. Managers will detest losing control. But this builds long-term internal capability.
Treat all T&M staff as headcount, just like you would contractors.	Use Purchasing data to convert T&M hours into either FTE or headcount.	Puts a cap on unfettered use of T&M staff.	Reduced headcount underspend.	V high. Purchasing data is rarely set up for this kind of thing, the calculation is arguable and there's a simpler and more obvious alternative.

(continued)

TABLE 6.2 (Continued)

Doing something about it	Mechanism	Effect	Benefit Metrics	Difficulty/Speed
ALTERNATIVE: Use Total and Unit Cost of Labour instead of headcount.	Aggregate all headcount and non-headcount Resource Augmentation staff costs and stop managing against headcount (see Ch. 14).	Gives more freedom to managers but also enables targets to be set against Unit Cost of Labour.	Total and Unit Cost of Labour reductions.	High. Requires big cultural change and a rethink of the control agenda. But makes complete operational sense.
Make it difficult to engage staff onshore when the same role is available offshore.	Tighten governance for onshore hires and loosen it for offshore.	Brings about swift increase in offshore third-party staff.	Reduction in unit costs (also known as a positive rate variance).	Low. This is not difficult to set up or enforce. There will be cultural resistance, but the benefits show rapidly.
Rationalize supplier numbers: maximum of five.	Run a comprehensive selection exercise, granting multi-year exclusivity.	Simplifies and strengthens vendor relationships, generates discount for volume and certainty.	Reduction in unit costs (also known as a positive rate variance).	Medium. Process can take a long time, with multiple vested interests fighting their corner. Still worth it.
Flip it around. Make it easier to hire employees (within limits).	Reduced approval chain for employee hires, subject to an approved workforce plan.	Gives managers freedom to operate within the constraints of the plan.	Reduced lost productivity days.	High. Again, control agenda concerns must be addressed, but this helps to reward those who plan in advance.

(continued)

TABLE 6.2 (Continued)

Doing something about it	Mechanism	Effect	Benefit Metrics	Difficulty/Speed
Reshape governance from its current preventative focus.	Develop a different approach to governance entirely. Give managers more latitude, but with much stronger after-the-fact controls for divergence.	Managers will like this, and approval cycles will be greatly reduced.	Process overhead, productivity improvement.	High. This is not easy to do, and you'll need reserves of patience to get there. But the enabling effect is transformative.
Make internal skills building an organizational priority.	Create mass pre-emptive upskilling and reskilling programmes based on company needs.	Reduced reliance on RA staff	Lower Total Cost of Labour	High. Only really works if staff are sufficiently mobile to be deployed where needed. Who's actually achieved this?
Make stewardship part of the incentive package.	Incorporate hiring employees, developing them and helping them move an incentive element.	Managers have a reason to act differently. More focus on internal development.	Reduced RA numbers and total cost of labour.	High. Culturally difficult to achieve without strong demonstration of business value.
Take scaled control of commodity hires so that managers can spend more time doing what they were hired to do.	Exempt certain high-volume, high-turnover roles from hiring approval. Create rolling pipeline of pre-approved candidates on a no-regrets basis.	Reduces hiring delays, speeds up onboarding.	Higher productivity, lower process overhead, lower total cost of labour.	Medium-high. Hiring managerial resistance to loss of control can be offset by trust in a stream of high-quality, pre-screened candidates.

(continued)

TABLE 6.2 (Continued)

Doing something about it	Mechanism	Effect	Benefit Metrics	Difficulty/Speed
Too many third-party staff? Then train employees to take these roles on, especially if those employees are in roles that are phasing out.	Use skills adjacency methods to identify likely future reductions that could be re-skilled into new roles.	Huge plus for employee loyalty, builds a more broadly skilled workforce, and a big money saver.	Avoided severance, lower unit cost, productivity gains and more.	High. Hard to spot real redeployment opportunities, requires mindset shift in managers and also in some parts of HR. Enormous financial plus though.

None of these are easy, although some are easier than others. In Chapter 9 we will look at how you go about overcoming resistance in its many forms, so we'll park that for now. The key here is whether the prize is big enough and attractive enough for Finance to be interested. The fact that you present your ideas in terms that Finance will get gives you a high probability of being able to generate their interest. To keep it, ask them now for their help in turning the metrics into numbers. Don't feign total ignorance of course, but I think that one of the things SWP does is that it gives other functions the chance to shine at their core competency. At this point, your business case should become a shared venture: you provide the expertise, they provide the financial and estimating knowledge.

Your job is to provide realistic expectations of when each of these things could be delivered. Before you provide them, do this. Whatever cautious timeframe you have in your head, double it; whatever quantities you have in your head, halve them. Most things will take much longer than your optimistic head will tell you, but don't worry. In most large organizations, the likely benefits over time will still be astronomical, perhaps seemingly nonsensical. This is normal. It's also why you must – must – not only agree with Finance exactly which benefits should be attributed to the SWP approach but have a clear and auditable approach to attributing them. I'll return to this in our next chapter.

Don't present your plan to the CFO, at least not until someone in Finance has positioned it with them first. Make it your aim to go into any meeting with the CFO knowing that they have already decided to say yes. That's what we did, and that's exactly how it panned out. Finance was a constant presence and source of advice throughout the process. Were our benefit estimates astronomical? Absolutely. Were they nonsensical? Absolutely not.

A critical thing to remember in all of this is that most of the measures I listed here are only made possible through the use of SWP to create those earlier Moments of Likelihood.

But wait, I hear you say. Not everyone has a third-party workforce problem, so how does any of this help me?

Internal workforce benefits

Now, I know that my big SWP moment came from an unusual angle but that doesn't make the solutions irrelevant for the internal workforce. Seven of the solutions I've listed above are all about internal staff. If you had zero internal staff, you'd still be able to use them and make a significant difference to your bottom line.

Let's remind ourselves of the table of issues that I listed out in Chapter 4, but let's now apply potential actions and mechanisms to address them. Again, the critical thing here is that SWP is creating a window of opportunity for you to do something more meaningful than before.

TABLE 6.3 Internal workforce benefits

Issue	Mechanics	Effect	Benefit Metrics	Difficulty
Skill shortages	Create mass pre-emptive upskilling and reskilling programmes based on company needs.	Reduced reliance on RA staff.	Reduced external costs. Fewer hiring cycles and overhead.	Medium. Only really works if staff are sufficiently mobile to be deployed where needed.
High turnover rates	Fixes not really enabled by SWP.			
Low staff engagement scores	Fixes not really enabled by SWP.			

(continued)

TABLE 6.3 (Continued)

Issue	Mechanics	Effect	Benefit Metrics	Difficulty
Lengthy time to hire	Create rolling pipeline of pre-approved candidates on a no regrets basis.	Longer-term view reduces (but doesn't eliminate) last-minute hiring panic.	External staff marginal cost; reduced overtime; reduced time to hire; faster time to productivity.	Medium-high. Hiring managerial resistance to loss of control can be offset by trust in a stream of high-quality, pre-screened candidates
Prolonged onboarding	Rolling candidate pipeline also enhanced by pre-screening and pre-initiation.	Reduces onboarding time dramatically.	Faster time to productivity.	High: There's a cost to pre-screening that needs to be proven by productivity gains
Ageing workforce	Large-scale succession planning, mentoring, knowledge transfer, retirement preparation	Younger managers emerge as successors	Younger staff attrition cost reduction	Medium to high. Not everyone will embrace the idea, so gains may be very isolated.
Piecemeal Hiring	Longer-term hiring plan, including projected attrition for key roles.	Reduced gaps in backfilling, swifter hiring.	Reduced sourcing overhead, faster time to productivity.	Low to medium. Not necessarily easy, but very attractive to Talent Acquisition.
Low early career staff retention	Fixes not really enabled by SWP.			
Use and retention of external staff	Everything in the previous table!			
Ineffective internal mobility/ redeployment	Establish cross-organization internal mobility or redeployment function.	Reduced backfilling gaps, fewer redundancies, stronger Employee Value Proposition.	Marginal cost of exit and hire vs reskilling.	High. While not easy, the financial and reputational value is huge.

(continued)

TABLE 6.3 (Continued)

Issue	Mechanics	Effect	Benefit Metrics	Difficulty
Limited diversity & inclusivity	Fixes not really enabled by SWP.			
Rollercoaster funding	Set floor employee percentage and establish third-party drawdown facility.	Avoids hiring and reduction cycle.	Severance and hiring cost avoidance.	Low to medium. The facility can be time-consuming to establish, but if part of a broader vendor strategy, not a major barrier.
High-cost location ratio	Build offshoring programme around location strategy in plan.	Stronger offshore presence.	Unit Cost of Labour margin. Reduced property costs.	Medium. Offshoring still offers some rate advantages, but these are diminishing.

Now you will see that I've said 'Fixes not really enabled by SWP' in some places. You might not agree with me but if I apply my own Window of Opportunity principle, I can't honestly say that SWP creates a larger one for those issues to be addressed. In conjunction with other approaches, maybe; on its own, no.

Surely it's not just about the money?

Well no, it isn't. The people benefits – greater retention, improved in-house skills, increased internal mobility – are valuable, but less tangible. It doesn't mean it can't be monetized, but it makes sense to address those that are more easily monetized first.

An enterprise as wide-ranging as this requires a whole collection of people and things to come together. We're about to go into the chapter that explores this in much more detail. But this is the keystone – engaging and winning over Finance really can buy you love.

REFLECTIONS

- **Multiple worker types make up your total cost of labour.** Don't just look at employees and contractors as sources of value.

- **You have to marshal your facts to win over sceptical Finance stakeholders.** Remember, you're the upstart function, but you're also the workforce expert. Make that expertise clear.

- **Don't hold anything back.** Make your case and your solutions as comprehensive as possible to show that there's a range of phased solutions that can realize value now and in the future.

- **Be humble.** Enlist Finance's help and endorsement. Use their numbers, their assumptions, their techniques.

- **Let Finance convince the CFO.** They will be better at it than you are.

- **Your solutions toolkit is larger than you think.** Get creative.

- **Apply the Window of Opportunity test.** If SWP is an enabler, it's an SWP benefit. Otherwise, not.

- **Finance backing is a catalyst and an essential.** But you all know that already.

Notes

1   Bersin, J (2014) The extended workforce: A new paradigm for HR, Deloitte Insights, 20 February, https://www2.deloitte.com/us/en/insights/focus/human-capital-trends/2014/extended-workforce.html (archived at https://perma.cc/RH5E-FW39)

2   Gartner (2013) Extended workforce management: Leveraging the power of contingent labor, Gartner Research, https://www.gartner.com/en/human-resources (archived at https://perma.cc/V69M-BQ8W)

3   Edwards, D (2025) Interview with Geoff Mullen, conducted on 4 March 2025

07

Lining up the anseriformes, aka getting your ducks in a row

Having the right people on your implementation team

Senior-level sponsorship and advocacy is essential – ideally C-suite. On top of that, ensuring the implementation is a jointly held objective across numerous areas is required – rather than it only being the responsibility of the implementation team. Thereafter [it's] crucial to hold people accountable for their contribution towards delivering the implementation.

ANONYMOUS PRACTITIONER

In this chapter we're going to start working through the process – odyssey, ordeal, trench warfare, joy are all alternative descriptions – of turning the potential of SWP into an operational reality. Much of the book has so far essentially created the value argument for SWP and you'll have seen already how wide-ranging its view of the organization can be. It's hopefully already clear that to bring something like this to life, you're going to touch a lot of different business areas, each of which will play roles that are either active or passive but which cannot be ignored.

You need to get your ducks (anseriformes) in a row, which means making sure that you have set yourself up successfully before you start. And you start with the people you need to be a part of your implementation team.

It takes a village – but which villagers?

I'm not going to say that SWP is the ultimate exercise in collaboration because that's bound to embarrass me when something even more collaborative comes along. But it's beyond question that collaboration is the difference between getting it to work and getting it to work well.

I'll come to such non-trivial functions as Finance, Supply Chain, C-suite and the actual business itself, but first we must look expressly at the multiple elements in HR that we need to bring together.

HR has its silos too, you know

That shorthand that I talked about in Chapter 5 also extends to departments. People speak about HR as if it is a single, amorphous blob of perceived transactional necessity and not a lot else. Pay and rations, as some might put it. Yet all functions have their own federations and rivalries too. I remember a particularly poisonous relationship that existed between Finance Technology and Finance Change in a former life: we were all part of the Finance Function, working for an especially avuncular CFO, but the rivalry was particularly intense, so much so that at a function talent contest, the jury was lobbied hard by the Head of Change not to award first prize to anyone from Finance Technology because it would not be a good look. And so it was that my passionate rendition of 'Try a Little Tenderness' failed to win me the iPad that it so richly deserved. But I'm not bitter.

My point – of course – is that you shouldn't assume that everyone in HR will even get what you're trying to do, let alone understand their part in it or go along with performing it.

Again, it was Paul Habgood who set out the practical challenge perfectly:

> 'The reality of a lot of HR teams is they think North to South in a [functional silo] and not East to West as a team... We have one... throwing over the fence at TA... and TA gets the impossible task of finding 400 pink squirrels and we still haven't solved our problem... It's like, how do we change the conversation to harnessing the entire power of HR... rather than each CoE just going off to work out what they're [each] going to do?'

Got it in one. SWP provides an opportunity for all the respective partner functions to maximize their own excellence. For that to happen, they need to be involved. Doing what?

THE ROLE OF THE HR FUNCTIONS IN IMPLEMENTING SWP

If we accept the premise that the value in SWP lies in how you execute the plan that it creates – and I hope you do – then these functions have to work out how to do that. The only point in working out how you will execute a workforce plan after the planning part has already been established is if you don't want to see any value for at least a year, because it will take you that long at least to design and implement the kind of changed behaviours that make having a larger Window of Opportunity at all useful.

It therefore follows that Fulfilment Channel Implementation must be one of the fundamental and concurrent workstreams of your implementation programme; not as individual elements, but as a collective. Otherwise, you're simply perpetuating the siloed mindset. This is not an easy thing to achieve but, for now, let's just focus on the HR functions that we'll need.

THE USUAL SUSPECTS

- **Talent Acquisition (Permanent).** Of course. The idea of TA non-participation or collaboration is not even up for debate, surely. You're still asking TA as a function to look beyond the next three, six, or even twelve months and to take positions on how it will source the next-generation workforce. What channels will it use; which of the techniques I described in Chapter 6 will they pick up and run with; what is the flow of instruction, data, approach and approval that could or should be changed? Are there alternative sources – not just Recruitment Process Outsourcing – for groups of hires? The list goes on.

- **Learning and Development.** Of course, again. The arguments for upskilling and reskilling people have, I think, already been made here and certainly elsewhere. But L&D functions don't always see themselves as change participants; actually, none of these functions do, frequently leaving it to a separate HR Transformation team of change agents to bring it about. I don't believe that's foolproof, however. If you introduce change managers into situations such as these, they will understandably seek to shorthand some of the activities and processes to a level that is portable and explainable to leadership. The trouble is that, in implementing this kind of change, the devil really is in the detail and only those in the respective functional CoEs can be expected to know that. There is a place and a need for change management nevertheless, but it's very specific. By the way, this doesn't relate just to L&D: it just felt like a good time to say it.

- **Whoever is responsible for Internal Mobility.** This can sometimes be a function in its own right (infrequent), a part of another function (more often) or even an ad hoc, side-of-desk activity spread across a number of HR Business Partners (unfortunately not uncommon). At the risk of stating the obvious, I'm not in favour of the last of these. For this fulfilment channel (which is what it is) to work, it needs to be able to operate across the whole organization and not just a subset of it.

- **People Analytics.** Essential. They're the ones that are going to feed your operation with insight, but also with the means of knowing how you're doing. Do not pass 'GO' without them.

THE LESS-THAN-USUAL SUSPECTS…

- **HR Business Partners.** So, you plan to strategically workforce plan every part of your organization single-handed? Oh, I see: you believe your leadership will cough up the budget for, well, exactly how many people to do this for you? Nope and nope again. You're going to need to use people the company already has, perhaps in ways that they're not used to. People who work with the business. These will be your eyes and ears; they just don't know it yet.

- **Total Reward.** What do you mean, really? Of course they need to be in. If you want to know what your workforce solution might cost you, how inflation might erode hoped-for savings, how the changing nature of compensation and recognition might grant you that crucial tactical advantage in securing or retaining the people you want – never in doubt.

- **Policy and Proposition.** Sometimes it's located in HR Operations, but it essentially boils down to whoever devises and enforces the rules. What's considered fair, legal, appropriate. It's likely that approaches you devise won't necessarily conform with some of those rules.

- **Organization Design.** I've included definitions in these next two items because I surely can't be the only person who hitherto didn't understand the distinction. Galbraith describes this as 'The process of configuring an organization's structure to support the execution of its strategy by aligning tasks, roles, systems and processes with its strategic objectives.'[1] In other words, if the business strategy involves changing the nature of the work, then organization design is likely to have a say in how that work is organized. You can't just plan a workforce without their having considered if the workforce change is the right one organizationally.

- **Organizational Development.** Described as 'a planned, organization-wide effort to increase an organization's effectiveness and health through planned interventions in the organization's processes, using behavioural science knowledge.'[2] You might conclude that this is an extension of the SWP Practitioner's role. OD practitioners might, however, argue that SWP is an extension of theirs. I think there's a symbiotic, frequently blurred relationship between the two. Indeed, many HR functions may not even have such a team. But since so much of SWP adoption is about behavioural change (oh yes it is), if this capability is available to you, get them on your team.

- **Employee Relations.** My work experience is that it's the part of the business that you don't think about that will eventually give you a nasty shock. You can create the most immaculate framework and see it all go up in smoke if you've failed to bring employees and their representatives along with you. ER will help you navigate your way around the traps into which you might otherwise fall.

Before I go on to non-HR team members, you'll notice that, in seeking to define the right HR representation in an SWP implementation, I've included representatives from pretty much every part of HR. It's not overkill, more a reflection of the fact that many of these different teams often operate independently. It's through the practical application of SWP that they can be brought to see how they interlock.

A PRACTITIONER SAYS...

'If you're going to get the best out of SWP, you've got to have all of those fulfilment functions on side with you and part of the implementation from the start.'

So this is an HR project then? We'll get into some of the politics around that in Chapter 9, but for now the answer is: No, Of Course Not. All along we've been talking about the importance of engaging multiple parts of the business if this is to be successful. So who do you need that isn't from HR?

Essential non-HR implementation team members

This breaks quite neatly into two distinct parts: the people who are going to run the project itself, and those non-HR functions you need in your team.

ESSENTIAL PROJECT TEAM MEMBERS

- **Agile Coach.** What? Why is an Agile Coach even remotely important to a project whose connection with technology is minute?

  a. Most people associate Agile with technology development, which is where it seems to have its origins.[3] That doesn't make Agile irrelevant for something like implementing SWP. It's a programme of work with a set of key workstreams, but within each workstream is a series of products – workforce plan, workforce plan approval process, plan change control, and many more besides – each of which will have multiple features (a workforce plan approval process will have multiple components, for example). By breaking them down this way, what feels like an almost unmanageable scale can be made to feel simpler.

  b. Taking that approval process as an example, the development of this might be handled as a series of small sprints in which approvals through the different layers of an organization might be structured and optimized. The Agile Coach can help you to define the small increments involved, ensure you demonstrate them and their value in short sessions, guide you to receive and absorb feedback and iterate on the back of it. They can also ensure that you're not delivering everything in one go at the end (often to mixed reviews). Instead, you're building momentum all the way. This used to be called 'quick wins', although Agile gives that term more structure, rationale and form.

  c. The issue with Agile in non-technology situations is that people aren't always familiar with how it actually works. I remember somebody telling me they were flying to London to spend a week on sprint planning, which is somewhat oxymoronic. Your coach will keep you honest about what you're doing and will push you to understand how making small improvements can realize value that can be presented and celebrated.

   d. One other thing. An Agile Coach is likely to sit outside of HR and can consequently cut across rigid or siloed thinking. That's a good thing.

- **Scrum Master.** If you're doing Agile (and I strongly suggest you do), you'll need a scrum master – the engine room of your implementation that will organize the events where you define Programme Increments and Sprints. They're also vital in helping your team to stick to the Agile approach.

- **Benefits Management.** Remember that Rowan Atkinson sketch from Chapter 3? Well, another line from it was, 'How Would We Know When We'd Got There?'[4] Well, how will you? In the last chapter, we identified a range of potential benefits – financial and otherwise – which can arise from taking specific actions that are enabled by SWP. So, exactly which events trigger benefit realization? When do they realize? How do you ensure there's no double-counting? How do you account for them? All this and more will keep this person fully occupied.

- **Programme Leadership.** Now it's the turn of Agile practitioners to be astonished. Doesn't Highsmith effectively argue that coordination and oversight traditionally done by programme management are effectively delegated to teams?[5] Well yes, but there's also plenty of arguments out there for the need for programme leadership to coordinate multiple teams and maintain alignment to broader goals.[6] I subscribe to the latter view. I've also called this programme leadership and not management.

ESSENTIAL NON-HR FUNCTIONS

- **Financial Planning and Analysis.** I've deliberately broken Finance into two parts for this purpose. FP&A are your natural Finance partners: the clue is in the title and, provided you can demonstrate value (as we discussed in Chapter 6), they will see their involvement in the programme as more than worthwhile.

- **Finance Business Partners.** FBPs may be more sceptical, especially at the sharp end as opposed to the leadership one. They have day-to-day challenges to contend with: worries about controls, overspends, trends and so on. If you're reengineering fulfilment processes (as SWP invariably leads to doing), then the FBP is going to point out where that might be difficult to bring about.

- **Strategy.** Seems obvious, right? Yet how many of you SWP Practitioners out there attend regular strategy team meetings? How many of you observe strategy building sessions or even communicate with strategy setters? How strategy develops and how you respond and contribute to it are crucial in creating traceability between the business strategy and workforce-driven outcomes.

- **Business Operations.** The critical connection with your business leader. If they don't like what you're doing, one word in their leader's ear is all it could take for a refusal to participate or to drag their participating feet. Besides, they're very much the operational glue that drives both business as usual (BAU) and change within a department. They know how the place runs and their nous is every bit as important to you as their buy-in.

- **Supply Chain/Vendor Management.** One of the Big Three B's – Borrow – is almost always managed exclusively by Supply Chain, often a group apart yet with much to offer by way of commercial insight and operational necessity. No SWP implementation should take place without them.

- **Real Estate.** Also known as the Always-The-Last-To-Know team, they're constantly chasing their tails to provide unplanned facilities for planned workers.

By having all these areas represented 'inside the tent', a part of your implementation team, you're not only drawing on their wealth of knowledge and individual expertise; you're also creating a sense of shared ownership and buy-in that they can share with their leadership.

There's one person I've not really mentioned: you. Because it's your leadership – yes, you are the programme leader – that will inspire all the implementation teams to keep their eyes on the prize, that vision that we talked about in Chapter 5. You need to constantly reinforce the 'why', and not just because that's a good thing to do.

This is not just a project team that you're creating; your goal is to build not just cooperation, but 'allies and partners' (as Jane Datta, ex-NASA, put it) for whom this becomes **the** way of working – sharing innovations and ideas in a virtuous cycle of continuous improvement. It's not just a project.

REAL-WORLD EXAMPLE
Jane Doe – unifying disparate SWP efforts

Context and challenge

Jane joined a global organization where each business unit ran its own 'workforce planning', typically using isolated Excel spreadsheets with no enterprise-level governance. Different divisions wanted different levels of detail (e.g. engineers needed meticulous data for a 10-year horizon, while HR or finance might only plan a few years out), causing fragmentation and inconsistent data.

Approach

- **Single Governance thread:** Jane identified and assembled capability leads from each business area, forming a central governance group with a genuine mandate to decide on build/buy/borrow/bot solutions.

- **Toolkit and Common Language:** Jane introduced a starter toolkit to ensure everyone used consistent definitions around skills, gaps and targets – even if some units needed deeper detail than others.

- **Incremental Implementation:** Recognizing that some teams required *extreme* granularity while other areas could be more flexible, Jane tailored the process to each group's comfort level.

Outcomes

- **Consolidation of scattered SWP pockets:** By uniting them under central governance, the organization reduced duplication and unnecessary hiring.

- **Improved internal mobility:** A shared view of the workforce allowed faster, cheaper redeployment of talent rather than external recruitment.

- **Stakeholder buy-in:** Presenting reliable data and success stories (e.g. quick redeployment or upskilling) encouraged reluctant leaders to trust the centralized approach.

Key takeaways

- **Central governance:** Form a strong governance board to unify siloed SWP efforts.

- **Common frameworks:** Even basic standardization fosters consistent language and data sharing.

- **Tailored rollout:** Different divisions need different detail levels; starting with a flexible toolkit is crucial.

Let's just suppose you've already considered all these people: how will you get them onto your implementation team? Are you just going to give them a call and have them come running towards you? It doesn't happen that way. These are all busy folk; you're going to need someone senior to make it clear just how important this project is for them to take notice. You're going to need a sponsor.

'Sponsorship, sponsorship, sponsorship'

I have already said that introducing SWP into an organization is a little bit like dipping your finger into a large pond. As soon as you do that, ripples start to fan out. At some point, every part of the pond will have been rippled by your finger. It's not an overreach to suggest this. If you haven't felt this already, just consider how SWP might affect your organization and you'll soon get the analogy. Are you going to be the one to bind together the organization and galvanize it into concerted and coordinated action? No, you're going to need some leadership muscle that can see the big picture, can understand how SWP could impact it and wants it to do so.

Back in Chapter 3, we talked about SWP needing a bit of a catalyst to come into being – a cause or an issue. That it makes SWP sound almost parasitical is neither here nor there. If there's a cause that SWP can help to enhance, then great. If it's a cause dear to the heart of the CEO, better still.

Jane (case study) was greatly aided in her work by having a CEO who saw SWP as a crucial delivery vehicle for their desired transformation:

> '*So… because we're going through such large transformation and our CEO is very clear on the direction of travel, it's made it easier for me to come into a role like this because the foundations have been set.'*

I once approached a CHRO seeking their sponsorship for the SWP implementation I had been tasked to deliver. 'You can have my name if you like,' they said, 'but I don't see what good it will do. Having my name doesn't mean that everyone will sit up and take notice.' I'll leave you to decide what to think about that response, but my own view is that a project of this breadth and ultimate scale is a whole lot more difficult to achieve without someone very senior being prepared to not only be in your corner but to also fight it. CHRO, COO, CFO, CEO – any of those will do and the more the merrier. A joint statement from those first three that says 'this stuff matters to us as a business' may not throw every door open in a heartbeat but knowing that those people are behind what you're doing helps a lot.

GETTING CXOS INTERESTED

You may wonder therefore how you get those people interested in the first place. Well, it's a bit like painting a room (as I've discovered to my cost). Applying the paint – getting the buy-in – is the last, arguably most straightforward step. The real work lies in the preparation, such as the things we've described in Chapters 4, 5 and 6. Don't just think that doing those things will be enough either.

When someone looks to sell something substantial to a customer, they build a communications plan. Who do the decision-makers listen to? Who do they pick up the phone to ask? That plan helps them to get the decision they seek.

AN EXPERIENCE: NAVIGATING BUY-IN

When positioning programme management software in a very large engineering company, we realized that the buying decision would emerge through the graduate intake network. Director A would receive our product demonstration and listen to what we had to say. As soon as we left the room, Director A would pick up the phone to Project Supervisor B, several levels below them, to get their views. Why? Because A and B were part of the same graduate intake 20 years ago, would meet up regularly still and respected each other's views. B gave A a view from the front line and an opinion unvarnished by hierarchical niceties.

So, before we stepped into the office of Director A, we had spent a lot of time getting to know B and positioning our product with them first. It didn't guarantee us the sale, but if A liked what we had to say, B was already primed to reinforce A's sentiment.

This is no different. Strategic Workforce Planning requires tactical nous as well. You are an influencer and you will need to identify and persuade your potential sponsor's influencers, trusted advisors and friends that this is a good thing for them to support. Hopefully that won't be an argument that you have to win but don't assume that the support for your implementation will come gift-wrapped.

Talking about influencers brings me to something dear to my heart. Much of what I've talked about so far involves people at relatively senior levels of an organization; people with a big-picture understanding of the business and a perspective that is not afforded to everyone. That is not the way most of the people in your organization see the world, which is why I must mention Steve Hackett.

What Steve Hackett taught me about stakeholders

'Supper's Ready' is a song by the English prog rock band Genesis. Widely regarded as their masterpiece in a canon lasting over 20 years, it is also over 20 minutes long.

The climactic section (called As Sure as Eggs is Eggs (Aching Men's Feet) – no, I don't know why either) is soaring and uplifting, especially when seen and heard live, as I did at a concert by their former guitarist, Steve Hackett, almost 50 years after it had been recorded. It really was quite something.

Almost 50 years earlier, a fan approached Steve after a live show and told him that, during that final section, they had seen God. 'I'm glad you saw God,' said Steve, a laconic individual who lets his guitar do most of his talking, 'because I was just trying to play the right notes.' I wrote to him to ask if this was true and he cheerfully obliged.

I'm not ashamed of repeating the story, because it offers a very useful maxim: namely, that however grand or wonderful you might think something is, others might see it very differently. Not just a few others, either. Most people in your organization are just trying to play the right notes, not because they're incapable of seeing the bigger picture but because that's not what they're paid to do. Your grand visions will only mean something to them if they make a positive difference to their working lives. Their sponsorship of what you're doing will be forever unspoken and it will never appear on any slideshow or email to everyone, yet it will be the most important sponsorship of all. Why? Because unless it works for them, unless it helps them in some way, they will simply ignore it.

Even well-planned change initiatives can falter if they do not secure employee buy-in.[7] They are eroded by a failure to embrace change,[8] not in any manning-the-barricades, *Les Misérables*-style act of defiance, but through sidesteps, disuse, discovery of other ways to do things that suit them better or, most damning of all, by simply continuing to do things the way they always did.

If this critical group is to embrace the change, you need to embrace them. Your last and most important team member is the Voice of Your Customer. These are the managers who have to endure the current hiring process; the staff member who throws their hands up in despair at the minefield through which they must tip-toe in order to get a training place; the procurement officer who is overwhelmed with requests for third-party contracts because it's easier to get that kind of resource through the door. In solving the bigger picture problem, you need to understand the smaller ones that make it up. You can't create the Mona Lisa without obliging paint.

Don't just go for token representation in your project team; draw on people from multiple parts of the business and from multiple layers. Their voice must be heard at every stage of your process. A word of warning though: they won't be easy to recruit to your team. The uncomfortable truth is that they will view your efforts to engage with them politely but with considerable scepticism. They will believe they have been here before and saw little benefit arising from this kind of reaching out.

You're ready to start, right?

Well, kind of. You've identified the problems you want to solve. You've created a vision of how things might work to solve them. You've methodically established the potential benefit to the organization of doing this. You've won people over and you have assembled a team of all the talents.

REFLECTIONS

- **You can't implement a plan in isolation.** Fulfilment isn't a downstream project – it *is* the project. Getting the right people in the room early avoids siloed solutions later.

- **Do you know who your fulfilment channels are?** Take a blank sheet and write down all the teams, departments or individuals who might play a part, however small, in executing the workforce plan. Then circle the ones you've actually spoken to.

- **Sponsorship is more than a name at the top.** Real sponsorship comes from those who can galvanize, build trust and clear roadblocks – not just from formal titles. That said, you need a strong sponsor for when the going gets political (and it will). If everyone has an equal voice but no one has authority, you're in trouble.

- **The Voice of the Customer must be heard.** The success of your implementation often lies not with the C-suite but with the people trying to 'play the right notes' while everything changes around them. Not token people or those who once worked on the shop floor five years ago, but people with real, lived experience of the day-to-day pain points. If you're solving the wrong problems, you'll implement beautifully and achieve very little.

- **Are you ready for some doors not to open?** Even with C-suite backing, not every team will be won over immediately. That's fine. Build proof, show value and let success travel by word of mouth. It usually works better than waving a mandate around anyway.

So, what next? Anyone who's been through this process will tell you that that question is not as easy to answer as it might seem. But heck, let's try to answer it anyway in the next chapter. Brace yourself.

Notes

1   Galbraith, J R (2014) *Designing Organizations: Strategy, structure, and process at the business unit and enterprise levels*, 3rd ed, San Francisco: Jossey-Bass
2   Cummings, T G and Worley, C G (2014) *Organization Development and Change*, 10th ed, Stamford: Cengage Learning
3   Dingsøyr, T, Nerur, S, Balijepally, V and Moe, N B (2012) A decade of agile methodologies: Towards explaining agile software development, *Journal of Systems and Software*, 85(6), pp. 1213–21
4   Atkinson, R and Curtis, R (1980) Sir Marcus Browning MP. Performed by Rowan Atkinson [Audio recording] In: Live in Belfast. London: Arista Records
5   Highsmith, J (2009) *Agile Project Management: Creating innovative products*, 2nd ed. Boston: Addison-Wesley

6 Project Management Institute (2017) *The Agile Practice Guide*, Newtown Square, PA: Project Management Institute

7 Kotter, J P (1995) Leading Change: Why transformation efforts fail, *Harvard Business Review*, 73(2), pp. 59–67

8 Armenakis, A A, Harris, S G and Mossholder, K W (1993) Creating readiness for organizational change, *Human Relations*, 46(6), pp. 681–703

08

Turn and face the strange

Bringing about changes

You have to change in this space. You've got to think about the way your workforce, the way you set up your operations, your organizational structure has to evolve.

ALAN SUSI, S&P GLOBAL

Implementing SWP is an act of change. A rather large act. Unless you're a change practitioner, this can be a rather alien world of Gantt charts, RAG statuses, pilots and deliverables. This book won't help you to understand those, but hopefully they are secondary to the key issues to consider. For me, they are these:

- what makes this kind of change challenging
- where to start
- how to organize
- creating governance
- knowing if you're getting anywhere

That's what we'll cover here. But first, a confession.

When I was around 11 or 12 years old, I was a trainspotter.

I'm not sure if this is a peculiarly English thing, but it basically involves looking out for a train engine that you haven't seen before and either writing its number in a book or crossing it off a list of numbers that are known to exist. I don't know if crossing off the numbers of train engines is something that pre-pubescent boys in general find irresistible, but I know that I was not alone in doing this at that age. Only later did I discover that the soccer ground whose distant roar I could hear from about half a mile away on a Saturday afternoon held more emotional appeal, despite being equally inconsequential.

I like trains, as does my friend Simon. A one-time high-flying IT executive, he now spends much of his retirement learning to be a specialist carpenter restoring dilapidated old railway carriages to a pristine, 1950s-era condition.

Simon's pastime is a leisurely one. Hand-picked wood is lovingly trimmed, fashioned, sanded into the shape pre-ordained by blueprints and then varnished into gleaming excellence before it is expertly affixed to the carriage undergoing restoration, anchored in a covered workshop, where it clicks seamlessly into place alongside all of the other wonderfully crafted efforts of the other volunteers.

Implementing SWP in an organization is a little bit like restoring a railway carriage. But only a very little bit.

To start with, your carriage will be out in the open, exposed to the elements where a sudden rain shower or storm might undo considerable amounts of the work you've already done. There are no blueprints, so you have to work out what needs to be created and how it's going to fit. The materials you have to work with are of varying quality and sometimes not known until you've taken them out of their packaging. You've got to strip away parts of the carriage that don't work anymore. Oh, and the train is moving, quickly, to its destination that it must reach on time. Oh, and there are passengers in the carriage, expecting to be served their tea and cakes as though nothing else is going on.

And yet, in spite of all this chaos – or perhaps because of it – SWP must not only be implemented but trusted to work. This chapter looks at how you might do that.

Let's start at the very beginning?

One of the most frequent questions posed by people who are about to start introducing SWP to their organization is where on earth they're supposed to start; this is often compounded by their being given no choice in the matter. Several of the advertisements that I've seen for SWP leaders aren't really for SWP leaders at all, at least to begin with. No, the initial ask is actually for someone who is going to implement SWP for them. This is why it's a good idea to have a few questions up your sleeve when going into an interview for such a position. You'll find some clues in the preceding chapters.

I always find it fascinating how, in many of the interviews I've attended, the hiring manager feels they have to explain to me the circumstances around the appointment, when you would think they had a whole advertisement to explain that. But that's typically what happens, accompanied by some diplomatic attempts to describe some of the rank organizational chaos that may have preceded the decision to hire. In Chapter 3 I talked about there sometimes needing to be some kind of crisis that might precipitate a hire. That's not necessarily a bad thing, because this is a big undertaking that doesn't need to be triggered by anything terribly trivial.

That's not the issue. The issue is that the hiring manager has already decided what kind of implementation they want.

Here are just a few examples of phrases that you might hear:

- 'We need to implement a framework by Q3 across the business to address an audit concern.'
- 'I'm looking for someone who is okay with scrappy.'
- 'We've already established a team and have a set of OKR's for you to deliver.'
- 'Once you've helped us sort out our Resource Management setup, we can move on to implementing SWP.'
- 'Erm… well, we're working on securing the funding for a project, so you'll be an individually contributing disrupter within our existing business-as-usual setup, which we think could be jolly exciting.'

Maybe you've heard something similar.

It's not for me to tell anyone where in the process they should start; they don't always get the choice, but it's worth remembering nevertheless what this ultimately is – a process. In its basic form, the process of workforce planning is devastatingly simple:

The object of the exercise is to get from its beginning to its end. Now, this sounds about as simple as asking someone to move a piano from one room to another, until you discover that the piano is in a room in London and needs to be moved to a room in Bogota.

Wherever you find yourself starting, all roads lead back to that process. The only question is whether you get to nail the process – I prefer operating model – before you implement SWP or afterwards. It's too simplistic to say that one of these is necessarily more painful than the other, because they both have their downsides:

FIGURE 8.1 The devastatingly simple process

TABLE 8.1 The pros and cons of process vs implementation

Process first, implement second	Implement first, process second
PRO: Done right, it ensures that there is nothing stopping you from executing the strategy more effectively.	PRO: You get something up and running fast, even if it's just part of the framework: it's a quick win and you can always fix any issues afterwards.
PRO: Scaling up can be a more measured, managed process than a big bang.	CON: You never get to fix the issues because other stuff gets in the way.
CON: People might become impatient for some results, because getting it right can take time.	CON: It's highly unlikely that anyone will think things are better; all you've done is give them more work to do with no gain.
CON: Done wrong, you can still run into roadblocks down the line and that will make it take even longer.	CON: You could burn out everyone – including yourself – by trying to put in place something that is bound to be incomplete and therefore frustrating.
CON: You could encounter an insurmountable showstopper: what will you do then?	CON: You could encounter an insurmountable showstopper: what will you do then?

The duplication at the end is deliberate. Making the right choice here matters and it's not just down to what sounds like the right thing to do. With the right sponsorship and support around you, implementing first and sorting out the process later could well be the right thing, because it can show a committed sponsor-CEO just how advanced (or not) an organization is in its thinking and behaviours and spur them into backing the project even further.

If I had a Bitcoin for every time someone has warned me about boiling the ocean, I'd still have no idea what Blockchain actually is, so I was spoiled for choice when it came to choosing quotes from those I have spoken to on the topic. This one – describing an SWP implementer's attempts to implement first and address the process second – is by no means unique:

> 'They tried to force the philosophy, kind of, boil the ocean in a way, try to support all business units... and pushed a little too hard and burned out a couple of HRBPs... it all kind of went down in flames from there.' – Anonymous Practitioner

One of the more maddening aspects of SWP is that there is invariably no absolute right or wrong answer to almost anything; my own belief is that I would far rather make sure that I have unblocked every dam before I start pumping vast quantities of water down the channel I've created. It also has the virtue of really binding in tightly all those different fulfilment partner representatives, because you're not the one who is going to come up with the end-state processes – they are.

REAL-WORLD EXAMPLE
Start somewhere – Jill Dobbe

Context

Jill launched SWP at a global Fortune 100 company and now works at Orgvue, where she helps organizations use technology for SWP: 'I find that each time, leaders first want a "push the button solution".' They countered with an end-to-end pilot – tiny in scope, but complete in method.

What Jill has seen work

TABLE 8.2 The Jill Dobbe Principles

Principle	Explanation
Start small	Don't attempt to 'boil the ocean'. Trying to include every worker type or tackle all data issues up front can stall momentum. Begin with what you have.
Pilot before scaling	'Start somewhere – just start... If you try to start at the beginning with all of it, you probably won't get started.' Contained pilots give traction without overwhelming the organization.
Embed learning into each cycle	'The value is in the learnings... from the first cycle to the second... to the fourth.' Each cycle should refine both process and assumptions.
Balance finance involvement	The best implementations involve finance listening and contributing, not dominating. 'Too much' or 'not at all' both undermine success.
Secure sponsorship for the long term	'Of course it has to have sponsorship... and leadership commitment to the three to five years to be able to make it work.' A rolling plan enables agility when markets shift.
Show progress	Learning alone won't convince hard-nosed stakeholders. 'Preciseness of the projection', 'closing demand-supply gaps' or 'influencing cost or decisions' are vital proof points.

Cultural context matters

Jill highlights the structural and cultural differences between the United States and elsewhere. 'In the US we can say, "you're employed today and tomorrow you're gone"... Elsewhere, we need to be more strategic and more thoughtful because it takes longer to make change.' This means the approach to workforce planning – and how long it takes to show value – must be adjusted accordingly.

Lessons you can lift

- A tiny, complete pilot beats a giant half-built programme.
- Finance partnership is a spectrum – absence or domination both fail.
- Prove the operating model first.
- Your licence to operate renews each cycle – show precision gains or cost influence every year.

Jill's view on getting started

'Start somewhere – just start. Talking forever kills momentum.'

'If you try to start at the beginning with all of it, you probably won't get started.'

'Start with what you have and then build from there.'

Let's get to work(streams)

The detailed model that I drew in Chapter 5 has to be brought to life and that means creating something that will actually work, is well-informed and will be accepted. As somebody put it to me:

> *'When your deliverable stops being PowerPoint and starts being something that actually affects the business, the game changes. The theory is neat and tidy, but the practice is different.'* – Naima Robenhagen Burgdorf

This is neither a quick nor an easy thing to do and that means setting some expectations from the very beginning. I make no apologies for peppering this chapter with quotes from other practitioners, but bear with me while I give you another one, exactly as it was said to me by Naima again:

> 'Believe it or not, it's the thing around leadership teams and organizations being like, "yeah, we wanna, we wanna get to the summit and we, we want that picture, that selfie with the flag that we plant on the summit." But then, like, "oh, oh, we have to, we have to train for that? And we have to hire Sherpas and we have to have the gear and we have to, oh, we have to, oh, we have to go all the way and put in, like, the ropes that are attached to the eyes and then we go up the mountain? No, we don't, we don't actually want to do that. We just want the picture".'

So before we go any further with the sombre warnings, exactly what is the mountain that needs to be climbed and how difficult is it?

My dog, Dylan, is a 15-inch high Cavachon; he is not a big dog. So when I – being somewhat bigger – take him for a walk, I seem to have all the advantages when it comes to deciding where we are going to go. Yet that walk will abruptly halt if Dylan decides that he doesn't want to go any further. With all four heels dug in, refusing to shift, he defiantly dares me to try. There is no way that he will move unless I pick him up or head home.

Now imagine that I have five or six Dylans, all joined together. If one or more of them decides they want to stop, we won't get very far.

Then imagine that I have not one string of five or six Dylans, but five or six strings. Not only does this make for a lot of complexity, it also requires me to carry an awful lot of poo bags. This is what you're trying to make happen when you implement SWP in an organization. Without the poo bags.

So let's try to create some order out of this apparent chaos. You're not trying to assemble a train carriage and you're not trying to boil the ocean or walk multiple pooches. These are the pieces that need to have life breathed into them:

1   Having something that will tell you what is going on with your people (that's your people analytics).

2   Having some idea of what the business wants to do (that's your Business Operations and Strategy folks) and how that's gathered and processed.

3   Consuming the other inputs that will help your personal filter room to start providing some output and insight.

4 Deciding how you're going to convey what you've learned.

5 Determining how you'll then settle on a workforce plan (and why).

6 Having some idea of how you're going to maximize the value available from this longer Window of Opportunity (this is down to your fulfilment partners).

7 Having some idea of how you will assess and manage progress.

8 Knowing how you will handle deviation and necessary changes.

Now you might cry foul, because I've been pretty flippant with the well-established staged process model for workforce planning (strategy, supply, demand, gap analysis, execution, monitor). It's not that I'm not taking these things seriously, quite the opposite, but absolutes are strangers to this SWP world and you have to set your sights realistically to begin with. Put simply, this will not work the first time you try it. Nor will it probably work a lot better the second time. And since these things tend to run in annual cycles, there's a certain lag between attempts.

My son's girlfriend unwittingly provides a good analogy here. She's a marine biologist and she takes small pieces of coral, attaches them to something called a star frame, places the frame in the sea and, bit by bit, the coral pieces grow until they fuse and form something cohesive and strong. Your project will succeed through a similar kind of organic growth: you have to fertilize it just enough so it can grow.

We've already looked at item 1 – the people analytics piece – in Chapter 4 and this is fundamental workstream for your project: let's call it Data and Tooling for the sake of simplicity and let's add item 7 – monitoring progress – to that stream as well.

Items 2, 3 and 4 inhabit the space of darker arts – the actual practice of Strategic Workforce Planning itself – and is an obvious workstream. Less obvious is the grouping of 5 and 8 into a Governance workstream, but it is in this space, the one where rules are set, decisions argued over, positions taken and authority stamped, that some of the toughest debates and frameworks need to be forged.

Fulfilment is a workstream in its own right and it's where you'll find multiple strings of joined-together Dylans. It's essential to have it as one workstream, not multiple function/silo-based ones. It's vital for them to continually calibrate and align, including your supply chain/vendor procurement function. One of the fundamental transformations you're bringing about is the definition of fulfilment as an alliance, not a set of separate solutions.

Your final workstream – it can be two – is programme management and benefit tracking. The first is obvious but the second is a must. Be laser-focused on the value points, the moments of crystallization, the way they're accumulated, verified and publicized. Yes, publicized. Communications is a critical element of change management in a project such as this. The very fact that it can take 80,000 words to explain SWP is surely proof enough of the need for a comms-centred approach. So, to summarize:

SOME ESSENTIAL WORK STREAMS

- Data and tooling

- SWP Practice

- Governance

- Fulfilment

- Programme, communication and benefits

As I will say repeatedly, other approaches are available and you have to use your judgement to decide what's right for you.

We talked about data in Chapter 4; we'll consider tooling in Chapter 15 and we will talk a lot more about practice in Chapters 10 and 11. Benefits will come to the fore in Chapter 12 and I've already outlined the kind of things you can do from a fulfilment perspective in Chapter 6 (although we'll return to some of those things shortly).

That leaves us with Governance. Strap in.

Order, order

Governance in business process management refers to the assignment of decision-making responsibilities, the definition of roles and responsibilities, and the establishment of rules, policies, and procedures that guide the execution and evolution of business processes.[1]

There are other, let's call them more prosaic, definitions:

> *'Governance is the organization of management. It refers to the goals, principles, organization charts that define who can make what decisions, as well as the policies and rules that define or constrain what managers can do.'* – Paul Harmon[2]

I suspect that people will side with one of these two definitions more than the other. It's a corporate truth that, in seeking well-managed business operations, almost anything of significance that someone wants to do in a business requires someone else to tell them that they can do it. The effectiveness of that form of governance is not the topic here. SWP is not going to overturn decades of carefully constructed governance merely by turning up.

So this is a non-exhaustive list of questions which, for me, mark the minimum level of diligence you should undertake. Our next chapter deals extensively with the objections that people raise and the change resistance they put up, so try not to throw up your hands in horror just yet.

What do you intend to happen as a result of an SWP being produced?
Yes, the hard ones first. It goes to the heart of your purpose in deploying SWP – is it to enable more optimal fulfilment, to manage costs, to test strategy feasibility, all of the above or none of them?

How is the plan to be approved?
How granular is your organization? Are there multiple airlocks through which the plan must pass before it reaches someone who is sufficiently empowered to say yes or no? Is it a central process or a federated one? (Hint: if you're in a federated company, let them decide their own approval governance; that way, they remain accountable for it and you don't.)

What criteria should be met if your plan is to be approved?
This will help to define whether your organization is really after a genuinely Strategic Workforce Plan or an Operational one. Even a subtle difference – like meeting a fixed budget target versus aiming to reduce unit costs by 5 per cent over three years – can reveal what kind of plan the business really wants. But there will be a range of others, such as advancing your diversity agenda, reducing (or increasing) external staff or offshore ratios or maintaining a flat total cost of labour.

How would you ensure that a team which planned 'well' benefited from doing so?
Crucial for you to provide both incentive and penalty for (respectively) active or passive participation. We'll look at how this can be used to

especially strong advantage in our next chapter. Clue: it also involves the use of governance.

What further benefit might there be for a team that executed in line with the plan?

The precursor to this of course is deciding what 'in line' might mean. At its simplest it might mean that the headcount or cost numbers stay on track. But there might be other behavioural outcomes that you're looking to achieve. Let's suppose that your Supply Chain team has crafted special, exclusive deals with a third-party supplier that are a lot cheaper per person per day. You want those deals to be exercised and not just gather dust. So make it worthwhile to hire people through that channel.

What tolerances would you allow for deviation from plan, and what would you do if those tolerances were breached?

Too often, governance can be mistaken for slavish adherence. Giant claxons sound and squads of senior managers descend on a hapless unit that has deviated by so much as a single headcount from what they said they would have. Is that the kind of governance that you want to have? Or might it be better to accept that things don't always go to plan and allow some latitude before you bring down the iron railings and the heavy mob? If so, what should that latitude involve and can you be clear about what might happen if someone took excessive advantage of it? Some governance – often hiring governance – talks a tough game but meekly steps aside in the face of the flimsiest argument. Is that going to be you?

How would you know tolerances were being breached or neared?

A brilliant example of how people analytics could be deployed to illustrate not just whether a unit was running hot, but also why.

How would you manage changes that needed to be made to the plan?

Generalfeldmarschall von Moltke (Chapter 2 – remember him?) was clear that plans change and you have to adapt them. What's a good change and what is not? How will you decide which is which and what will you do as a consequence? If your process is going to work from end to end, you need to know.

How would you ensure there remained an adequate controls framework if you altered approaches to hiring?

A good way to ensure that people will turn against you will be if you propose removing certain approval rights or controls without providing proof positive that controls will persist. Risk and financial controls can't just melt away; you need to show how and where controls continue to ensure people are doing the right thing.

This is just a flavour for you to think about and act upon as you develop your implementation project. By nailing these issues early, the process you pilot will successfully absorb into your pilot unit, which will become the champion for other units to follow.

Don't drop the pilot

If you want a champion, they need to have a good reason for championing you. You'll do that by demonstrating that the process you are building will enable them to address a specific challenge that they face. We're getting ahead of ourselves a little bit, because I want to handle resistance in our next chapter. However, not everyone needs persuading about the potential value. So if you have those in your business, work with them but, crucially, do so to solve a problem they have along the way. After all, you're doing this for the good of the business, aren't you?

A word of caution though. Make sure the process really works. You'll be under pressure to make advances, but here's what one practitioner said to me:

> 'We did two or three pilots at the tail end of last year... I would have waited a bit longer...[to] get some of the foundational basics more established before trying to demonstrate value quickly.'

How do you know it's working?

Check, check and check again. Check within your project team members. Check with friendly colleagues in Risk, in Finance, in the business units themselves. Describe your ideas and get their feedback. Prototype your options: do they work? What falls over? How do you fix them? Hold a Show and Tell every two weeks in front of senior stakeholders. Even if you're demonstrating nothing more than a new sound that goes 'ting' – provided that 'ting' can be shown to be taking you successfully towards your end goal, then you are building or maintaining a sense of delivery momentum. Success breeds success, as they say.

You won't get it perfect – and that's the point. You're building something adaptive, iterative and collaborative. If what you've done so far gets you onto the mountain slopes, the next chapter is about what happens when the mountain pushes back.

REFLECTIONS

- **SWP implementation isn't linear.** It's carpentry on a moving train, with paying passengers on board.

- **There's no perfect starting point.** But there's always that best next step.

- **Process or implementation first?** Either can work. What matters is clarity, sponsorship and adaptability.

- **Fulfilment isn't a bunch of separate channels.** It's an alliance that must be aligned and actively managed.

- **Communication is your ally.** Keep showing progress, even if all you've got is something that goes 'ting'.

- **Governance matters.**

- **This is like coral.** Frame it right and let it take hold.

Notes

1 Dumas, M, La Rosa, M, Mendling, J and Reijers, H A (2018) *Fundamentals of Business Process Management*, 2nd ed. Cham: Springer

2 Harmon, P (2008) Process Governance, *BPTrends Advisor*, 6(3)

09

Siren voices

Resistance, lack of interest and incentive

When people say they can't plan the future, I ask if they're going anywhere nice on holiday. Then I ask: where, who with, when, how are you getting there? Suddenly they can answer everything. It shows they can plan; they just haven't invested the same thought process at work.

PRACTITIONER LEGEND LINDSEY CLARKE

The last time I counted, I had amassed 1,109 quotes from 58 separate contributors, the largest portion related to this chapter's themes about pushback. They are, however, themes that run throughout the entire book; much of making SWP operational is about winning over people who don't always want to be won over. In more conventional books this is called stakeholder management and I don't propose to try to teach anyone a thing or two about that, but I'm beginning to think that there's an entire book waiting to be written about overcoming resistance to SWP. In a broader book such as this, this chapter on resistance can only scratch the surface.

I believe the term 'stakeholder' can be drawn very widely here. If your employees aren't feeling the value from SWP (even if they wouldn't call it that) then maybe you're not reaching the parts of the organization that you need to reach.

If only this was the sole origin of potential pushback or resistance. There's a bit more to it though than that, which is what we're now going to consider. So I distilled the comments I'd received into some recurring paraphrases and funnelled them into a word cloud. This cloud paraphrases the most common things I heard practitioners say they are told. Some are blunt, some more nuanced – but together they illustrate a consistent backdrop of hesitancy, confusion and territorial friction.

FIGURE 9.1 SWP Objections Word Cloud[1]

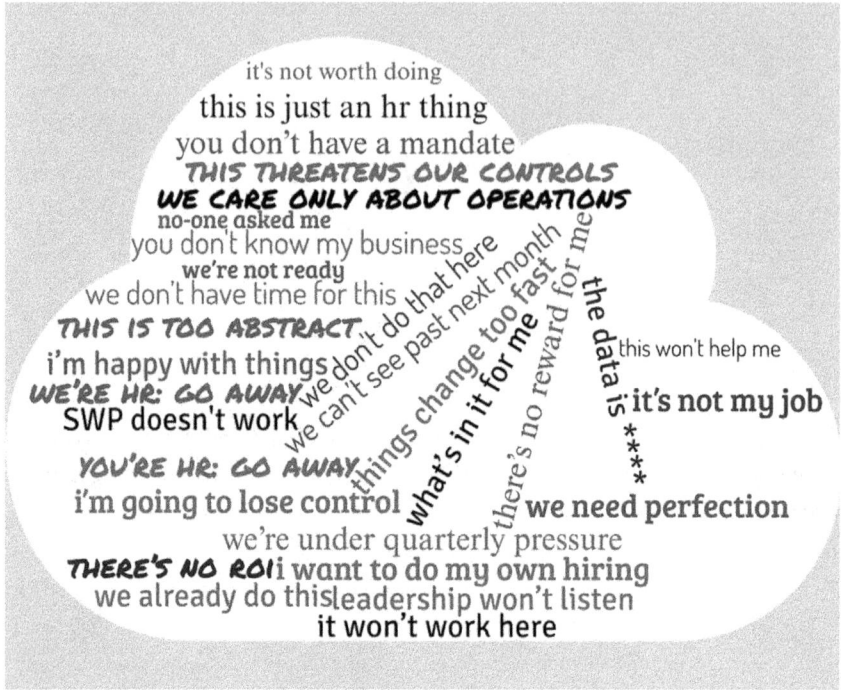

Here's the list.

REASONS (NOT) TO BE CHEERFUL – BARRIERS AND RESISTANCE

- **Short-termism and urgency**
  - We can't see beyond next month
  - Things change too fast for us to plan
  - There's no immediate ROI
  - We don't have time for this
  - We're under quarterly pressure
  - We're focused on ops, not strategy

- **Mindset and capability gaps**
  - We're not ready
  - We need a perfect forecast
  - Planning feels too abstract
  - It's not my job to think that far ahead
  - We've tried SWP before: it didn't work
  - That's not how we've done it
- **Misunderstanding or misclassification**
  - We already do this
  - This is just an HR exercise
  - This won't help me with my day job
- **Ownership and territory**
  - You know nothing about my business
  - I'm going to lose control of things
  - I want to do my own hiring
  - This threatens the controls we have in place
  - I'm happy with how things are
  - You don't have any mandate with me
- **Organizational or structural resistance**
  - It won't work here
  - Leadership won't listen
  - We don't think it's worth doing
  - We don't trust the data
- **Motivational or political dynamics**
  - What's in it for me?
  - There's no reward for long-term thinking
  - Stop this now: no one asked me
  - You're HR: go away
  - We're HR: go away

Now, none of these phrases are new. But what's interesting – *really* interesting – about this list is how very few of them relate to process, tooling or data. They're mostly human, emotional and cultural. Not all of them, but many more than I expected. We should also recognize – as if you hadn't already – that some of these paraphrases are really saying something starker: we don't want to do this.

Some practitioners liken introducing SWP to trench warfare: every objection must be battered down – often repeatedly, with different people (and sometimes the same people) – before you make real headway.

There is no blanket answer to every challenge; sometimes the best approach is to back off altogether if the resistance is strong. As one practitioner puts it:

> 'I'm not going to force SWP on someone who isn't ready. We decided we're not asking a fish to climb a tree anymore. If it's not the right environment, it's not going to work, so why waste time?'

So let's start digging into these different themes and look at ways you might be able to break down a barrier or two.

Addressing resistance

Short-termism and urgency

- We can't see beyond next month
- Things change too fast for us to plan
- There's no immediate ROI
- We don't have time for this
- We're under quarterly pressure
- We're focused on ops, not strategy

This essentially falls into two distinct themes:

1 Our only focus is quarter-end.
2 We've got no idea what might happen in the longer term.

QUARTER-END FOCUS

> '[Leaders rarely] get rewarded for time spent on strategy... even top execs are
> basically focusing on quarterly operations. It's not malevolence – it's how they're
> measured. SWP struggles if you can't get them to carve out time for five-year
> thinking.' – Jordan Pettman

It's true as well as completely understandable. Thirteen-week cycles, and at the end of each lies the expectation of outcomes, results and progress. 'The tyranny of the urgent', as someone described it.

But that tyranny can be counterintuitive. 'Quarterly report pressure... drives knee-jerk cuts,' says Jill Dobbe of Orgvue; 'you need a rolling three-to-five-year plan to absorb those blips instead of lurching.'

Someone I worked with put this into context a few years ago. 'If you look at our investment funding over the past few years,' they said, 'each part of the business will complain that it's pretty lumpy, causing them to go through a regular and depressing cycle of hire and fire. However, the total funding for the company over that time has been pretty much the same. So how is it that we're having to fire ANYONE? And how is it that 50 per cent of our workforce therefore has to be external, costing us a fortune?'

Jordan Pettman, one-time SWP Guru at Insight222, echoes this:

> 'There's so much change hitting every industry that if leaders only do short-run
> operational reactions, they'll sabotage long-term viability. This is exactly where SWP
> must pay off.'

And if you think this is a statement of the obvious, then you tell me how many permanent staff were let go in one part of the business while people were being hired in another.

The longer-term approach is therefore to take the average total people requirement over the period, allow for some degree of flex that can be accommodated by temporary staff – say 10 per cent – and that gives you the permanent establishment that you'll work with.

Is it that simple? Well no, because not everyone is interchangeable, because some people will be in the wrong place at the wrong time and because getting people from one part of the business to another may require retraining, which itself takes time.

> 'Finance wants immediate cost results, but developing an upskilled workforce might take a year. So we keep reminding them, if we do short-term cuts, we might harm our pipeline's capacity. There's always that tension – quarterly cost vs. long-term readiness.' – Dibyendu Sharma, Unisys

But by taking this longer view, you can manage the workforce differently, as a workforce for the whole company and not just for one part of it. And that's interesting, because that's who your workforce's employment contract is with, although you wouldn't always know that. How is this good for quarterly outcomes? Well, you can expect to see a reduction in overall unit labour costs because you'll be using a more regulated level of external staff and you can expect to see reductions in the number of people being made redundant overall – always assuming, of course, that this is a course that you're prepared to stick to for at least a couple of years to allow it to mature.

You might also want to consider changing your resource management model.

HYPOTHETICAL EXAMPLE
Creating an enterprise-wide talent bench

Problem

It's not uncommon for large enterprises to have federated, semi-autonomous divisions where people who do the same or similar things are scattered across them.

It's still not unusual for each division to maintain its own job-description library and career frameworks.

When fresh orders arrive, each business looks only at its own headcount and, if short, hires externally, often at a premium.

Given the pace of change, you might sense a looming technical skills crisis but have no enterprise level view of what skills you have or how they're being deployed.

Possible intervention

- **Reduce complexity.** Distil career development frameworks and job profiles to one common core skillset/task set framework.

- **Lift people out of silos.** Remove common capabilities from their divisions into a central Centre of Excellence.
- **Run as an internal consultancy.** Common talent sits in a central talent pool and is assigned to projects and tasks across any division. Skills are matched to work; divisions no longer own the majority of the people.

Potential impact

- A single pool can minimize any immediate skills shortage crisis.
- Visibility into actual skills allows rapid redeployment.
- Upskilling bridges domain gaps while allowing fundamental skills transfer.
- Costs fall (fewer premium hires).

Key takeaways

- Job description overdose hides capability. Standardize first.
- Talent benches give large organizations resilience and agility that silos cannot.
- Skills portability and targeted reskilling beats 'hire more' reactions and can defuse looming shortages.

As for the argument that you can't see beyond the next three months, well I'd refer you to the peerless quote at the beginning of this chapter. And if that doesn't work, then I have two questions for you:

1   So will you be making and selling exactly the same in three or five years as you are making and selling now?

2   (Assuming the answer is 'I very much doubt it') So what do you think's going to be different?

And let the conversation begin.

Mindset and capability gaps

- We're not ready
- We need a perfect forecast

- Planning feels too abstract
- It's not my job to think that far ahead
- We've tried SWP before: it didn't work
- That's not how we've done it

I believe the first three have been answered elsewhere in this book already:

- We're not ready – in Chapters 3 and 8, where we note the importance of organizational readiness.
- We need a perfect forecast – in Chapter 2 where we recognized the need to navigate uncertainty and Chapters 4 and 8 which emphasized the need to act with imperfect data, because perfection simply isn't out there.
- Planning feels too abstract – the adapted definition I suggested in Chapter 2 – rendering the workforce fit for the purpose of executing business strategy – offers a practical response to this suggestion.

But the last three – ooh yes.

IT'S NOT MY JOB....

There are circumstances where this is a completely acceptable answer. Take this example from Dirk Jonker, CEO of technology vendor Crunchr:

> 'Fulfilment centre leaders plan hour by hour. Hourly plans roll up into half-day plans, those into day plans, week plans, and that's their world. When HR walks in talking SWP – automation in five years, skill taxonomies – they get an allergic reaction. These people will never debate the impact of automation three years out; it's outside their scope. HR has little to do in that short-term horizon.'

However, if that's not the kind of operation you're managing....

Yes, it is your job. If you're a manager, you have been entrusted not only with the responsibility for getting something done but with a responsibility for the stewardship of the part of the business for which you are responsible, however small that might be. Or do you plan to simply muddle on through for the next however many years and hope that you have people who can maybe cope with whatever turns up then? Don't be surprised if the next restructuring announcement comes as a total shock.

WE'VE TRIED SWP BEFORE: IT DIDN'T WORK.

Yes, so have I. I remember the first time I was asked to participate in the exercise. Someone gave me a very large sheet of paper drawn into quadrants, with a block for future challenges, one for the effect on the business, one for what skills we'd therefore need.

Yes, I've only mentioned three quadrants. We did the first two quite well, considering we'd never done it before, but when we got to box number three we just came to a halt. The leap to come up with a set of skills without data, technology or advice to guide us was simply too great. Besides, we were really asking the wrong questions. In this next disclosure from an active practitioner, the challenge of having been there, tried it, dismissed it was all too stark.

REAL-WORLD EXAMPLE

A legacy of failed attempts – a practitioner's story

This practitioner wanted to remain anonymous. They recently joined this US-based consumables/medical organization of over 5,000 employees.

Something I didn't anticipate coming into this role was the negative perception people already had of workforce planning. We've failed with it three times:

- The first attempt was all very theoretical and academic.
- The second was 'busy work': job families, 'critical role' exercises that just annoyed everyone.
- The third was almost solely about skills which, on their own, are [a] nebulous thing.

Business leaders put in the effort and got nothing back, so now they [plan] on their own with their own tools. One HR partner said, 'our leaders won't participate with HR at all'.

I realized I had a branding issue to fix before I had any chance of getting this off the ground. I started a listening tour to feel the scars. One leader was polite but the real message was, 'Don't talk to me about this anymore'.

What should they have got? A plan they can execute and monitor, so that six months later we can look back and ask, 'Was that decision right? If not, change course.' The purpose of workforce planning is to inform a business decision and have a measurable outcome. They'd never seen an outcome.

So I follow the enthusiasm: deliver for two or three units first, show tangible value, then approach the sceptics with a finished product instead of another data request. We're building a single metrics set – cost of workforce including contingent labour, spans and layers post-reorg, thresholds that trigger action.

[This] reputation problem bleeds into people analytics too: leaders ask for more dashboards, but when we come back with planning questions, they push us away. PA can't just be 10 pages of dashboards; someone has to say which metric is flashing red and what the decision is.

You can see how these objections bleed into each other, but an overriding plea comes through: put yourself in the shoes of the people who are actually running the business and look at those things that are troubling them. Make something – anything – work for them and earn their confidence and trust. We'll talk about this a lot more in Chapter 11.

THAT'S NOT HOW WE DO IT HERE.
I see. How's what you're doing now working out?

Motivational or political dynamics

- What's in it for me?
- There's no reward for long-term thinking
- Stop this now: no one asked me
- You're HR: go away
- We're HR: go away

The messages are clear:

- I'm terribly important
- You are not wanted here
- What's in it for me?

I'M TERRIBLY IMPORTANT
If you've assembled layers of sponsorship and engagement, the likelihood that someone will feel they have been ignored is a relatively small one. However, there will always be someone – or someone new – who will not be aware of what you've been putting together and you should arm yourself with a briefing pack for anyone for whom what you're doing is new news. **Rehearse this,** preferably with an already-friendly stakeholder who will be happy to point out the glaring holes in your presentation (yes, there will be some). Better still, hold an all-day or a half-day objections workshop in

which you develop the full range of arguments against what you're doing and the answers that will allay any concerns.

YOU ARE NOT WANTED HERE

If that's the vibe you're getting, either from HR itself, or because you are from HR, you're entitled to ask why that is. Either you're a threat, or you're perceived as a nuisance. In either situation, your response needs to be the same. Do something that will make their life easier, make them look better, or preferably both.

We're HR...   In this situation, you pose a threat to the established order of things and to existing ways of working. One example?

> 'Our country Talent Acquisition Partner speaks to their business leader every week to find out what hires they need and which ones we need to cancel – we don't need anyone else asking them the same questions, you'll upset them.'

Let's unpack that one. What this says to me is this:

- The TA Partner has a close and frequent working relationship with their customer.
- The TA Partner hasn't been given any long-term view of likely need, so they **have** to speak to the customer weekly to avoid being overwhelmed suddenly by a barrage of requests.
- Hiring is reactive and there's no evidence of any pipeline in operation.
- There's a lack of certainty about the need – hence the cancellations.
- The TA Partner probably feels overworked and frustrated.

Back to that Window of Opportunity diagram from Chapter 1. With a better view of the long term, the TA Partner can map out a hiring campaign that's primed to bring candidates on stream within a given time box. It won't be exact or perfect, but the purpose of the weekly call is no longer to pick up the latest box of surprises, but to review the plan against the current state and to agree on any adjustments. That's the TA Partner now feeling able to do a much better version of their job. SWP is an enabler for a variety of people to bring to their job the excellence they know that they can.

You're HR...   In this case, you might be tempted to say that yes, you are HR but you're different: well, they all say that. The more powerful approach, however, could be something like this:

NO WIN, NO SEE

'Yes, you're right, our reputation isn't great is it? But the only reason anyone brings SWP into any company is to help the business, or there's no real point to my being here. So you have nothing to lose and everything to gain from my trying to make a difference for your part of the business. I want you to feel that HR might be of some use after all, but I won't impose some random solution upon you and I won't try to manufacture a success that isn't there. If I can't make a difference or if I fail, I'll go away.

So, to start with I have just three questions:

1   What's causing you the biggest worries about the next three or so years?

2   What's the single biggest workforce issue that you'd like to get fixed?

3   What's the biggest objective this year for you, professionally?'

Now we're jumping ahead a little to Chapter 11, where I want to dive more into the questions that will help you to elicit both a response and the chance to make something good happen. You'll notice, though, a couple of things about the questions:

- The answers might well have nothing to do with SWP…yet.
- They're personal. You, not your business. You. Because caring about your business really entails caring about you.

WHAT'S IN IT FOR ME?

Well, in the absence of the killer response that we'd all like to give – 'continued gainful employment, how does that sound?' – we need to be inventive. That said, this might be exactly what's at stake. The arrival of a new leader who is passionately in favour of – well, anything that you had previously been pushing back against – is likely to bring about a rapid change in your attitude, unless you have a mountain of evidence to support your opposing position and/or no fear of losing your job, for whatever reason. Most of the time, you'll have neither of those.

It's not an absolute that to land SWP successfully you have to be prepared to solve a whole bunch of issues that are nothing to do with you – but it can certainly help. The answer to those three questions I posed just now will tell you a mountain's worth of information about how you need to orient your approach.

You might argue that all you're trying to do is make the business leader you're dealing with look good or feel good, which is frankly a bit cynical, surely. Well, yes and no.

If my customer – for that is who they are – isn't feeling the value from what I'm doing or is struggling to find anything positive to say either to their boss or my boss (which is worse), then I'm not helping. So yes, that's what I'm doing; and no, there's nothing cynical about that, because there will be a consequential win-win-win: for the business, for the customer and for me.

Let's look at a more complex example.

FROM PREVENTIVE TO DETECTIVE HIRING CONTROLS

What do your hiring managers complain about the most? This could make any of the lists in this book seem tiny by comparison, but I'm fairly confident that high up on everyone's list will be the frustration with hiring pretty much anything or anyone. The approval chains, the headcount checks, the organizational design charts, all of which have to be gone through even though the budget was agreed at the beginning of the year.

'For goodness' sake,' said one hiring manager to me (only they didn't say goodness), 'just let us get on and hire the people we need when we need them and get rid of all this approval nonsense. If you discover that one of my people has hired at too high a rate, just tell me and I'll speak to them. But for goodness' sake (they didn't say it then either), let us get on and do our job.'

So what would you do about that? Well, you could say this:

'Alright then. You can hire all the people you want based on the blanket approval we'll get for you. But you'll only get that approval if you can show me a workforce plan for the next three years that leadership are happy with, and you'll only be able to hire that way for as long as you stick to the trajectory of the plan and if you go about that in the right way. Otherwise, you'll be back into approval hell once more until you sort yourselves out.'

I've deliberately left a few gaping holes here that we'll gradually fill up, here and in the next couple of chapters. One of those holes or counterarguments can be found in this last group of objections below.

Ownership and territory

- This threatens the controls we have in place
- You know nothing about my business

- I'm going to lose control of things
- I want to do my own hiring
- I'm happy with how things are
- You don't have any mandate with me

Here, we have two main objections:

- You're diluting our ability to govern (aka control)
- Get out of my way

YOU'RE DILUTING OUR ABILITY TO GOVERN

A move from preventive to detective hiring does indeed change the control agenda, assuming that controls are predicated on stopping bad things from happening. It's therefore natural to fear that those things will break out everywhere if you remove those checks. The hardest part of one implementation in which I was involved was convincing all relevant parties that their respective control agendas were not compromised by the altered fulfilment approach I was advocating.

Put simply then, you need to convince people that the controls that existed previously are altered or changed, but not simply canned. Let's take the preventive-to-detective hiring example.

I'm sure you can spot the difference. Critical to the challenge about controls is that those business areas that do the right thing – we'll come to what those are in Chapter 10 – have clearance to hire without needing permission to do so. They don't avoid scrutiny: it merely takes place after the hiring, not before, and the incentive to do the right thing lies in what will

FIGURE 9.2 Detective hiring: same controls, different place

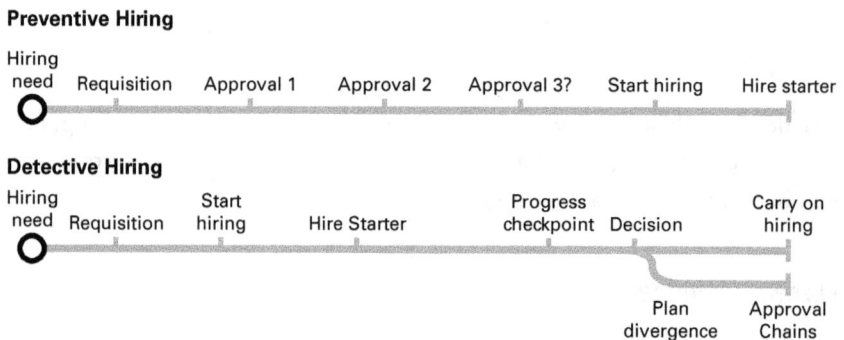

Preventive Hiring

Hiring need | Requisition | Approval 1 | Approval 2 | Approval 3? | Start hiring | Hire starter

Detective Hiring

Hiring need | Requisition | Start hiring | Hire Starter | Progress checkpoint | Decision | Carry on hiring

Plan divergence | Approval Chains

happen if they don't – a return to a tougher form of governance than they had experienced previously.

There's also one other prerequisite here, which is that the plan has already been approved. What's the basis for approval? It can be whatever is right for the business, be that meeting financial, productivity, demographic or diversity goals and many more besides. That provides the anchor for the license to hire; it also requires robust monitoring and retrospective governance to ensure it remains on track, of course.

GET OUT OF MY WAY

Many years ago, there was a song called *The Hole in The Ground*, which was all about an officious 'man in a bowler hat' telling a workman that the hole he was digging was all wrong: the wrong place, the wrong shape.[2] The end result of this officiousness was that the man in the bowler hat ended up in the hole. Now this passed for funny in 1962, although you can make a couple of more cutting observations: the long-held and largely British obsession with class differences, and the simple truth that people just don't like being told what to do by anyone who presents as knowing their job better than they do.

Chapters 10 and 11 are all about the strategic workforce conversation and how you might go about engaging with the business but, for now, it's important that you understand this much: if you don't have something valuable to offer to the business or if you can't demonstrate that value, then you ARE in the way. You have no mandate at all to saunter into someone's office claiming to be able to solve problems if they will only listen to you. You must not just show humility; you need to feel it. So what are you going to do? Plough on regardless? Or are you going to ask the fundamental question: what's keeping you awake at night? The renowned thinker and speaker Amit Mohindra nails it:

> 'At some level, people are anxious to hang on to their jobs and are focused on their little world within the organization. It's natural, then, that their personal agendas come first. When someone shows up with a more general optimum at odds with their local optimum, they feel threatened. This is the basis of some of the resistance towards people analytics and SWP.'[3]

Address that and you will go far.

REFLECTIONS

- Most resistance isn't stupid. It's scared, overloaded, bruised, or just focused on something more urgent.
- When people say 'we can't plan', they often mean 'we don't trust that planning here gets us anywhere'.
- Resistance is rarely about the process. It's about the people. Don't sell a framework: solve a problem.
- Objections are clues: listen to them.
- You won't earn trust with slides or systems. You'll earn it by making someone's job easier, bit by quiet bit.
- If you can't show that you're useful, then you're the one in the way.
- Start where ther's pain, not just where there's appetite.

Notes

1 Edwards, D (2025) *Word cloud on Strategic Workforce Planning challenges,* Created using WordCloud.com, Unpublished image
2 Rudge, M and Dicks, T (1962) *The Hole in the Ground* [lyrics and music] Performed by Bernard Cribbins, London: Parlophone
3 Edwards, D (2025) Interview with Amit Mohindra, conducted on 1 May 2025

10

What has SWP ever done for us? Part 1

Ultimately, delivering value is all that matters, but you've got to talk first

They want to solve the world problem with it instead of, 'Let's start with something, show value, build capability, and scale.' If you start small and drive it forward, you can rally people around success.

TECHNOLOGY VENDOR SVP

There is very little that lights up the SWP Practitioner's eyes more than when their work results in something good. It is the elixir upon which they thrive until they find themselves drinking from the fire hose, with executives from across the business clamouring for their help.

That first win can be where the value proposition takes root. Over the next two chapters, we'll look much more closely at how that first win comes about, starting with something really simple: a conversation.

So where *is* the beef?

I've already said (in Chapter 5) that the value in SWP comes not from SWP itself but from the actions you take in executing it, like the ones I listed in Chapter 6: but which do you choose?

Take a look at the bottom half – the action half – of this splendid diagram from Adam Gibson.

There are a couple of things to say about it. First, it's a really good diagram that captures the logical flow any good SWP Practitioner should understand and follow (which is why I haven't tried to reinvent it); second, its message is vital – the workforce plan only matters if it helps the business to achieve something it cares about. Third, don't worry about the top half just yet because we'll come to that; and fourth, it will be clear that no single diagram will represent the different problems a business needs solving – there will be dozens, maybe hundreds of them. If you try to rationalize how all of those workforce plans at the bottom of Figure 10.1 look like when combined, your brain will freeze, possibly for good.

FIGURE 10.1 Strategic alignment of workforce plans[1]

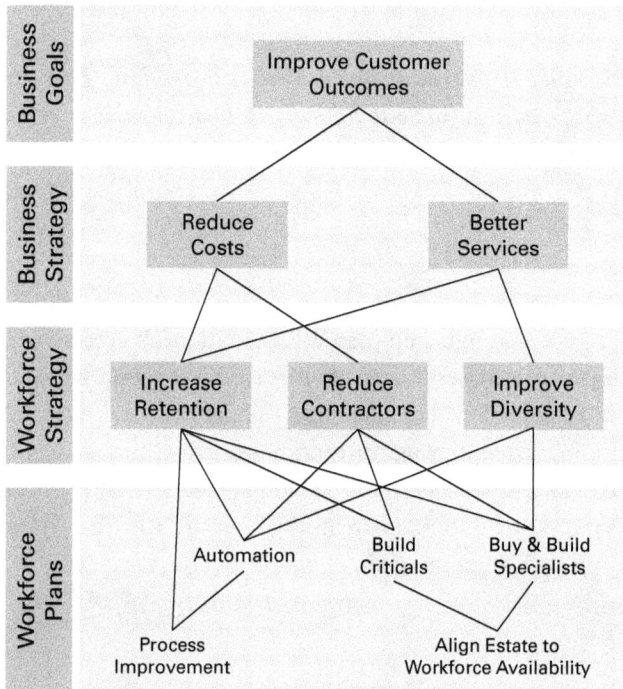

I used to be a reporting system consultant for a long-gone computerized finance system and, when presented with a report request that required configuration, I was already visualizing the steps I would take before the request conversation had finished. You'll find this same phenomenon occurring to you in your work too.

And that leads me to ask you to consider the kind of people you need to have permanently in your operating team.

Born to run – your SWP team

> 'The big mistake HR makes is marching up to business leaders and asking, "How many people will you need in your bakery in three years, on a Saturday?" It's nuts. Ask what will change in the business, not a fake three-year head-count.' – Dirk Jonker, Crunchr

My favourite ever boss – who would wince at the thought of being anyone's favourite – always insisted that we make the complex simple. SWP is simple, as is what the SWP team does:

- understand now
- learn about the future
- determine risks
- propose solutions
- coordinate actions
- follow up
- repeat

There are other tasks as well and there are other actors in the process; for now, we'll just look at your side of the operation.

Who does what?

SWP Teams tend not to be very large, but the people you have in them will be key to ensuring that these stages are well executed:

- **Understand now.** This is where your People Analytics colleagues shine. You need them to give you more than just a set of dashboards – where are the fires? What industry norms are breached and where? What's the level of data confidence? What's the margin for error?

- **Learn about the future.** In Chapter 7, I described HR Business Partners as your eyes and ears – the group most likely to pull together the intelligence that will help you to build solutions. In some larger companies you may have a dedicated team known by a range of different titles – Workforce Consultants, Workforce Strategy Partners and so on – but what unites them is that they are expert interrogators and coaches who are fully conversant with the different fulfilment options that are available, which enables them to guide business units as they plan. A lot of the time, of course, it's just you.

- **Determine risks.** We've already covered (in Chapter 3 and elsewhere) the criticality of workforce risk in SWP. You won't have anyone dedicated to this, but this is where the collective knowledge of your Workforce Strategy Partners and People Analytics Advisers, together with your own judgement, will be invaluable.

- **Propose solutions.** Your consultant/strategy partner, if you have one, should be the connective tissue between the different fulfilment teams that enables them to propose a selection from the 9 B's that we laid out in Chapter 5, where I also said that the magic happens when those levers are used together.

- **Coordinate actions.** It's extremely rare for the SWP practitioner to play an active part in actual solution delivery. SWP is an enabler of action. That said, the experience you will have gained from enabling these actions over time can and will equip you to offer advice on execution cadence, governance and the like.

- **Follow up.** Have we achieved what we wanted? Is the benefit that we anticipated visible, recognizable, calculable? In a perfect world, someone in your team will be pulling together these myriad metrics to give you an evidence base. We'll be covering value measurement in Chapter 11.

So that's what you might do and who, if you're lucky, you might have doing it. So let's now consider the many ways (yes, there's always more than one way) that you might go about actually doing this.

It's good to talk

> *'We turned it into a really informal, consultative chat instead of an intimidating, rigid process: just talking through future needs. We captured their input without bombarding them with frameworks. That helped us get more honest insight.'* – Jo Thackray (ex-Sage plc)

Striking up a conversation is hard. I am full of admiration for those people who spend their days cold-calling people in the hope that they might generate some kind of sales lead. I had to do it as part of my job once and I was woefully bad at it:

> *Me:* Hello, I'd like to tell you about how you could save time and money using project management software.
> *Prospect:* No thanks.
> *Me:* Oh, alright. Bye then.

It really was that excruciating. Fortunately, there's an acceptance on the part of most people in a business unit that you're looking to do something helpful for them. Here are some of the ways in which you might find yourself putting a meeting into the diary.

Routes to your customer

- **You're part of the annual business planning process.** If so, congratulations. You, or someone before you, has worked tirelessly to pull some form of SWP into the annual process from which it had previously been excluded. You'll be expected.

- **You want to raise the implications of strategic developments with an unsuspecting business leader.** This is bold, but laudable. You're either connected to the Group Strategy team or you've been reading around the subject on a STEEPLE crusade and you've spotted implications for a business unit.

- **You've identified some workforce risks in a review of analytics and want to explore them.** Again, it's potentially risky because a) the business might not see it as a risk, or b) they'd already spotted it and don't need your help, thank you very much. Which is not unlike me and my cold-calling misery.

- **You've issued a quarterly strategic review and you've been asked to advise a unit on its implications.** We're moving into high-end practice here. You've done your STEEPLE analysis, you've read everything going on LinkedIn and you've been attending regular strategy meetings as a guest, which gives you enough to proactively share your opinions about the meaning for the workforce.

- **You're launching SWP (or relaunching it) and reaching out to business units to spark the conversation.** This is probably your entry point. It requires a modest, yet assertive pitch ('There may be nothing that I can do to help you, but I'm pretty confident that there will be something') and there's rarely any unit head who is so thrilled with their workforce status that no one could improve upon it.

- **You've been asked to help a unit with their workforce strategy.** Practitioner heaven – you're in demand and all you have to do is pitch up, unroll your script, open up your bag of tricks and you'll have them begging for more. Or will you?

It's one thing to talk about how you'll weave your magic in meetings such as these but it can be quite another to have to do it for real. It's what happens in the room or on that call that matters.

Preparation is everything

> '*I found a route in so people would see me as enabling them, not treading on their patch. Actually, it's easiest if they feel they own something and I'm just helping.*'
> – Joe Heppenstall, QinetiQ

Anyone who doesn't fear an engagement with a unit head – certainly the first, second and maybe even the third time – has either faced down a pride of angry lions in their past or is being very naïve. I always worry that I will somehow fail my next audience. This is partly due to acute imposter syndrome and the learned understanding that you are only as good as your last performance: it can take months to recover from a bad one.

Everyone has their checklist and their way of approaching things and they will all have their merits. Some of the questions I ask myself before meeting a unit head will include:

- **Why are we meeting now?** Is there some event that's triggered this? What kind of meeting might it therefore develop into? If it's been initiated by the customer, then they're seeking your help. If you've initiated it, then you're pitching (at least partially). If it's part of the planning cycle, then you want to escape the implied formality and focus on how the customer is feeling.

- **What do I know that could be of interest?** Again, we're using our understanding of the general company circumstances and of the potential risk factors that you can check off. If there's a cost reduction imperative, what's the grade mix, the resource mix, the unit cost? If an ageing workforce is a general characteristic, is that the case here? Is attrition running hot in certain countries or age groups? If younger talent is leaving after, say, four years then what's the implied development cost that just walked out of the door? If the impact of AI is the concern, what evidence might corroborate or confound it? Does the World Economic Forum's 'Future of Work' have anything to say (apart from it's very heavy because it's over 200 pages long)?

- **How are their people feeling?** You might think that I'm drifting into HR Business Partner territory here but all I want to do is understand what we're dealing with and, of course, cement the notion that this is a collaborative exercise in conjunction with other parts of HR and not just yet another siloed HR activity.

- **Do we know which parts of the workforce are the most critical?** One of the fundamental challenges for a practitioner – and I've certainly not been great at this – is to get into the work itself. In Chapter 4 we looked at how segmentation helps reveal what's truly critical in a workforce. But let's consider what segmentation looks like when it's rooted in operational truth.

GETTING INTO THE WORK

Marc Sokol and Beverly Tarruli[2] give a superb example of this, the highly irreverent précis of which goes like this:

> Q: Hey, what's the most critical part of the workforce in a low-cost airline?
> A: The cleaners.
> Q: You're kidding me, right?

> *A: Not at all. You thought I'd say pilots, didn't you? Well, pilots are very skilled people, that's true. But all pilots are of a minimum, very high standard. Whereas the cleaners can vary a lot from one team to another in how quickly they can clean the aircraft and it's that speed which determines how fast you can turn the plane around for its next high-volume, low-margin flight.*
>
> *Q: Could you tell me some more?*
>
> *A: Sure, call me after I've finished my cleaning shift at the airport.*
>
> My challenge to you is this: exactly how well do you know how your workforce actually works? And when I say that I don't mean that you need to understand how to write a software program or assemble an engine. Your job is to connect the workforce to what your strategy requires of it.
>
> Marc and Beverly call this out as well. If you're looking at a different market sector – a different customer demographic, for example – do you have the workforce that can address it? That can understand it? That can conceive, design, build, package, market and sell to it? What does that entail?
>
> This is why it's often not enough to talk about just skills, and I know only too well the current burning desire to build skills-based organizations across the globe for as far as the eye can see. But what's the name of the skill which will deliver that understanding – empathy? My good mate Alicia Roach asks which organization is ever going to tell TA to hire 300 empathies. That's about as useful as asking them to find you 300 pink squirrels.
>
> One more thing: Marc and Beverley go on to say that the airline in question, having recognized the value of the cleaners and optimized its quality, then moved on to focusing on the quality of in-flight attendants, especially regarding their emotional intelligence, since that can have a disproportionate effect on brand perception. The criticality didn't remain static. That's why segmentation matters.

- **What do the people analytics tell us?** I think there are two sides to this question:

   a. What generic structural issues exist (such as the ones I outlined in Chapter 4)?

   b. Given what we might know about the company's strategy or the unit's goals, what indicators suggest there may be trouble ahead?

So, for example, an IT division that's looking to boost its automation capability might be alarmed to learn (and yes, they may not know) that the attrition rate of automation engineers is four times the company average; that 90 per cent of that is happening in the 18–34 age bracket; that 100 per cent of it involves people with an average tenure of three to four years and 100 per cent is taking place in low-cost locations, which is where the division plans to base the majority of its staff in future. This layering of the analytics reveals a significant threat to a fundamental pillar of the unit's future strategy. But I suspect most of you knew what I meant before you even got to the example…

- **What is this business leader most worried about?** Drawing on our themes of resistance in the last chapter, you need to make a concerted effort to put yourself into your customer's shoes. Perhaps they're new to the position and looking to establish themselves; perhaps it's an era of unprecedented change (but when is it not, these days?).

There are loads of questions like this and you need to decide which ones work best for your customers and their context. But there is one more thing that you should do if you are to have added credibility: you either have to adopt total humility and acknowledge your lack of familiarity with their world, or you must remember to speak a different language entirely.

Talking Suffolk to my mum – the many tongues of business

> 'SWP lives at the intersection of HR, Finance and line management. If you speak only in HR terms, Finance tunes out. If you focus only on financials, HR may feel it lacks consideration for people…which impacts culture. Meanwhile, line managers are focused on day-to-day execution. You have to act as a translator – bridging perspectives so that each function sees the value in their own terms.' – Jeff Mullen

My Mum is 91. Like me, she comes from Suffolk and the people there have a particular set of accents and phrases. 'Sloightly on the huh' is Suffolk for 'that's not straight'. It doesn't mean much beyond that community but, of course, that's my point. When I go to visit my Mum, my vocabulary changes along with my accent. Similarly, when you meet with someone from Finance, or from the Business, or even someone from HR, you need to change your language. You might also want to adjust your approach:

> 'We started with a robust structure but ended up softening it – turning it into a more informal approach and adapting it for each function. Some wanted the structure; most needed a more conversational style. We just changed our approach depending on the stakeholder.' – Jo Thackray, ex-Sage plc

Is that easy to do? Absolutely not and you'll probably experience some awful died-a-death-on-stage moments when the approach you believe will work fails completely. I certainly have.

Okay, so you've got your team; you've done your preparation. It's time to walk down the corridor to start the conversation.

Talking the talk

> 'I worked with a brewery and I didn't drink beer – didn't drink at all. It was St Patrick's Day, everyone was on Guinness and I was sipping Coke. The CEO asked what I was drinking; I told him, and he let fly a stream of expletives. Then he put me on a development plan: for a full year I had to go out 'in trade' every week, stand with the reps, visit pubs, learn the product – yes, even learn to drink it. The lesson that never left me is this: understand the business, first its product, its customers, its margins – then weave your HR or workforce-planning themes into that conversation.' – Jean Blackstock

Friends of ours have just become grandparents, just as Finony and I did 10 years ago. They, like us, watch their children from the side, often struggling with things that they struggled with too. But they're not exactly the same. Sometimes they can help with something they too have experienced, but a lot of the times they can't. There is no certain path through parenthood, no manual to follow. Similarly, there is no perfect script for an SWP conversation. What follows then can only be a guide to some of the things that I and others find works in some circumstances – but be aware that one size definitely does not fit all.

Leading the conversation

These guidelines are just that, nothing more. However you approach the conversation, I believe there's always a clear sign that you've had a good one: you'll feel drained afterwards. Whatever your style, whatever questions you ask, your internal CPU needs to be operating at 100 per cent of its capacity, around one simple question: how does this translate into workforce solutions?

ALWAYS BE HUMBLE – FIND OUT HOW THEY ARE

It really doesn't matter how many times you've held these conversations. You're there to serve, coach and advise the business – maybe challenge it – and you should never take anything for granted, whether it's your first meeting with someone or your fiftieth. Good friendships and relationships at work are priceless – they smooth frequently rocky paths and they enable empathy and mentorship that are essential antidotes to often-difficult experiences. But they are work relationships; few of them endure past your employment and they are entirely secondary to your colleague's personal circumstances.

You might say that this is basic common sense: of course it is, but that doesn't mean that you always remember that.

KEEP THE SPOTLIGHT ON THEM

You're unlikely to encounter a business unit head asking you how the latest workforce plan is coming on and it follows that, even if they do ask, they won't want a monologue from you. A much-admired boss of mine once said, 'David, you'll never hear anyone say, "That was a great speech – I wish it had been longer."' He had listened to some of mine.

You're there to find out how their business is faring and what their challenges are. By all means, if this is your first encounter then establish your credentials, your right to be in front of them. That will range from an extremely simple, 'I don't know if I can help you but I'm going to do all I can', through to your rattling off a long list of awards you've won and blue-chip companies you've worked for (although I wouldn't).

So how are they doing? What's on their worry list right now and for the future? You must be able to sift those in-meeting and be honest about which things you can help them with and which things you can't: you'll earn respect for that.

WHAT'S IMPORTANT TO THEM – WHAT ARE THEY TRYING TO DO?

Even if you already know what they're trying to achieve, still ask the question, a) to reinforce the narrative you believe to be the case and b) to tease out any dissent, deviation or variation in desired outcomes.

WHAT ARE YOU TRYING TO DO?

Call it sales, consulting, whatever – get all the pain on the table, take them down and then bring them back up with the solutions they will choose. Yes, them, not you. You're getting them to formulate the answers, because they will then own them more than they would had you just handed solutions to them.

GET ALL OF THE BAD STUFF OUT THERE

Your audiences have already voiced their own worries. Translate these into risks, so that you normalize the problems into a single, manageable list of issues in a consistent format.

You should then follow with those that you've identified in your preparation – geopolitics, C-level strategy, etc. Wherever possible, bring those risks into their world. Are tariffs impacting global supply chains? What does that mean for them?

> 'Early on, we just proactively produced a lot of reports on what could go wrong, focusing on major risks because our culture is risk-averse. That got the C-suite's attention, and eventually we had enough credibility to run a yearly five-year forecast.'

ESTABLISH HOW STRATEGY WILL BE ACHIEVED

Your audience will already have most of the answers to your questions; your task is to ensure the workforce element is not seen as just an afterthought. But first they need to tell you which strategic levers they expect to pull to meet their ambition. These can be a whole range of things: develop new product, invest in technology, alter a manufacturing process. There could be any number of things on that list: the important thing to establish is which levers are the most important.

Here's a greatly simplified example:

In this example, I've asked a business leader to score the extent to which a lever will bring about the desired goal, using a simple scoring system where 1 = minimal and 5 = huge.

Simple? Yes. Simplistic? No – in the absence of limitless resources, business effort is necessarily prioritized. This approach doesn't aim to definitively prioritize how strategy will be achieved; instead, it points to the most likely routes the business will take – it's a bit like the distinction between beyond reasonable doubt and the balance of probabilities in a courtroom.

TABLE 10.1 Example scoring of strategic levers against business goals

Lever	Enable business capability	Support new business growth	Improved user experience	Total
Simplified processes	3	2	5	10
Platform standardization	2	1	4	7
AI development	4	1	3	8
Digital transformation	3	1	4	8

Don't overthink this – if that's where the sentiment is, start with that and see where it takes you.

DETERMINE THE WAY IN WHICH WORK MIGHT CHANGE
Again, you won't get perfection but, a bit like the quote I shared at the beginning of Chapter 9 about holiday planning, your audience will have more of an idea than they think.

Again taking the simplification of processes as an example, you could argue that if they don't yet know what that might look like, the chances of it delivering for them are slim.

EVOLVE THE CONVERSATION FROM WORK TO CAPABILITY
By building this gradual story of the things that will bring about change, how those things will affect the work, you will almost naturally ease into an understanding about the kind of worker needs there will be and how those needs will alter from where they are now. While this may sound a lot easier than it can be in practice, presenting the logic of the approach to your audience in this way will make the process more accessible.

The aim is not to generate a 'how much' – for anything that is longer-term, the 'what' is far more important.

'Does that mean you'll need more of x and less of y?' is the kind of question designed to elicit answers. If you've guessed right, good for you; if not, well you'll be given the correct answer there and then.

ELICITING ANSWERS BY ASKING GOOD QUESTIONS

In this hypothetical example, an IT function wants to use agentic AI to handle and resolve 80 per cent of all Level 1 and Level 2 support calls by 2028.

The question is this: *What are the function's future skills needs going to be?*

This is probably too big a leap for a leader to make and could, if asked, cause them to push back.

The following aren't perfect examples, but an illustration of the questioning technique that you *could* adopt instead:

- So describe to me what you think this future level of AI resolution would look like.

- How much does AI resolve today?

- But there would still be a degree of human intervention in future, right? AI won't solve everything.

- How would that human aspect differ to what it looks like now?

- Do you think it's realistic for AI to solve 80 per cent of these calls, or will you really have to staff for a lower percentage?

- Is the likely change a straight pro-rating, or is it more nuanced than that?

- Will these human agents also provide supervisory cover for the service in general, or will that require a different team?

- Can our existing people do the kind of work you'll want from them in future? What would it take to get them there?

It's more intensive, but it's more likely to bring your business head closer to an answer than they might otherwise have reached.

In summary

There's no clever macro-laden spreadsheet that sits behind what we've covered here. Instead, there is a simple, conversational technique that is founded on showing and accepting vulnerability, asking questions and an iterative process of relationship-building, listening and building trust.

In Part II, we're going to cement that understanding, inject a sense of urgency where it's needed, translate the needs into actions and see how those actions will, over time, create momentum that can propel SWP into the operational DNA of your organization.

REFLECTIONS

- **You need good people around you**, either in your team or indirectly willing to help you.

- **This is a people business.** Not in the HR sense, but in the listening, nudging, interpreting and asking-the-right-question sense.

- **You've got to get into the work**, knowing enough to ask the right questions, or asking enough questions so that you know enough.

- **You'll need to prepare.** Not just with data and charts, but with context, insight and understanding.

- **Language matters.** If you go in speaking 'HR' to Finance, or 'Strategy' to Ops, you'll lose them before you've even started.

- **Tools are just tools.** They help but, as my Finony would tell you, you can have the best tools and still be useless at home improvements. A table can help guide a conversation, but it's no substitute for the conversation itself.

- **You won't get far without segmentation.** Understanding which roles are truly pivotal (and they're often not the ones you think) changes the whole conversation.

- **Help your audience arrive at the answer** and they might just do something with it.

Notes

1 Gibson, A (2021) *Agile Workforce Planning: How to align people with organizational strategy for improved performance*, London: Kogan Page
2 Sokol, M and Tarulli, B (2025) Strategic workforce planning and organization development: Combining different types of expertise to drive meaningful change, *Organization Development Review*, 57(1), pp. 9–15

11

What has SWP ever done for us? Part 2

It started with recruitment only... two years later those who once pushed back now come to me asking for help.

ANONYMOUS (BUT HAPPY) PRACTITIONER

Let's pick up from the last chapter and move from the initial conversation to starting to make things happen, building momentum as we go.

Rather than tell you what happened in Chapter 10 – because you may just have finished reading it and would question the purpose of so doing – I thought I would let this short case study summarize it for you:

REAL-WORLD EXAMPLE
Lindsey Clarke – driving SWP in a resistant organization[1]

Context and Challenge

Lindsey leads SWP in an organization where projects can last for decades – meaning little short-term accountability.

She faces intense resistance – from leaders who claim they 'can't plan next year', from people fearful that SWP's data will reveal uncomfortable truths, and from a matrix structure that fosters bureaucracy and 'ownership' disputes over people.

Approach

- **Segmentation/pivotal roles:** She introduced a workforce segmentation system that identifies 'pivotal' roles, setting a firm rule that business can track.

This pilot gave them a metric to buy into and refined their understanding of which roles have a disproportionate impact if gapped; it also helped them recognize it is not about seniority.

- **Opportunity statements:** She pushes teams to phrase issues as 'opportunities' rather than 'problems', expanding innovation and broader solutions.
- **Holding up the mirror:** Lindsey is unafraid to highlight operational or structural flaws, even when HR leadership reacts negatively. She stands by data, keeps an audit trail of actions, and refuses to issue half-finished analysis.

Outcomes

- **Gradual mindset shift:** Senior leaders started seeing the value of labelling certain roles 'pivotal' and building succession for them first. They began self-correcting mis-labeled roles.
- **Ownership:** With simplified, segmented data, directors realized, 'If I claim this role is pivotal, I must fill it quickly', prompting them to act.
- **HR involvement:** Lindsey's team still leads SWP directly but is slowly enlisting HRBPs, rewriting processes so that HR can't sidestep SWP requirements.
- **Persistent friction:** She continues to meet turf wars (matrix structure, annual budget constraints), but each SWP cycle fosters more buy-in and clarifies the 'no-later-than' accountability for key roles.

Key takeaways

- **Data + hard conversations:** Real SWP means pushing stakeholders out of comfort zones.
- **Small steps:** Workforce segmentation and pivotals proved a gateway pilot, giving tangible metrics that overcame initial cynicism.
- **Unwavering integrity:** Lindsey copes by staying true to her values, refusing to water down essential truths – even if it provokes healthy conflict.

I did a little dance after I spoke to Lindsey, despite being a very poor dancer. You see, her story is a textbook example of the conversation we've already explored, enhanced by her own take on how criticality can be determined and her implacable approach to spelling out hard truths. I wouldn't recommend spelling out hard truths the first time you talk to someone, though – unless you're Lindsey, that is.

Her example is the very essence of creating a small win from which favourable momentum can grow. It's the first element of what I want to explore in this chapter, along with how you develop buy-in, ensure you've done enough to keep building on it and – now this may seem a little radical – how you start to plumb into the broader business strategy.

Win small

> 'Attempting to start [SWP] for the entire enterprise all at once is doomed to failure. It's just too heavy a lift. Attack point problems instead and scale through what you learn with the rest of the organization at the right speed.' – Amit Mohindra (ex-Apple).

Now you might not agree with this sentiment from one of the most respected thought leaders in the business, but Amit has a point. If you try to implement a company-wide framework, then you'll get exactly that: a framework that does nothing in particular. And if you try to do what you've always done, you'll get what you've always got: a process of limited value. But this is counter-intuitive for an organization that's just hired you (hopefully at great expense, because believe me you'll earn it) to magic all their problems away: I said plenty about that back in Chapter 3.

So, the whole point about the conversation that you developed in Chapter 10 is to identify that small item of change – that critical segment of the workforce – that people need to zone in on and, once you've done that, you'll have to make them want to do it. Here's one way:

> 'I introduced a concept called panic early. It takes three months to hire, nine months to reach proficiency, so you need to panic now. Operational leaders are brilliant at today's fire, but that skill set isn't naturally going to step back and look nine quarters out – you have to grow that planning muscle.' – Oliver Shaw, Orgvue CEO

Is it reasonable or even fair to induce a sense of panic (if that's the right word to use)? Well, I was at an offsite recently where the team leader pointed out that, in previous such events, their team had held earnest debates, made some excellent points and produced some brilliant ideas; but they had failed to agree a set of actions. So perhaps panic has its uses. But whatever it is that you do, your ultimate responsibility is as an enabler of decision-making and action. Put another way...

You don't make the decisions

At the same offsite, I took a chance by laying out how I was going to structure the workforce conversation, setting out the steps I was going to follow (looking a lot like Chapter 10). I also made it very clear that it was highly unlikely that we would arrive at many answers by the end of my session. 'That's fine,' said one of the more outspoken attendees, 'if we can identify some more, some less of and some stay the same, that will be so much further than we've got before.' I hadn't reached the point where I was going to tell them that. A phrase in government that you may have heard is, 'advisers advise, ministers decide'. You're the adviser in this.

> 'The practitioner's role isn't to dampen expectations; it's to say, 'This is what could happen' and then let the business debate the recommendations. [For example] no one person can forecast the true impact of AI – you need that discussion at the senior table.' – Sadhana Bhide, Pearson

After that, they'd set their own objectives and it was a case of walking them through until I could introduce them to the multiple B options that we explored in Chapter 5.

In that same chapter, I also said that the magic came from how you blended those different options. So what does that blend look like? What is that secret sauce?

Optimizing fulfilment

I'm looking for some kind of analogy that can help to explain the reason why you might want to blend different fulfilment options. Here goes.

Christopher Nolan's film *Dunkirk* is a disorienting one to watch, because it tells three stories, each of which is running over a different timeline within the film. That makes it quite difficult to understand – right up until the one, solitary moment when all three storylines converge for a split second, before continuing on their way at their different paces. While not the perfect metaphor for what optimized fulfilment might look like, it does reflect the idea that your fulfilment approaches are at their most optimum when they converge and not just when they're all running at the same, uncoordinated speed. That said, it is not an easy thing to describe, let alone make happen.

Why would you want to optimize your fulfilment? It's hard enough to just fill some of these critical positions without trying multiple routes simultaneously. Where's the value in that? It's time we re-introduced the S word: <u>skills</u>.

Why companies don't grow new skills first

If an organization is to remain competitive and at the leading edge in its sector, it will strive to be among the first to adopt new skills or expertise. I don't think that needs any peer review – it's a statement of the obvious. But it is also understandable why large companies may not want to make speculative investments in equipping staff with those skills until there's some evidence that they will actually be of any use. You can burn a lot of cash that way, if you're not careful. The acquisition or development of new skills is therefore pre-ordained to lag in those companies.

But you can also understand why, for the exact same reason, third-party staff vendors would make that investment. These vendors are used because they have those skills already, so they are frequently the first port of call for a company looking to stay ahead and hedge their internal learning utility risk. Long before companies are willing to take a chance, these vendors will be recruiting staff at scale to preserve their value proposition.

All of this makes complete sense, so you might be forgiven for wondering why I'm dwelling on it for so long. Well, the problem is that this acquisition of skilled people at what will be a premium rate is rarely accompanied by a corresponding plan to part company with them as soon as they can be replaced by a stream of talent available on the open market. There are four good reasons for replacing them:

1 **Cost.** There is a cost to continuing to use them when it's no longer essential to do so: they remain at a premium.

2 **Capability depletion.** Your company never ingests the capability to generate similar intellectual property of its own.

3 **Vendor risk.** The vendor may want these people back for something more lucrative elsewhere, which leaves you – where, exactly?

4 **Employee neglect.** What message are you sending your own people if the headline roles and projects are always taken by external staff? That doesn't match up to the career-enhancing promises of your Employee Value Proposition.

It surely makes sense, therefore, to find replacements, either by training your existing stock of internal staff or hiring new ones, but there's a problem: it's harder to do those things and it takes time. Why harder? Well, it takes time to get approval to hire (unless you've done something like that which I suggested in Chapter 9) and training someone – which takes time – isn't the same as their becoming operationally ready – which takes longer.

None of that makes it any less desirable, since there is much to be said for a loyal employed workforce, especially one that is receiving skills training and other forms of personal development. Optimized fulfilment is therefore desirable and arguably necessary.

How optimizing could work

I say 'could' because you're probably ahead of me already. It's three straight-forward-sounding steps:

1 plan to engage external staff for a fixed period, which is determined by the time it takes to

2 create a training campaign to generate internal replacements, identify suitable candidates, train them and help them to attain sufficient accreditation to be deemed operationally ready; and the time it takes to

3 establish a targeted hiring campaign aimed at attracting emerging talent as it enters the market.

This will vary from one set of capabilities to another, which means a series of different hiring cycle journeys. That sounds highly complicated but, if you think about it, we have lots of different hiring journeys already; it's just that

FIGURE 11.1 Optimized fulfilment

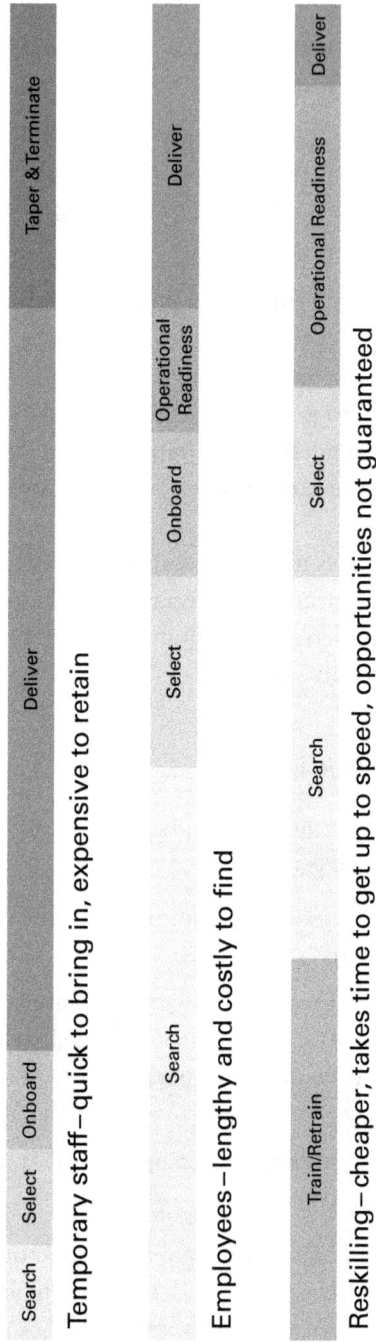

Search	Select	Onboard	Deliver	Taper & Terminate

Temporary staff – quick to bring in, expensive to retain

Search	Select	Onboard	Operational Readiness	Deliver

Employees – lengthy and costly to find

Train/Retrain	Search	Select	Operational Readiness	Deliver

Reskilling – cheaper, takes time to get up to speed, opportunities not guaranteed

they exist in different fulfilment silos and don't connect with each other. Now THAT's complicated.

This kind of interconnection would have been simply impossible only a few years ago, but a range of different technology offerings now enable journeys such as these to be estimated and created with growing accuracy. We'll be discussing technology in general in Chapter 15.

Optimized fulfilment could be seen as the highest form of end product possible from a strategic workforce plan because, in its best form, it seeks the best route to delivering the capability needed to execute strategy and because of the high-functioning collaboration it entails from multiple fulfilment channels. Such collaboration simply won't happen overnight, or even over several nights. Fortunately, there's also plenty of scope for individual channels to optimize independently; that's just as well, because there are extremely sound reasons for doing so that include your own continued licence to operate as a practitioner.

Individual optimization – stepped benefit realization

Since I first raised the possibility of extending the Window of Opportunity in Chapter 1, I've sought to emphasize that the extension is about more than creating extra time to do the same old fulfilment things; it's about doing things you couldn't previously do. It won't come as a surprise to learn that doing things differently will happen more quickly in one channel than in another. This is good, because it gives you the opportunity to lead with an early win through one channel while holding out the prospect of further wins down the line as other channels start doing things more creatively. This renews your licence to operate and develop the remaining channels. I've chosen to call this Stepped Benefit, although you could call it a number of other things as well.

This is all very well, but what can this kind of stepped benefit generation look like?

BENEFIT STEP 1

What: Switch third-party staff locations to lower-cost ones and mandate low-cost from now on.

How: Tell your supplier that that's what you want. Yes, that's it.[2]

Why that would work: The era when everyone had to be co-located has thankfully been consigned to the same bin as those wonderful conference phone units that never quite seemed to work properly. Collaboration tools are anything but perfect still, but thankfully many of the reasons often used in the past for not doing this – language difficulties, communications channels, cultural bias (yes, we should include that) – no longer apply.

What's it worth: Quite a lot. Rate differentials can still be considerable, especially in more commoditized roles, which is why finance as well as software development sectors flourish in lower-cost areas.

How do you measure the benefit? Simple cost accounting. Ask your friendly local finance partner to explain the difference between rate variance and volume variance – yes, seriously pick up the phone and ask them. It gives you a good excuse for getting in touch. When they answer, tell them you want to be able to show that the cost of buying in the same number of external staff as the business has been buying is less than it was when you started. That's something that your actions have influenced. You don't want to be held accountable for the business deciding to buy in more of these people because they're cheaper: that's a problem the person on the other end of the phone needs to talk to the business about.

How soon can this come on stream? It's probably the first thing you can do.

Next benefit steps

There is no one sequence of benefit events such as those in Chapter 6 – be they cost, agility, lead-time, whatever – that will enable you to get from a small start to a grandstand finish. That first step that I just described may be of no value to you because either a) you have no third-party staff or no need of them, or b) you have already offshored as many people as you possibly can anyway. For each unit you get the chance to work with, the combination will differ as much as the sequence.

But there is one item in this collection of benefits that we've not yet talked about: ironically enough, it's what drew me into this profession in the first place and it's the keystone of Chapter 1.

The trouble with redeployment

What, I hear you say (okay, I don't, it's a book), about what I talked about in Chapter 1, about the person who might lose their job for no good reason? I talked about this some more in Chapter 3. I like to call the redeployment of people in those situations a fulfilment channel too, although it is a more complicated one because, for it to work well, you need to have visibility of both likely reductions in one area and likely matching openings in another, in more or less the same timeframe and the same locality, all of which can be pretty serendipitous, albeit less so in a large organization where turnover is more obliging. Consequently, that window of opportunity is likely to remain relatively small because aspects of this puzzle – particularly likely reductions – rarely come into focus until pretty late in the cycle and it's likely to be a job more suited to resource managers looking to plug an assignment gap at short notice.

But it's not impossible, and SWP can contribute significantly in some circumstances. Big tectonic shifts happen and these are definitely opportunities to plan a more strategic approach or, at the very least, to show what's possible.

Big shift redeployment

Early in my SWP career, I and my peerless visionary colleague Tom Carrigan (whose capacity for vitriolic despair is a thing of unmatched beauty) experienced this at first hand and it provided us with gold-standard evidence that redeployment at scale is possible.

REAL-WORLD EXAMPLE
Redeployment in action

Background

Following the 2008 financial crisis, The Royal Bank of Scotland received large amounts of UK Government aid; the European Commission mandated, as a consequence, that RBS should divest itself of over 300 of its branches, to be rebranded as Williams & Glyn.[3] There followed huge amounts of investment to create separate systems and processes so that this separated bank could then be sold. This is all well known in the UK business sector.

What was less well known was that there was a torrent of RBS staff flowing out of the bank into this new one, with Tom and I both actively engaged in trying to identify candidates in the old bank for open positions in the new one.

RBS tried to sell this new bank with no success and sank an alleged £1.8 billion into the process.[4] They then announced that the split was being cancelled: the challenges in separating the systems were just too great.[5]

A great screeching of tyres

This came as a shock, especially to those who had decided to move across to the new bank; what they had hoped would be a career propellant suddenly became a potential career terminator. What followed was a bit like one of those old cartoons where characters run into a tunnel towards the light at the other end, only to come running back out of it again when they realize that the light is coming from a train hurtling towards them.

All of a sudden, Tom and I became very popular, trying to re-home people in the old bank. Between us and our small team, we managed to re-home about 250 people, not into the roles they had previously had, but into other roles in RBS.

Why was this significant?

Well, up to this point there was a generally accepted wisdom that you couldn't take somebody in a given role – project manager, for example – from one part of the bank and plonk them into the same role in a different part because they wouldn't have experience of it. So my learning was this:

1 People are transferrable. If they are good at what they do, they will be able to do it in several different contexts, which they will pick up quickly enough.

2 If you have the redeployment capability established, you can move mountains with it when it's needed; bigger ones still if you have time to prepare for it.

3 We did this with next to no data and without any of the technologies now available to us. To bring these matches about, people had to speak to people and I believe that the human interaction will remain essential, transcending the productivity benefits that those technologies can deliver.

There's also a point 4, which is this. Perhaps it's just me, but I get the sense that an organization can be extremely direct and effective in a crisis. Things suddenly happen at speed, rules and regulations of little consequence are bypassed because they just get in the way. There's also a sense of togetherness, of shared purpose and intent that isn't always evident at other moments.

Yet, when the crisis dies down, the togetherness often recedes; the rules return. When that happens, redeployment snaps back to somewhere near its original inelastic state. The moral of that tale is that you may have to repeat a success several times before people take its value seriously.

Win small – on repeat

> 'My philosophy… is this: To agree to do workforce planning, it's built on 100 wins… And that's typically evidence-based… It's that hundredth time that they have the trust in you to do the right thing… Once they see small progress each time, they're way more open to continuing the bigger journey.' – Alan Susi, S&P Global

I am spoiled for choice with case studies that illustrate how this gradual approach of accumulation can be a solid route to the successful embedding of – for now, I'll keep calling it this – SWP. Before I do, however, I want to pick up on a phrase in the quote I've just provided – 'typically evidence-based'. What evidence? What base?

Getting the credit

The benefits list in Chapter 6 included a list of metrics that could be used to measure benefit and I've also talked in this chapter about rate and volume variances, all of which are perfectly good things to talk about. Indeed, talking – having that conversation – is one of the things that many people cite as being something for which SWP can act as the catalyst.

That's all very well but telling your CFO during the budget setting season that you deserve another year's budget to generate further conversations is one of the less compelling arguments I've heard for extending your licence to operate. A stack of stakeholder testimonials is good but being able to attribute savings to what you're doing is definitely better, and attribution is another matter altogether.

You're going to want a good, committed Finance partner working with you because a) attribution will only come your way if they say it does and b) because a common question you'll hear is, 'What happens to the money that I save if I do this?' You need to answer that question.

The legend that is Adam Gibson said this to me:

'First piece of advice: Dave Ulrich once told me, "Invite a Finance person to lunch; they'll accept because they have no friends". It's half-joking, but the idea is, if you befriend Finance, you can solve each other's problems. They want more certainty in the budget gap. You can bring a workforce angle: "We'll hire at this rate or reduce at this rate, so your cost line is more predictable". They love that, because it means fewer shocks.'

Getting Finance on this is worth the price of a lunch, because they will navigate you through the attribution minefield.

Cost savings come in two forms

It's important to understand that you have two very different kinds of cost saving:

1 **Cost reduction.** What you are now doing with your workforce costs you less than it cost you before you started doing it. You employed someone on a lower grade because you did a Bend exercise that suggested redesigning work more suitable for a more junior member of staff after the previous, more senior incumbent left.

2 **Cost avoidance.** This is the finance equivalent of saying, 'you dodged a bullet there'. Put as simply as possible, your SWP approach and/or your improved fulfilment options allowed you to divert the business from something that was going to be costly. This doesn't have to be anything clever. It can sometimes mean slotting someone at risk of redundancy into a different role or, as in Figure 11.2, where the difference is not in the budget but when and how Finance and SWP/Fulfilment are brought in. On the left is what often happens. On the right is what could happen through better engagement.

What you might also notice from this diagram is that this is the practical expression of feasibility, which turned up in the reimagined Dowding system

FIGURE 11.2 Cost avoidance in action

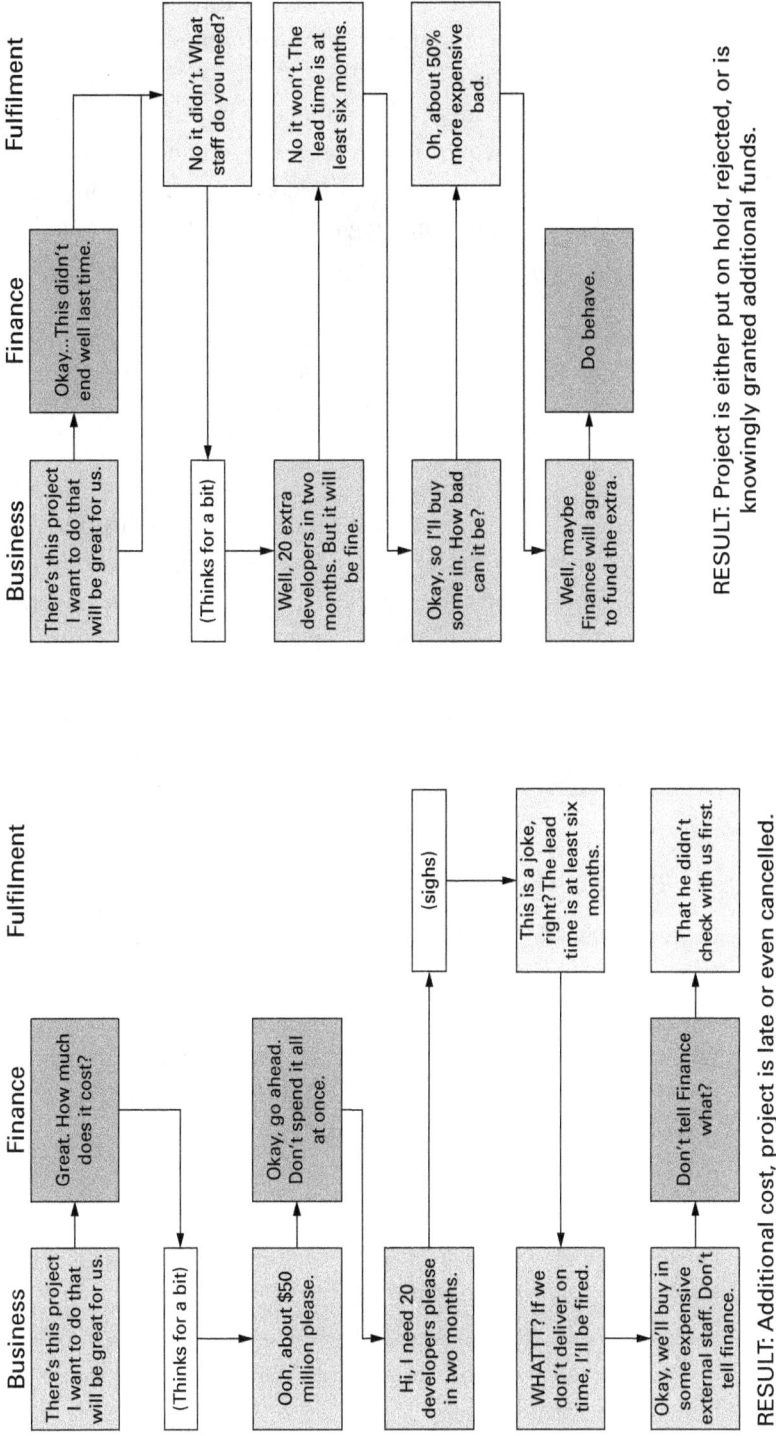

Business — Finance — Fulfilment (first flow)

- Business: There's this project I want to do that will be great for us.
- Finance: Great. How much does it cost?
- Business: (Thinks for a bit)
- Business: Ooh, about $50 million please.
- Finance: Okay, go ahead. Don't spend it all at once.
- Business: Hi, I need 20 developers please in two months.
- Fulfilment: (sighs)
- Fulfilment: This is a joke, right? The lead time is at least six months.
- Business: WHATT?? If we don't deliver on time, I'll be fired.
- Business: Okay, we'll buy in some expensive external staff. Don't tell finance.
- Finance: Don't tell Finance what?
- Fulfilment: That he didn't check with us first.

RESULT: Additional cost, project is late or even cancelled.

Business — Finance — Fulfilment (second flow)

- Business: There's this project I want to do that will be great for us.
- Finance: Okay…This didn't end well last time.
- Fulfilment: No it didn't. What staff do you need?
- Business: (Thinks for a bit)
- Business: Well, 20 extra developers in two months. But it will be fine.
- Fulfilment: No it won't. The lead time is at least six months.
- Business: Okay, so I'll buy some in. How bad can it be?
- Fulfilment: Oh, about 50% more expensive bad.
- Business: Well, maybe Finance will agree to fund the extra.
- Finance: Do behave.

RESULT: Project is either put on hold, rejected, or is knowingly granted additional funds.

diagram in Chapter 5. By extension, we can therefore legitimately argue that we're contributing to business strategy by identifying workforce-related risk to successful project delivery.

Cost reduction is, of course, very popular with Finance colleagues and understandably so, but I would argue that cost avoidance is equally valuable for your businesses and here's why: the corollary of avoiding making a damaging spending decision is making a better one instead – one that delivers better delivery, improved productivity and so on.

It's also extremely useful for growing your own reputation as someone who enables better-informed decision-making. That reputation relies on your being able to rustle up the evidence. You have to capture it.

Recording those little wins

Keeping a record of these incremental gains matters, not just for your own sanity, but for renewing your licence to operate when the next budget cycle comes round. Time spent agreeing precisely how it will be recognized is some of the best time you will spend. It places you on an unarguable footing: it is your evidence.

How you do this is, of course, up to you. But some things will be necessary for you to agree with colleagues whether this is a benefit for your programme or for someone else's. Here's a list of what you could use:

CAPTURING BENEFITS

- **In-scope activity.** These should be the projects that you have initiated to bring about this particular benefit, e.g. Frankfurt Engineering Reskilling Project.

- **What is not in scope.** Make sure there is a catch-all here: your programme may expand and you want to make sure that anything that you've not explicitly declared in-scope is still counted.

- **Benefit evidence.** What are the data points that show some kind of change? An example might be a renegotiated vendor contract that's been made possible because of the longer-term demand view you've created. What systems will you use to capture the evidence?

- **Outcome and usage.** What were the pre-determined rules for the treatment of reductions: are they made available for funding other work, do they go towards a budgetary target?

- **Target onstream date.** When do you realistically expect these benefits to start flowing? Vendor renegotiation can take ages, for example.

- **Benefit status.** Some brilliant colleagues of mine developed a grading mechanism for individual initiatives that categorized each of them from being a loose idea all the way through to having been executed and credited, a little bit like you might score a sales pipeline. It's a really good way of keeping people on track.

- **Benefit category and origination.** This kind of thing covers multiple benefit types, as we have already seen, involving multiple different teams and disciplines. Make sure that both are categorized and identified so that each area can communicate their impact through their own reporting lines.

Done right, you will build a ledger of unimpeachable evidence of your achievements, evidence that you can then use for the inevitable pushbacks and political challenges, about which we're going to talk in the very next chapter.

REAL-WORLD EXAMPLE
Jane Doe – navigating new strategy

Context and challenge

Jane's organization is about to roll out a fresh corporate strategy, yet no dedicated workforce planning function exists. Responsibilities like future skills forecasting get scattered across different roles. Jane sees an opportunity to embed SWP thinking into the new strategy but worries she doesn't have the mandate to do so.

Approach

- **Tag-teaming on future skills:** Jane and her colleague, John, split tasks: John focuses on immediate skill analysis, while Jane looks for ways to connect that to succession and leadership discussions.

- **Succession planning as an in:** By asking leaders, *'What do you need in your people to deliver the strategic objectives?'* she begins bridging strategy and workforce needs without a formal SWP banner.

- **Low-key 'elbowing in':** Jane contemplates whether she should push more aggressively to insert workforce feasibility questions into strategic forums, acknowledging that small interventions build credibility.

Outcomes (so far)

- **Rich insights on skills:** Even a few open-ended questions in succession planning revealed crucial skill gaps.
- **Growing confidence:** Realizing she *can* nudge leaders to consider workforce risk encourages Jane to engage more directly with future strategy rollouts.
- **Steady but piecemeal progress:** Without a specialized SWP function, the approach is fragmented, yet each success fosters trust and may lead to a more consolidated SWP practice over time.

Key takeaways

- **Using existing HR processes:** Succession planning or performance reviews can serve as stealth SWP vehicles.
- **Small wins, big credibility:** Proving value in small pilot areas can pave the way for broader, more formal workforce planning adoption.
- **No one-size-fits-all:** In an organization lacking a formal SWP role, *any* chance to link strategy to people readiness is worth exploring – even if it's incremental and 'under the radar'.

REFLECTIONS

- **100 small wins.** Pilot segmentation efforts or succession-focused conversations can turn initial resistance into active engagement.
- **Fulfilment optimization isn't all about cost.** It's about better decision-making, smarter trade-offs and long-term resilience.
- **Redeployment is a fulfilment channel.** It may take a crisis to show what's possible, but one of those shouldn't be necessary.
- **Benefits can come in steps.** Early wins (like vendor rate shifts) can buy time and goodwill to pursue more complex, strategic initiatives.
- **Attribution matters.** Starting conversations is great, but you'll need evidence (and ideally a supportive finance partner) to secure continued investment.

- **Cost reduction and cost avoidance both count.** Understanding and articulating both will strengthen your case.
- **Capturing benefit requires discipline.** Setting scope, dates, categories and statuses in advance helps you protect the credit when it comes.

Notes

1 Edwards, D (2025) Interview with Lindsey Clarke, conducted on 14 February 2025

2 In case you feel I'm being overly flippant here, there are plenty of vendors who can do exactly this, quickly.

3 European Commission (2009) State aid: Commission authorizes UK support to Royal Bank of Scotland with conditions to limit distortions of competition, Press release IP/09/1787, 30 November, https://ec.europa.eu/commission/presscorner/detail/en/IP_09_1787 (archived at https://perma.cc/HVY5-LRVB)

4 The Week (2017) EC sounds positive note on RBS plan for Williams & Glyn, The Week, 28 February. https://theweek.com/75166/ec-sounds-positive-note-on-rbs-plan-for-williams-glyn (archived at https://perma.cc/E256-UZQL)

5 Finextra (2016) RBS scraps W&G carve out; writes off £345 million spend on spin off, Finextra, 5 August, https://www.finextra.com/newsarticle/29270/rbs-scraps-wg-carve-out-writes-off-345-million-spend-on-spin-off (archived at https://perma.cc/JMJ3-44XZ)

PART THREE

How to land it

12

Politics – will the force be with you?

'We always check if leadership is willing to act on whatever results we find. If they say no, then you don't have an SWP problem, you have a politics, governance or incentive problem. No point doing deep analysis if they already know the answer they want.'

ALEJANDRO GIORDANELLI, MERCK KGAA

Reading the room

Don't get carried away

The Charge of the Light Brigade first fascinated me when I came across a Readers' Digest version of the book, *The Reason Why*, by Cecil Woodham-Smith[1] at my grandparents' house. I loved the way the author weaved the story of feuding cousins, class-led prejudice and British military incompetence into a story that read more like a novel than a piece of dry history about one of Britain's most notorious military calamities. But most of all, I was fascinated by the story of Captain Louis Edward Nolan: his story is more instructive for the SWP Practitioner than you might first think, so bear with me.

Nolan was a well-known junior cavalry officer who had written 'an important, even ground-breaking'[2] book on cavalry tactics[3] prior to his appearance in the Crimean War in 1854. He had strong views and was very critical about what he saw as cautious cavalry leadership in the first major battle there.[4]

At The Battle of Balaclava, Nolan delivered an order to those two feuding cousins, one of whom – Lord Cardigan – happened to command the Light Brigade, the other – Lord Lucan – being his commander. The order, from commander-in-chief Lord Raglan, instructed the cavalry to 'advance rapidly' and to 'try to prevent the enemy carrying away the guns'.[5] Unfortunately, neither Cardigan nor Lucan knew which guns Raglan was talking about (they couldn't see them), to which Nolan interjected, 'There my Lord are your enemy, there my lord are your guns', pointing directly down a valley at the end of which were large numbers of Russian guns pointing directly back at them. By the time Captain Nolan realized that these were not the guns he should have been pointing at, the cavalry was already charging and he was about to be the first of 247 people to die.

So what learning is there from this for the SWP Practitioner apart from the obvious don't-go-charging-at-a-bunch-of-loaded-cannon-on-a-horse one?

- **You don't know what you don't know.** You may think that you're in possession of all the facts but others may have a big picture that's even bigger than yours.

- **Yours is not the only option.** You're working in a large business where there are a lot of clever people. You're just one of them.

- **Don't insist that people look your way when they're more concerned about something else.** You're only going to annoy people if you do that: read the room.

- **However wrong your leadership might be, they're still in charge and you're not.** Adapt to the prevailing power dynamics and accept that they're there for a reason.

That said, you are not there to keep the peace: raising uncomfortable truths is part of the job. Just don't expect an avalanche of thanks: there are pitfalls to doing it.

Things may not work out as you expect

A colleague and I recently agreed that sometimes, when you raise concerns, you feel a bit like the little boy in the Hans Christian Andersen tale who pointed out that the Emperor was wearing no clothes.[6] I was curious: what happened to the little boy as a result of his calling this out? Well, so far as I could tell, nothing at all. The child has no name and isn't mentioned again in the story. What **is** mentioned is that the Emperor keeps on walking. Translated from the Danish, it goes like this:

> 'That made a deep impression upon the emperor, for it seemed to him that they were right; but he thought to himself, "Now I must bear up to the end". And the chamberlains walked with still greater dignity, as if they carried the train which did not exist.'[7]

Your leadership may acknowledge that you have a point, but they won't necessarily a) thank you for raising it or b) stop doing whatever it was that they were doing, because losing face may be more harmful than pretending not to be bothered.

Getting heard

Getting heard at all

Back in Chapter 2, I considered the relatively low corporate level a lot of practitioners occupy. They don't typically report into the CEO; they don't frequently report into the CHRO either. Getting valuable messages to that level may be an impossible task in itself. Here's a practitioner example:

> 'The first SWP plan I wrote here never got beyond my HR director because they said, "it basically says we're ****". It doesn't: it shows the risks and needed actions. If you can't look in the mirror, that's not on me... There's a fear of accountability right in HR.' – Anonymous Practitioner

I understand that frustration, because I've experienced something very similar when producing a report that either takes an excessively long time to reach senior leadership – by which time it's old news – or it never gets there. It's too easy to lament a CHRO's unwillingness to see what you see. But maybe your writing didn't help. They don't want 10 pages on top of 20 others.

Those 10 pages may still be needed – demanded even – by a unit manager who wants evidence to back up your summary. You need them too, but you have to put yourself in the CxO's shoes to eliminate your own possible bias; these days you have a clever little helper to do that for you.

Every little AI helps

We'll be talking about artificial intelligence at greater length in Chapter 15 but I just want to show you how I might use AI to generate a summary report for a CxO. By the way, I think this is a totally legitimate thing to do and the sooner we all get comfortable with the idea that it can make us all more productive instead of somehow being cheating, the better. There's nothing remotely cheating about using AI since much of the art – for now at least – lies in the kind of instructions you give it.

CREATING AN EXECUTIVE SUMMARY

1 You could just type into the prompt space of your engine of choice,

Produce an executive summary from this report.

You will get back a perfectly functional summary that is perfectly generic and as likely to hit the spot with your CxO as it is not. You're not asking your engine to think terribly hard about what might help to register a direct hit.

2 Here's an alternative instruction:

You are the CxO <amend as appropriate> of Company X. The company is currently experiencing considerable competition from Far East newcomers to the sector while there is considerable market stagnation, especially in Europe. Your workforce is aging rapidly, especially in some core technologies. The introduction of tariffs in the United States is problematic for the company because most of its revenue growth has been in that territory. You are under pressure from shareholders to revive the company's fortunes and not just through a cost-cutting death spiral. You are also notorious for being very demanding for clear, crisp messaging. Produce the kind of executive summary you would want for yourself from this document and set out those aspects of its content that you believe to be missing for it to be fully informative.

NB. Large language models aren't always current, so you'll need to feed in recent context – such as tariffs – yourself.

You're on your way to producing something that will resonate with your CxO by virtue of putting it into their own context. This may be an iterative process, but experiment with it.

Is this the guarantee that your messages will get through? No, nothing guarantees that, which is why it's so important that you have a story that matters to a CEO and you know how to tell it.

Telling the story

> 'We're the storytellers that help people connect it all up... If we sound like the analytics team, the business switches off, so we adapt our language to what resonates. Ultimately, we're nudging them to make the right decisions and de-risk the business.' – Consulting Partner

It may come as a surprise to some that storytelling is a word frequently used when describing SWP practice. Surely it's all data, analytics, formulae and other similarly worthy stuff. But we've already seen how, almost uniquely outside of the CxO meeting room, the practitioner can be the focal point for a collection of different inputs that need to be woven together. This requires you to connect all of the points on the journey.

Remember Adam Gibson's splendid chart in Chapter 10, where he drew connections from Business Goals through to Workforce Plans? Well, that chart multiplied many times over is the story that you need to be able to tell; but what works as a solution for one part of the business will probably not work for another. As I said earlier, each business paints its own masterpiece when it draws up its plans, but only you know that it's the *Mona Lisa* that you'll see when they're all put together. That is your power.

It is not, however, your key to the boardroom and we must again remind ourselves that we're not just trying to project the future workforce needs in order to achieve our intended strategy; we're also challenging our organizations to do things differently in a very holistic sort of way.

Power dynamics

In a recent LinkedIn article, David Wilkins of TalentNeuron said this:

> 'SWP requires the coordination of job architecture, skills intelligence, labour market data, people analytics, demand and supply forecasting, gap analysis, and gap fulfillment strategies. But in most enterprises, each of these pieces lives in different

> silos... Consider a structural rethink: Who owns SWP in your organization today – and
> are they empowered to drive it? Is authority for this work aligned at a high-enough
> level to coordinate all of the tech and process pieces or is decision-making
> fractured?'[8]

I don't think that any SWP practitioner would argue with this for a second; it's my own experience that a set-up which involves all of the respective talents (see Chapters 7 and 8) will deliver the most effective results. If I were being flippant, I'd suggest that David is saying, 'You just have to give me all the keys to the castle and we'll all live happily ever after'. Hmm. History is littered with cautionary tales of people who made such claims. His argument is more compelling than that, of course, in seeking alignment of ownership, architecture and authority. Nevertheless, much as we might like to change the world, deeper forces often block progress and we have to recognize that...

> 'Culture gets in the way. People might want to keep doing it the old way, or they
> have to weigh short-run goals. Then you ask if they truly want SWP solutions, or if
> they just want to keep the old system. That's an underlying political dynamic –
> how the org is structured, how leaders are rewarded – it's not malicious, it's the
> system.' – Guru Jordan Pettman

I'm going to return to that phrase, 'how leaders are rewarded' in Chapter 16, but for now I want to zoom in on what might be meant by 'the old system'.

Here's one example of what we all know happens. Let's just suppose that we have established the most beautiful SWP framework ever – it's light, it's relevant, it's adored in SWP communities up and down the land as the very model of a modern major-general, so to speak. Many parts of the business have already signed up to it and are feeling the benefits to their areas. They're hiring people without constraint because they're following the rules that people have agreed.

And then Finance, the CEO, or both declare a company-wide hiring freeze. Your framework just lost all credibility.

Professor John Boudreau of the University of Southern California is one of the shimmering demigods of HR thinking, so it was with no small amount of trepidation that I approached him for his views on the state of things in general and it was on this topic that he laid things out brilliantly. Here's some of what he said.

> I don't know that we need any more logical frameworks about how HR adds value or how investments in people pay off. I think that's all available. My own feeling right now is that that sort of thing is seldom really in the awareness of executives outside of HR and in many cases, HR is not in a position to bring that kind of insight to the executive levels... whether it be line leaders or C-suite leaders or boards or investors... the HR profession really isn't looked to for that kind of insight. So I think a lot of the logic, a lot of the evidence, a lot of the really good work that gets done sort of sits inside a bubble of people in HR talking to each other.
>
> You know the example of running into the hiring freeze or the hiring cap or the budget freeze when we had something we thought would be really good for retention, or maybe workforce flexibility, something like that and [there's] plenty of evidence to show that the very best performers out there would like to have flexibility of some sort and then the CEO says, 'but I want everybody back in the office', you know, for whatever reason they have, but it's generally not particularly well informed in terms of what we know about return-to-office, just to take that one example. And I think there's a lot of reasons why things like strategic workforce planning, people analytics, etcetera have failed to break through to become more like a financial perspective on the organization.
>
> You know that that every leader is expected to understand how finance looks at the organization and how money moves through it. Every leader is expected to have some rudimentary understanding of a common model about how money works, right? They you don't get to shop around and say, oh, I don't like the way my CFO is doing the financial analysis. I'm going to shop around until I find a CFO who will do it the way I like it or do it the way that makes me look good. But you can shop around for an HR organization and perspective that you like better. You know, I like the idea of HR as compliance. They keep all that legal stuff off my desk. Other than that, I'm going to run this business based on a financial model and therefore if I need the money, I'll put in a hiring freeze.

He's right, of course. So when HR pitch up with great ideas about doing something across a broad canvas, I'm not so sure we should be surprised by the reaction we might get.

The moral of the tale

Knowing that politics is an inevitable, unavoidable part of your terrain gives you some chance of navigating it. You may argue that this is better called stakeholder management, but I think this is somewhat more tectonic, which means navigation that is careful and considered, not bold and adventurous:

> 'In early stages, you might just do a small pilot or highlight a short-term risk. Once you prove it helps, people warm up to expanding SWP. If we jumped straight to a huge AI-driven complexity, it might fail culturally.' – Paul Habgood, Mercer

This a lesson hard learned and that's because there are still organizations out there that want to be able to say that they're doing this when all they've really done is create a function and a process (as I hinted at in Chapter 3). This can be unhealthy for the business and definitely unhealthy for the practitioner if, like Captain Nolan, the guns are actually pointing at them.

> 'When you first arrive, you're everybody's saviour. You're the silver bullet that's going to fix entrenched workforce problems and all the change fatigue.
>
> So you go in gently, because we need friends in every camp – Finance, HR, OD, L&D, Strategy, the unions, the lot.
>
> Then the discovery work starts. We mirror the problems back: "this process is broken", "that tech stack is obsolete", "the budget envelope makes the strategy undeliverable".
>
> The organization was invested in a miracle; what it gets is a mirror – and mirrors are inconvenient. Now you're the friendly critic nobody asked for.
>
> It's even worse in the public sector. Government demands we have a workforce plan because pay-bill is the biggest line in the budget, but there's no appetite for the hard work that comes after diagnosis.
>
> They...expect you to solve a 40-year structural problem in three months without upsetting anyone.
>
> That stakeholder swing is the emotional tax of this job; 50–70 per cent of your year is spent on engagement – updates, diplomacy, re-selling the vision to a revolving cast of executives – simply to keep the licence to keep doing the work.'
> – Practitioner legend Jen Allen

Politics can wear you down but – and we know this to be true – it's also part of the allure.

REFLECTIONS

- **Don't expect to be carried aloft by a grateful ExCo.** Uncomfortable truths can be too uncomfortable to be welcome.

- **HR is not seen as a natural source of insight like this.** You need to persuade people that you're a force for good.

- **Create a channel through relevance.** Don't just tell the CxOs everything you want to tell them: tell them things that they will care about.

- **Tell stories.** Weave together the multiple strands into a compelling narrative that no one could disagree with.

- **Read. The. Room.** Don't go charging in when no one else is interested.

- **Don't give up.**

Notes

1 Woodham-Smith, C (1953) *The Reason Why: The story of the fatal charge of the light brigade*, London: Constable.

2 Buttery, D (2008) *Messenger of Death: Captain Nolan and the charge of the light brigade*, Pen & Sword.

3 Nolan, L (1853) *Cavalry: Its history and tactics*, London: Bosworth and Harrison

4 National Army Museum (no date) Campaign journal of Captain Louis Edward Nolan, aide-de-camp to General Airey, Quarter Master General in the Crimea, 5 September to 12 October 1854 [Manuscript] Online collection, National Army Museum, London, Accession number: 1989-06-41-1, https://collection.nam.ac.uk/detail.php?acc=1989-06-41-1 (archived at https://perma.cc/N4Y7-PHCT)

5 Brudenell, A M (2008) Lessons in Leadership: The Battle of Balaklava, *Military Review*, March-April, pp. 77-84, https://www.armyupress.army.mil/Portals/7/military-review/Archives/English/MilitaryReview_20080430_art012.pdf (archived at https://perma.cc/56CH-ZT3T)

6 Andersen, H C (1837) *Kejserens nye Klæder* ['The Emperor's New Clothes']. Eventyr, fortalte for Børn, 2nd collection, Copenhagen: C.A. Reitzel,

7 Andersen, H C (1837) *Kejserens nye klæder*, Andersenstories.com, https://www.andersenstories.com/da/andersen_fortaellinger/kejserens_nye_klaeder (archived at https://perma.cc/T5MJ-N294)

8 Wilkins, D (2025) The strategic workforce planning gap: Why even the best struggle to connect strategy to execution, LinkedIn, https://www.linkedin.com/pulse/strategic-workforce-planning-gap-why-even-best-connect-david-wilkins-0mfne/ (archived at https://perma.cc/2MS3-98H8)

13

Strategy, scenarios, scale, scope... and Sheena

SWP on the grand stage

'Don't believe everything you read... few if any organizations are doing this as well as it could be done.'

ANONYMOUS PRACTITIONER

In Chapter 12 we completed a mini-trilogy focused on engagement, delivery and the navigation of political dynamics, all of which are essential components of the practitioner's craft. As surely as night follows day, we now turn to phrase books.

I would be reduced to tears of laughter reading about the celebrated book *O novo guia da conversação em portuguez e inglez,*[1] a Portuguese to English phrase book, gloriously liberated from any link to accuracy by the inability of its author, Pedro Carolino, to speak English. To overcome this mild inconvenience, he used a Portuguese to French phrasebook followed by a French to English one. Also published as *English as She is Spoke,*[2] the book contains such legendary and well-known English sayings as 'to craunch a marmoset' and 'Then he kicks for that I look? Sook here if I knew to tame hix.' Reading these again now has me gurgling like a toddler once more.

Another splendid example of not getting it right is the story of Major-General John Sedgwick of the Union army whose last words on 9 May, 1864 were, allegedly, 'They couldn't hit an elephant at this dist-'. This source of mirth is also, of course, a personal tragedy as well as a military one. He was 'one of the most experienced and competent officers in the Army of the Potomac... greatly respected and loved by his men.'[3]

Carolino also meant well but instead found himself ridiculed (and disproportionately famous); both tales offer pointers for the SWP Practitioner (and plenty of others besides).

Strategic Workforce Planning is less likely to feature in a small family-run business than in large, multinational, multi-faceted organizations of such bewildering, labyrinthine complexity that it is a given that even the most seasoned newcomer will need weeks, if not months, just to understand how it is structured and claims to work. Yet it is exactly this kind of environment in which SWP is expected to work miracles; it is no place for hubris, rigidity of thought or lack of clarity.

You're all individuals

In Chapter 2 I described data as being a bit like mercury; I want to give that a bit more of a pulse here. I'm as guilty as anyone in this business of looking at a big picture and taking that to be some kind of universal truth: 'oh, our attrition stats are awful', 'we face an ageing population cliff-edge', 'we're not retaining our younger staff for long enough'. There can be dangers lurking in a reliance just on the biggest picture.

HYPOTHETICAL EXAMPLE

The big picture may not be as big as it first seems

- An aggregated workforce plan suggests that next year there will be a net decrease in India of 375 heads.

- That is made up of 1,225 reductions and 850 additions. Great news – we don't need to let all of those people go? Hold on a minute.

- In those roles where there are either sizeable reductions or additions planned, we can see straight away that the planned additions exceed the planned reductions substantially (there are a couple the other way round).

- Applying that cap, the number of possible redeployments has already dropped to 480.

- Let's add another mesh to this sieve. What does adding the grade do for this picture? The opportunity total drops to 450.

- The data is starting to let us down now, because we have no information about whether there is a city match, a timing match and a departmental

---

match. That much salami-slicing still needs to take place before we really know the opportunity potential.

- You also know nothing about any individual circumstances that might restrict someone's ability to be redeployed. Individual life stories can have a profoundly degrading effect on what seems like a very solid number.

I recognize the contradiction with something I said just in chapter 12 – about you having the *Mona Lisa* view that no one else has. That is still true, but like any painting, da Vinci's great work is an aggregation – a collection of brushstrokes woven together. Similarly, an organization consists of many functions, individual in nature, each of which is peopled by individuals. Sweeping generalizations need to be handled with great caution.

So – big picture, little picture: where exactly do you take aim?

How strategic should strategic be?

To illustrate this question, here are quotes from three eminent practitioners in very similarly sized organizations. See if you can spot the difference:

Quote 1

'But I absolutely should not be doing strategic workforce planning in the individual business areas: it should sit at the enterprise. We should have an enterprise view.'

Quote 2

'We spent a ton of money with [a world-famous consultancy] building a multi-chapter playbook but the machinery was so heavy in use, it collapsed under its own weight. [One major division] literally became allergic to the term strategic workforce planning. We were told, "If you use that phrase, they'll throw up on you before you get out the door".' – David Shontz, ex-Nokia

Quote 3

'Some business units just aren't ready for a five-year strategy, so pushing a "universal" SWP approach was wasted effort. Now we only roll out to units that have a strategic outlook or are open to it, and that works better.'

About another 25 further opinions are available; however, the message for me is a very clear one: SWP – let's keep calling it that for now – will only probably land in a large organization of large divisions, not if it is done to them, nor even if it is done for them, but if it is done with them, which means you need to have a very good reason for darkening their door in the first place.

And I think that leads me to a difficult but necessary conclusion which goes beyond the inevitable one-size-doesn't-fit-all observation, totally legitimate as it is – namely that trying to strategically workforce plan an entire business at once or using the same approach, style and method is counterproductive. I may not be an academic but I can't possibly advocate (as I do in Chapter 4) the use of segmentation and micro-segmentation at a role or task level only to say that this should not apply when looking at an organization and its divisions. SWP has to be of value – and be seen **and believed** to be so – to the areas where it is practised.

Now to my knowledge there's no academic theory to back up what I'm about to say, but here's a hypothesis for you. Those parts of the business that either seek or welcome a strategic approach to addressing issues of workforce strategy and risk are quite likely to be of strategic importance to the organization as a whole. Why would you subject yourself to a great deal of analysis and crystal ball-gazing if you weren't? When I'm approached by a part of a business that's looking for help – yes, it happens – its strategic relevance is usually self-evident. It can be customer-facing or a vital infrastructural component; either way, its failure would cause the lights of the entire building to dim or go out altogether.

Before we move on, I would just endorse something that another couple of practitioners say:

Approach different functions differently

'We totally iterated the process function by function. Some love a structured approach, others respond better to a simple conversation. It's all about matching their style if you want to get a good outcome.' – Jo Thackray, ex-Sage plc

I don't want to talk about that

'In [Our Company], the financial pitch alone isn't enough. They care about operational aspects. But I've had other orgs where the financial argument was the key. Different cultures respond to different hooks, and that's part of the frustration.' – Naima Robenhagen Burgdorf, Ramboll

---

Put another way, don't sprint in with a slide deck and a bunch of spreadsheets just because a unit has got in touch. In the early days of SWP adoption we can tend to charge in excitedly, only to trudge away dejected when it becomes clear that that is not what is wanted here.

I would, however, pick up on that last little bit of quote – 'and that's part of the frustration'. What is? The fact that different teams have different priorities? The fact that yes, we're all individuals? These are frustrations? If so, they're frustrations that we have to embrace if we're to be taken seriously as experts who are there to help the business and not just process enforcers.

To further reinforce this, here are a couple of examples from people who have been there and done it in major-league organizations.

'So what we found in one of the organizations... it was easier to go business by business – because this was all pre-demerger. We looked at function level and actually got some quite good stuff. That was what I would call the little-s SWP.

Then we started to see there were some big S's that sat across the whole system. If you want to turn the company into something different – become more tech, more digital... In this instance and context, it was better if we tackled those things at Group level... We picked three big tickets and put them to the overall exec: if we don't tackle these at enterprise level they'll overlap, duplicate, conflict and be inefficient. We called them enterprise capabilities – fundamental to the future...

The exercise showed how people used the same words for different things. 'Digital' meant a million things to a million parts of the business. At enterprise level we said, if that's the capability we need, let's nail down where it's the same, where it's unique, and build separate cases for each.'

Viv Meredith – implemented SWP at AstraZeneca, GlaxoSmithKline and Anglo American

'In big European companies, we rarely do an all-enterprise plan. People break it down by function, by job family. Then we see if we can reconfigure the workforce, but even that depends on local incentives. So it's partial coverage. Some areas get a deeper SWP focus, others not so much.'– Anonymous practitioner in a European giant

---

A measured focus on those areas where you'll make a difference is desirable, but the second quote also makes a point about geographical differences that call for something more reliable than Snr. Carolino's phrasebook: what are the issues when you start to cross literal and cultural borders?

You're not from these parts, are you?

Now I'm going to mention my home county of Suffolk again. It's a very quiet place and not many people go there, so forgive the modest attempt to raise its profile.

Like many places, Suffolk plays host to many villages whose spelling is at odds with their pronunciation. As a teenager, I lived in Bromeswell and anyone who failed to talk about it as Brmswll (without the vowels) would immediately be marked out as a foreigner. Similarly, not calling Grundisburgh 'Grunsbrer' will earn you the silent treatment. These aren't just linguistic curiosities – they reflect deeper differences in regulation, strategic outlook and organizational culture that shape what SWP can even attempt. Universal strategy is a bit meaningless if spoken in a dialect no one recognizes – or maybe even wants to hear.

> 'In the US the conversation is very structural; in Europe it's people-y, welfare and engagement. APAC wants Moneyball-style analytics. One narrative does not win globally. You need a different dialect for each geography.' – Nick Kennedy, Workforce Planning Institute CEO
>
> 'Elsewhere they... need to be more proactive because it takes longer to make change, whereas in the US we can say, "You're employed today and tomorrow you're gone". That culture shapes how you introduce workforce planning.' – Jill Dobbe

Taking that last quote in particular, it's straight away clear that any kind of workforce planning in the United States may not need to be as nuanced as it is in many parts of Europe and elsewhere. Things like redundancy consultation periods, notice periods etc., change timing dynamics significantly. It's possible, although there's no direct correlative link, that much of the workforce planning technology available reflects this simpler landscape, since it emanates largely from the US. We'll be looking more closely at technology in Chapter 15.

For many practitioners, however, getting to grips with local regulation is unavoidable. Pity the first of two quite extraordinary people I want to spotlight. In different ways, both show how SWP can move beyond internal mechanics and into the realm of societal consequence – not as moral crusade, but as business necessity.

REAL-WORLD EXAMPLE
Selling the plan 60 times

Voluntary SWP adoption in a fully decentralized global humanitarian agency

Context

This humanitarian organization has over 60 country offices, each holding its own budgetary authority. HQ could recommend, but never mandate, HR initiatives.

Problem statement

Country directors complained of 'never having the right talent in the right place at the right time' yet saw SWP as another HQ fad.

Approach

1 **Pitch roadshow** – Head of SWP engaged individually with every country director.

2 **Three-slide rule** – Slide 1: local talent gaps and turnover risk; Slide 2: scenario forecast of programme disruption; Slide 3: low-cost SWP support offer (toolkit + analyst).

3 **Early adopter showcase** – Within four months, two offices piloted the framework and recorded a reduction in surge-hire costs. Their directors briefed their peers on the results in regional calls and meetings.

18 months later

- 42 countries embarked on workforce planning initiatives, in most cases self-funded and always on their own initiative.
- A rotating 'community of practice' call replaced top-down governance.
- Corporate HR used 'adoption density' as a leading KPI in board updates.

'I had to pitch to over 60 country directors individually and win their trust... however, once we had a few successful cases the word of mouth from one country director to another was the best "selling tool".

    We used one global methodology but adapted the content of the analysis and recommendations to the specific local context, engaging local HR for advice and ownership on the HR Action Plans.'

The lesson?

The time and effort spent in initial engagement is key to success in selling the initiative in a decentralized structure. One global methodology can be applied, but in the implementation the local context has to be considered when drafting action plans.

Now I'm going to stay with this remarkable practitioner for a bit longer, and the reason for so doing will probably be obvious. Humanitarian agencies don't typically follow a nicely smooth path; their very rationale is to respond to crises across the globe, crises that may emerge and develop gradually or which arrive with shattering suddenness. In such a world, scenarios are not just a nice-to-have; they are a matter of life and death.

Imagine

'It's about building the muscle to plan, not having a perfect plan.' – Viv Meredith

When speaking to Tobias Bartholome of the German airline Lufthansa, I learned a new word. In English, we try to come up with a new word that no one has ever heard before to describe something. German is much more sensible – it just bolts together existing words to create something recognizable (albeit rather long). *Scheingenauigkeit* is one such word. *Genau* means exactly, and *genauigkeit* means accuracy. We won't talk about what *schein* translates into but join the words together and you get 'sham accuracy'. It's an important point to bear in mind when talking about scenarios – even if you have just one of them.

The longer I've worked in this space, the more I realize that SWP is less about 'How many do we need?' and more about 'What will we do?' and that's what brings me back to our wonderful humanitarian practitioner again.

REAL-WORLD EXAMPLE
Scenario SWP for perpetual crisis

Planning amid pandemics, famines and conflicts

Context

The agency operated in a constant state of emergency – new disasters every quarter; funding swings tied to geopolitics.

Problem Statement

Traditional five-year workforce plans collapsed within months of approval.

Approach

1 **Crisis catalogue** – 15 archetypal events (e.g. category-5 cyclone, simultaneous conflict + drought) with historic staffing curves.

2 **Directional metrics** – Focus on demand trajectory (up or down) rather than headcount precision.

3 **Rolling review** – Annual for first two years, then biennial, combining bottom-up country assumptions with HQ geopolitical briefs.

Three years later

- After three cycles, staffing forecasts for major emergencies were within ±8 per cent of actual deployments.

- Funding proposals included pre-costed workforce scenarios, helping fundraising efforts and donors' approval.

'Crises were constant... You can't forecast them precisely, but you can model scenarios.'

The lesson?

Scenario ranges and a regular cadence of review trump single-number forecasts when volatility is permanent.

This practitioner's world may well be the very zenith of volatility, but global volatility in the 2020s is not confined to the natural world. The British Prime Minister Harold Macmillan was supposedly asked by a journalist what worried him: 'Events, dear boy, events', was the reply.[4] The events that impact business are rarely as seismic and vital as those humanitarian agencies must confront, but anyone trying to suggest that everything is smooth sailing needs to reflect on this current period in political, economic and social history for the more-than-occasional pushback example.

'We're not telling [the business], we're trying to get the right answer of what exactly your workforce and skills are going to be in five years... We're trying to get a platform that aims us to think about that and think about the scenarios... so that we can act on it. Otherwise we end up in distress all the time and just reacting to what's right in front of our faces.' – Paul Habgood, Mercer

That said, crisis responses sometimes showcase the kind of agility made possible by a Strategic Workforce Plan well-grounded in its willingness to embrace vague, its readiness to act in the downstream functions and in its understanding of what the workforce is capable of doing. We'll draw these threads together in Chapter 14, using an all-too-real-world crisis: the Covid-19 pandemic. What is clear to me is that the development of a planning muscle – that innate understanding of what the workforce is, could be and how it could be made to be so – will be seen as being more valuable over time than simply producing a plan for an extended period (as if that were itself simple, but you know what I mean).

Adam Gibson of EY talks about 'adjusting the sails en route to the island'. The less said about my own attempts at seacraft the better – I am a danger to others – but no doubt had I practised a bit more, my failings may have evolved into something more elegant. Gibson's point is that this becomes, over time, something that you feel and ceases to be something mechanical and stressful. 'If you don't do that,' he says, 'you're effectively drifting, hoping to bump into land.'[5]

Adam is an Advisory Council member of the Workforce Planning Institute. Nick Kennedy, the Institute's CEO, is more concerned that agility can be hindered by strategic inflexibility. 'Why does strategy stay frozen for five years,' he asks, 'when everything else in the enterprise is supposed to be agile? We're still treating strategy like stone tablets and that cripples the planning muscle.' Having been involved in a few annual strategic planning cycles – more of which in a moment – I'm not so sure I agree. Regardless, given that this book is about Strategic Workforce Planning, it's probably time we talked about that strategy bit.

Let 'em in – HR can enrich strategy

'What I love is the ability to connect HR to the strategy of the organization. Strategic workforce planning is one element, but the buzz comes from aligning people, skills and numbers to business intent – that's where I excel and I really enjoy it.' – Jean Blackstock

'Strategic [workforce] planning is closer to strategy consulting than to deep analytics.' – Dirk Jonker, Crunchr CEO

I wonder how many practitioners out there actually participate in the development of strategy or even get to hear of it until it's already become those tablets of stone that Nick Kennedy talks about. As I see it, if you know what the company strategy is, you can ask, 'Have we evaluated how feasible it is from a workforce perspective? Do we know the scale of change we need – reskilling, location shifts, time frames, the market for these people?' If the answer's 'not sure', then we need to dig in, because workforce is surely a significant part of the strategy, not an afterthought. Frustratingly, you only normally get one chance each year to jump onto the fast-moving carousel that is the annual strategy-setting cycle (in which we reset the three-year strategy…). Miss that chance and you're then having to play catch-up.

'Unless you're in the executive planning sessions, you're really out to sea.' – Cole Napper, Lightcast

Becoming a participant in the broader company strategy setup is rarely easy. Firstly, company strategies can be highly sensitive, frequently subject to closed-door non-disclosure agreements (NDAs). It can take a long time to persuade someone that you either deserve to be a member of that community or, more likely, can be **trusted** to be a member. You may need to use your own network of sponsors and friendly senior champions to prise open the door to be let in.

There is no one good way to show that you are worthy of inclusion – remember what I said in Chapter 9: you're (probably) from HR and, whether anyone likes it or not, that comes with baggage. How best then to get included? Well, imitation is the sincerest form of flattery, so do what they do and then go a little bit further.

Bringing horizon to the foreground

Every now and again, in one of the regular online practitioner community gatherings that bring people together, I see a presentation that makes me realize that I'm really not as smart as I'd like to think I am: something that offers a fresh way forward or one that is more powerful than anyone's tried systemically before.

This UK financial institution has concluded that its human capital, if not on a par with its financial capital, needs to be treated more seriously (a theme I'm returning to in Chapter 16). Its SWP team is not therefore a couple of people scratching away in a basement office; it's a substantial complement of almost 20 people, some of whom are essentially dedicated to horizon scanning – not just a quick look out of the window to see if it's raining (not easy in a basement office anyway), but a full-blown, in-depth assessment of icebergs that are dead ahead and farther afield.

Armed with this, they put themselves in front of business unit heads and ask them very directly: have you thought about what you will do if these icebergs come your way? Now, what they do with the answers is their business (no one's giving away all of their trade secrets in an open presentation, for goodness' sake), but I believe this kind of information is priceless. It's the very foundation of the situation analysis, the risks and scenarios that you can lay in front of your CHRO, Group Strategy, Finance, whoever you like, as proof positive that you're a player to be reckoned with. You're not a support act; you're one of the headliners.

I hinted earlier at SWP having a societal purpose; now some might shy away from such a notion, because some might feel uncomfortable about the suggestion that SWP has some kind of lofty moral ambition. But no. As they say in the films, this is strictly business.

Sheena and a whole new dimension for SWP...

Who is Sheena? Well, Sheena holds the British Empire Medal (odd, given that Britain no longer has an empire) for the most remarkable of initiatives.

The lockdown imposed on populations worldwide by Covid left many families cooped up in small homes or apartments, unable to buy many of the essentials for a variety of reasons. Sheena turned the empty vastness of the Edinburgh headquarters of the Royal Bank of Scotland into a giant distribution warehouse, begging, haranguing and demanding help from larger corporations to donate basic supplies that were then boxed up into subsistence packages for the city's more disadvantaged residents. With an army of volunteers and endless reserves of conviction and energy, thousands of families were kept going through her efforts with 6,000 meals per week.[6] Whatever the medal should be called, she deserved it.

Now you may think this is all very nice, but you need to also understand that Sheena is a pioneer in this workforce space. We're all talking now about skills adjacency – the idea that having a certain set of skills may therefore qualify you to make the leap across to a different opportunity. Sheena was talking about skills adjacency 10 years ago. Sheena knows her stuff and she cares about it. She currently has a great interest in generational shifts and, when speaking to her, I asked whether SWP should be paying more attention to them than they currently do. Here's what she said:

> 'That's exactly what I was trying to get across. Right now across the UK – and especially in Scotland – boys are facing the highest levels of suicide, the most serious mental health challenges, and disproportionately high rates of youth offending.
>
> It's not just that they're topping those charts – it's that the numbers are rising fast. Their academic achievement is falling behind, with some estimates showing under 40 per cent of boys meeting expected outcomes. They're trailing girls in workplace readiness by a good 14 per cent, and they're being heavily influenced by the wrong kinds of social media – content that's not only dismissive of women, but also convinces boys that girls are getting all the support, while they're being left behind. And they're rebelling.
>
> If this continues, I genuinely worry that in five years' time, the male allies we've relied on to support women's progress in the workplace won't exist. These boys – if they keep internalizing these messages and continue to feel unheard, unseen and like they're failing – won't grow into the kind of men who lift others up.
>
> But we can change that. Workforces have a real opportunity to be part of the solution – by bringing in visible role models, by adapting the language we use, by investing in training that supports boys to grow into emotionally strong, respectful men.
>
> I know women are still underpaid and underrepresented in leadership. But we won't solve that by ignoring the fact that boys are slipping. We have to look at both sides of the coin.[7]

Not many people look at things this way.

This language and subject matter are about as alien as was English to Mr Carolino. But I believe that the S in SWP stretches way beyond issues that are obvious and that they are relevant, not just because they point to possible future social disruption, but because they are a nailed-on risk to the business. As I've said a few times already, if not in so many words, we aren't really in the planning business: we're in the risk business.

REFLECTIONS

- **SWP is not uniform.** Don't try to make it so.

- **Embrace early workforce strategy adopters.** They're probably strategic thinkers.

- **Cultural differences aren't just noise.** They can be the difference between acceptance and rejection.

- **The real muscle in SWP** is the ability to adapt to scenarios, not just the ability to model them.

- **Societal issues are not nothing to do with us.**

- **We're in the risk business.**

Notes

1 Carolina, P J de (1855) *O novo guia da conversação em portuguez e inglez*, Paris: J-P Aillaud, Monlon e Ca

2 Carolina, P J de (1883) *English as She Is Spoke: The new guide of the conversation in Portuguese and English*, edited by J. Millington. London: Field & Tuer.

3 American Battlefield Trust (n.d.) The Death of John Sedgwick, https://www.battlefields.org/learn/articles/death-john-sedgwick (archived at https://perma.cc/5DGG-MYJP)

4 The attribution of this quote to Macmillan is not as rock solid as it might first seem, terrific as it is. A good examination of its origin can be found at Quote Investigator (2020) Quote origin: Events, My Dear Boy, Events. https://quoteinvestigator.com/2020/08/31/events/? (archived at https://perma.cc/9FLM-P8LP)

5 Edwards, D (2025) Conversation with Adam Gibson, EY, conducted on 18 February 2025

6 Jardine, C (2020) Amid the Covid crisis, some business executives are proving they are not all like Donald Trump – Christine Jardine MP, *The Scotsman*, https://www.scotsman.com/news/opinion/columnists/amid-the-covid-crisis-some-business-executives-are-proving-they-are-not-all-like-donald-trump-christine-jardine-mp-3013783 (archived at https://perma.cc/F8DM-TEP8)

7 Edwards, D (2025) Conversation with Sheena Hales, conducted on 21 May 2025

14

The challengeable orthodoxy of third parties, headcount and skills

A different take on who counts, how we count and what really matters

We're co-leading a contingent labour project, not really for us ... But now we truly understand the contingent labour process, the vendor management systems. And so when you do that, you've built a ton of trust.

ANONYMOUS PRACTITIONER

Why have we divorced skills from task? The first thing everyone does is map the workforce's skills. I don't care – start with demand; start with the task. We tried to do that in Police Scotland, or at least some of the L&D folk were doing it, and I asked them: 'I've just found a skills listing for police officers that includes "baking" ... and "basketball 1" and "basketball 2". Are these relevant skills for police officers? Have we ever deployed a polis [policeman] to the Great British Bake-Off in an official capacity?' If we have, fine, but I'd suggest that's not a skill set we need. Why is it on my system? Why have I got, as a result, 36,000 skills profiles, none of which seem remotely relevant when you look at the actual work?

JEN ALLEN, EX-POLICE SCOTLAND

This last phase of the book could be called Soapbox. It doesn't mean that I'm about to embark on one long rant but what follows may still feel like a long op-ed: there is a passion in the community that stirs some strong emotions – not just in me. Many of those emotions will be on full display in Chapter 17 and they make for compelling reading. Before we get there though, I want to focus on two things that we don't talk about enough and one thing we don't seem able to stop talking about: respectively, external staff, measurement and skills.

We need to plan for the whole workforce

The problem with third-party workers

Although he was present throughout much of *The Three Musketeers*, D'Artagnan was not himself a musketeer. In the story, he's perceived very much as an outsider, despite helping them at various points through Alexandre Dumas' epic tale. He's doing the things that they do but he doesn't wear the hat. When the three actual musketeers say, 'All for one, and one for all', they're talking about the three of them. You don't hear them saying, 'Us three and him (sort of) for one, and one for us three... and him, sort of', do you?

How many of this kind of worker do you currently have in your organization? Some of the people I've spoken to in compiling this book have only half-jokingly replied that they can't be sure how many employees they have, let alone anyone else. In Chapter 6, I offered my own definition of the main subtypes of third-party worker, which I defined as someone employed by a third-party company and who, as I said, 'will rarely be treated or seen as part of the company's headcount. More often than not, they will be managed through Supply Chain as a non-headcount expense, rather than through HR.'

I want to remind you of only one of these, the one that I think matters most here:

> **Resource Augmentation (RA).** A lot of people might describe these as Statement of Work staff... But Advisory staff do that too... The distinction is that these are roles also performed by the company's own employees, hence the naming. These staff are frequently co-located with employees and may report to an employee as manager.

Put simply: same roles, different badge and different treatment. These staff most closely resemble employees, and that's a problem.

So, what is the problem? As I see it, there are a few things:

1 As I've already said, they're not treated as workers. They're a purchase order, a statement of work that renders them abstract, an almost invisible form of workforce.

2 As I've already said in Chapter 6, they're usually engaged on a piecemeal basis by individual managers, they're flying below the financial approval limits that allow managers to sign off on their own, they're often renewed and they're not always working on a fixed price basis.

3 As I've said in Chapter 11, their unit cost is higher, you're not necessarily building your own capability if you rely on theirs, your vendor could move them elsewhere to your detriment and it sends a poor EVP message.

None of these things make them a bad choice. It's conceivable that a future of work in which everything is pop-up functions, short-term gigs and one-off deliverables would make RA much more desirable than large numbers of employees. That future is not implausible and certainly not wrong.

The pace of technological change is now so great that the era of L&D-led upskilling is perhaps no longer tenable for some functions, like technology. Can they reasonably be expected to keep up with that pace, or should those functions shrink dramatically to a core of company and subject matter experts, relying on RA staff vendors to provide people with cutting-edge capabilities? Looked at this way, RA may become a dominant labour source and not just a top-up.

All of this suggests to me that we should take the RA workforce much more seriously than we currently do. And it is almost always not a planned-for element of our workforce supply.

Why should we care about Resource Augmentation workers?

Well, not all of us should – especially if you don't have any. But any organization which runs change projects alongside its Business as Usual (BAU) activities and any organization that uses technology at any scale is likely to have them. I say 'likely' because it's quite possible that you probably won't know much about exactly how many you have.

This isn't just anecdotal, but it's echoed in the few studies out there. One such, by the consultancy Flextrack in association with PwC in 2023,[1] suggested that $352 billion a year was spent globally on what they called Statement of Work staff, plus a further $449 billion on what they described as Gig/platform staff.[2] The value of the whole extended workforce space was estimated to be $3.7 trillion in 2023.[3] These are non-trivial sums of money so we really ought to know who these people are, what they do and what they're doing.

But of course we know these things, don't we? Don't we?

The data issue

A reminder: RA staff are not workers or, to be precise, they are not head-count. They are an expense, a purchase order. Consequently, their data is typically managed through procurement systems rather than workforce platforms – unless systems access provisioning dictates otherwise. Some extended workforce systems are in use, but their usefulness varies wildly. That's because these systems are highly configurable and the configuration will be heavily influenced by the make-up of the implementation team.

Each function will naturally implement a system that reflects the issues of greatest interest to them. HR may wish to uniformly apply a job and skills framework to every worker, but if they're not an active participant in the implementation – not a given – then a different list may emerge, driven in part by the lists that vendors actively maintain and on which they base their prices (the rate card, as it is known).

Opacity is fuelled by a collection of other similar delights, such as a lack of distinction between Fixed Price and Time and Materials staff (see Chapter 6 for the distinction) or the project that the workers have been brought in to serve. There may be a hiring manager name but that isn't always the actual hiring manager, being instead the business manager for the unit who is administering the purchase order.

Even if all the datapoints that you want to see are available and even if all those datapoints have been accurately populated – two assumptions on which you shouldn't rely – it's quite possible that you'll encounter resistance to sharing it with you.

'I CAN'T TELL YOU THAT'

A quick diversion. Although everybody works for the same company, there is often a strong tendency to keep certain things from each other: 'I can't tell you that because it's commercially sensitive', or 'I'm afraid that this is under NDA so we can't tell you anything about it'. Many of the practitioners I've spoken to encounter this. There is an understandable desire to restrict access to sensitive information about redundancies or rates. There is very real legal and reputational risk at stake in the event of disclosure. But SWP Practitioners can't deliver a whole-organization view if major changes are withheld. I have found legal teams happy to suggest a balanced solution.

Is total workforce planning worth it?

So how insistent should you be about trying to create an entire workforce view? Well that depends very much on how much of the workforce operates under this broad RA umbrella, and that's not just driven by a fixed amount or percentage. Five per cent of a 100,000-person organization is a meaningful number. So is 500 if, in the course of any one year, 500 employees leave the company due to redundancy or because they were unhappy with career opportunities. On the other hand, a seasonal business, or one that is 'feast or famine' – where business can swing dramatically on a single large customer order – has no place maintaining a very high percentage of employees who could be laid off if the order is lost.

These are judgement calls that only you can make in the context of your own business. However, if there is even a degree of materiality to the RA element, then this group of staff should be treated with the same seriousness as any other component of your workforce and the function that procures them should be regarded as every bit as important a fulfilment partner as Talent Acquisition and Learning & Development.

There are two primary reasons for this. First, they are providing capability into your organization that you are using for business purpose. That is no different to any other class of employee. Your data should be robust and detailed enough to convey this message and it needs to be improved if it doesn't. The knowledge it should give you should enable you to make decisions about whether there is any risk inherent in the capability balance of your business.

The second reason for taking this seriously is that your spend on RA staff is, just like your spend on contractors, part of your Total Cost of Labour. And we need to consider why we don't talk about TCoL more often.

Measurement

> '*This year… we didn't issue head-count targets. Units got cost targets instead.*'
> – Anonymous Practitioner

Headcount flaws

We seem to be wedded to the use of headcount and I wonder why. It may be because this can be used (by some, not all) as a simple unit of measure for costing a function – a rule of thumb which says that one head costs $100,000 and that the need to reduce $10 million in cost therefore means that we need to reduce the workforce by 100. This is all very well *if* every head actually costs $100,000 – but we know that they don't. Nevertheless, 'trifles light as air are to the zealous confirmations strong as proofs of holy writ'[4] – a Shakespearean way of saying never let the facts get in the way of a good story.

And so it is ordained that a redundancy cycle is planned and pulled together to reduce the workforce by 100 people, regardless as to whether or not the average cost of the chosen 100 is actually $100,000, which it rarely is because managers will typically try to retain their best people in order to keep the show on the road. Consequently, the redundancies happen without making the hoped-for savings, leaving everyone unhappy.

Cost is a uniform measure (but not the only one)

It follows therefore that using the cost of labour as an alternative measure enables you to project workforce of all shapes and sizes on an equal footing. It also enables you to combine employees and all extended workers into a single view of labour cost. This allows you to consider the relative average cost of labour of one unit against another, which might provide leverage for alternative planning solutions, such as reducing reliance on more expensive RA staff in favour of employees, thus reducing unit costs and also reducing the potential need for redundancies when belt-tightening is required.

Headcount still has its uses, of course: a gradual return to the office is increasing the need for office planning and headcount – which pays no attention to the number of part-time workers there may be – remains a good barometer of need.

The point, of course, is that there is usually more than one lens through which the workforce can and should be seen. And yet for all this ambiguity and inconsistency in how we measure the workforce, there is one area where our conviction seems to be absolute – even if our clarity isn't. That area is skills.

Skilling me softly

> *'Skills? Absolutely freaking nowhere. It's another marketing wave. Ask a customer "skills of the person or skills of the position?" and they can't tell you. Everyone buys in because nobody gets fired for chasing the buzzword of the year.'* – A VERY senior technology leader

I know only too well the passions that are inflamed by this subject. It is undeniably the case that some organizations have embraced skills planning with missionary zeal and have shown some tremendous results. There are equally those who believe that SWP and a skills-based organization should have nothing to do with each other. Some of the quotes from my interviewees are blushingly strong.

Whole books on skills-based organizations are being written and companies across the globe are catching the same wave, concerned that a failure to know what people are capable of doing will leave them trailing in the race to capture the next wave of talent that can address the current extreme pace of change. We're going to talk about technology and AI in Chapter 15, so I won't dwell on that now. But to illustrate the conundrum, I want to use a couple of analogies and examples, one frivolous, the other very much less so.

Skills are sometimes unnecessary, sometimes invaluable

In Chapter 9, I referred to the song *Hole in the Ground* and how it reflected people's dislike of being told what to do. The poor official was only trying to ensure standards were being met.

Of course you need standards, but what skills are required to dig holes? Did John, the guy who dug the foundation for our house extension that was as deep as he was tall, possess Shovel Management to the required level? Sometimes, tasks are enough.

> *'What work actually needs doing, and what one or two skills are truly non-negotiable? If you've catalogued 20,000 skills, you've basically admitted you haven't a clue what matters.'* – Jen Allen

Everything has its place. My own experience is that business leaders are comfortable talking about skills but that future skills needs may be more easily identified through an understanding of the consequences for work, i.e. tasks. Many companies focus in on skills they deem critical for the future, drawing on their own sector knowledge and other sources, such as the World Economic Forum's massive Future of Jobs Report.[5] These projections can then be funnelled into overall workforce planning thinking to see whether workforce plans align with the broader thinking about critical skills trajectories, allowing corrective measures to be taken to maintain a longer horizon of ambition.

I promised an example of where skills knowledge was used to spectacular effect; this example, taken from the Covid pandemic, shows the approach at its very best.

REAL-WORLD EXAMPLE

Redeployment at speed – lessons from Unilever's talent marketplace

Practitioner: Neeta Saggar[6]

Context

In the pre-Covid years, Unilever began experimenting with a new way of managing internal mobility through a skills-based talent marketplace powered by AI matching. At the time, few organizations had heard of such a thing, let alone scaled it. But Unilever were clear: for such a system to succeed, it had to be anchored in Strategic Workforce Planning and closely aligned with business transformation goals.

What followed was a journey from pilot to enterprise-wide deployment, made possible by technology and by careful attention to business context, skills transparency and change management.

Challenge

When the pandemic hit, Unilever faced a dramatic demand shock. Its hygiene business was booming, while its food and restaurant channels slowed to a crawl. The company needed to redeploy thousands of employees across the globe, quickly, to maintain business continuity and do so without violating employment relations or triggering resistance.

Response

Unilever leveraged its existing talent marketplace infrastructure, already integrated with strategic workforce planning data. But success came not just from the tech but from how the redeployment was framed.

They launched a campaign: 'Raise Your Hand. Lend a Hand'.

Rather than forcing moves top-down, the redeployment was made voluntary, with employees shown opportunities that matched their skills or adjacent capabilities. Using multi-point skills data – from CVs, current and past roles, qualifications and expressed aspirations – the system could surface reasonable matches. Human validation then confirmed the options, and employees could opt in to new assignments.

This created an unexpectedly powerful effect:

- employees discovered latent strengths and new passions
- many stayed in their redeployed roles permanently

The approach built trust, avoided union confrontation and moved over 4,500 people in a matter of weeks.

Lessons

- *Redeployment at scale is possible but only with trust and transparency.*
  A tech-led redeployment might have collapsed under its own weight. By inviting rather than imposing, Unilever maintained goodwill and agility.

- *SWP must inform marketplace logic.*
  Talent marketplaces without clear signals from SWP risk being hollow. Neeta notes that many organizations launch marketplaces with no clear idea of which skills matter and therefore what to match against. Unilever's success came from its integration of SWP insight with technology.

- *Skills don't equal jobs; that's the point.*
  Employees were often matched based on skill adjacencies, not formal qualifications or job history. The project revealed how skills visibility unlocks new pathways, both for the business and for people's careers.

- *Simplification is essential.*
  Many firms get stuck in ontology paralysis – drowning in taxonomies and architectural debates. Neeta recommends beginning with end outcomes, not systems. 'Talk about the restaurant menu,' she says, 'not the kitchen'.

The thing that strikes me in this example has occurred to many others to whom I've spoken in the course of writing this book, which is that skills taxonomies and skills-based frameworks are a valuable component in determining what somebody is and what they can do. But it is just one component and it's one that is still very much in its practical infancy for most organizations.

Toby Culshaw, sage of longstanding, is more direct:

> 'If you're hiring [people] for their skills, you need to be hiring them against a skills-based taxonomy and a skills-based compensation framework ... their performance review should be a skills-based performance review... HR is nowhere near ready... and most businesses aren't designed around anything skills-based.'

The personal solar system

One of the first records I can remember hearing was of *The Planets* by Gustav Holst; it would have been around the same time that my mother got me out of bed at about 4 am so I could watch a very fuzzy black-and-white image of Neil Armstrong setting foot on the surface of the Moon. I've always been interested in the solar system, so perhaps I was naturally drawn to think of people and their attributes in a similar vein, rather like Figure 14.1.

Isn't this how people really are? Now, I could embellish this a little by introducing the concept of gravitational pulls that might draw certain attributes towards the centre; I could show how the orbit of smaller satellite objects might decay and I could throw in a comet or two to illustrate how visiting situations can suddenly become important. The thing is that possessing a skill does not indicate an ability, a readiness or even an interest in using it. Other things must line up before a possible fit becomes a genuine one. It's another way, perhaps, of illustrating the Chapter 12 example of how apparent redeployment opportunities reduce dramatically when confronted with the real world.

If you think about it, the humble CV/resumé embodies many of these attributes. If only there was a piece of technology that could take its contents and make something truly valuable from them. But wait: let's talk about technology next.

FIGURE 14.1 The whole person model

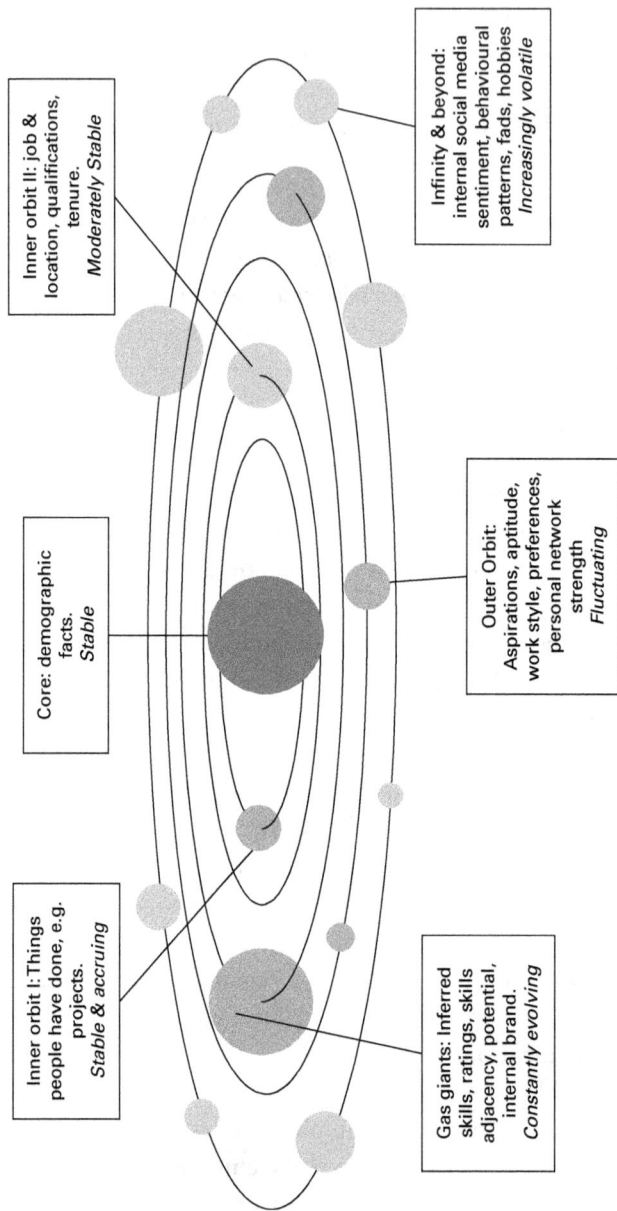

Inner orbit II: job & location, qualifications, tenure. *Moderately Stable*

Infinity & beyond: internal social media sentiment, behavioural patterns, fads, hobbies *Increasingly volatile*

Core: demographic facts. *Stable*

Outer Orbit: Aspirations, aptitude, work style, preferences, personal network strength *Fluctuating*

Inner orbit I: Things people have done, e.g. projects. *Stable & accruing*

Gas giants: Inferred skills, ratings, skills adjacency, potential, internal brand. *Constantly evolving*

REFLECTION

I don't believe in change for its own sake. Neither do I believe that any of the three pillars of this chapter – who we currently count, how we currently count them, what we currently choose to value – should be demolished. Each of them serves a purpose within a given context. It's just that people and people in business are so much more than individual dimensions. Our ability to perceive, to reason and to make decisions stems from being able to ingest multiple reference points of differing types and process them with extraordinary clarity. Surely looking at people in business through multiple lenses is some kind of equivalence to what we do naturally.

Notes

1 Flextrack Inc., PwC (2023) *Shifting Gears Again: Is your workforce ready for another disruption?* Flextrack Inc., Carey NC
2 Staffing Industry Analysts (2022) The Global Gig Economy 2022, in Flextrack Inc., PwC (2023). *Shifting Gears Again: Is your workforce ready for another disruption?* Flextrack Inc., Carey NC
3 Johnson, C (2025) Global gig economy reached $3.7 trillion, Staffing Industry Analysts, https://www.staffingindustry.com/news/global-daily-news/global-gig-economy-reaches-37-trillion (archived at https://perma.cc/UN9Q-9A2D)
4 Shakespeare, W (c.1603) *Othello*, Act 3, Scene 3. In: Greenblatt, S et al (eds.) (1997) *The Norton Shakespeare*, New York: W.W. Norton & Company
5 World Economic Forum (2025) Future of Jobs Report, Geneva. World Economic Forum
6 Edwards, D (2025) Conversation with Neeta Saggar, conducted on 5 June 2025

15

TechNo

*Technology and AI can enhance
SWP – but there's no panacea*

*The hardest bit of SWP is demand – understanding what the organization
will actually need. People try to get super-scientific: haul in 10 years of
historical data, run regressions, Monte-Carlo simulations. It still won't
predict the future. None of us are Nostradamus. We don't know if Covid
Mark 2 lands in six months or there's [going to be] a war in Fiji.
Technology's an awesome enabler; AI can accelerate the parts that can be
accelerated, but we still need humans to decide. If you push a magic button
and the black-box spits out a number, the first question is: 'Do we believe it?'
The conversation round the data – the messy bit everyone tries to skip – is
the value.*

ALICIA ROACH, CO-CEO, EQ8

There are a few things that you can currently guarantee at virtually any HR
conference: the keynote address will be about artificial intelligence; the
main concourse will be awash with technology company sponsors; and the
caterers will outdo themselves with canapé flavour combinations that you
never knew you wanted (because you didn't want them). Having heard a
lot about the first, seen a lot of the second and left untouched a lot of the
third, I want to consider three principal questions. First, whether existing
technology is a genuine enabler of SWP; second, what technology and use
might *become* a potent enabler; and thirdly, what AI means for the SWP
Practitioner.

You know the drill by now. I talk about something random before taking a 90-degree turn into what I really want to talk about. So let's talk about fish cakes.

Current technology as an enabler

It's just a fish cake

For most people in Britain in the 1960s, the freezer was a shoebox-sized compartment that occupied a small corner of the refrigerator. What therefore went into it was itself necessarily small and novel. Regular occupants would be a cardboard-packaged block of ice cream – vanilla, strawberry or raspberry ripple (no other flavours available then) – and fish cakes.

I didn't realize that fish cakes could be traced back to 1st century Roman recipes compiled by Apicius[1] but I was seven at the time so I wouldn't have been that bothered. I was more interested in the highly processed mash-up of fish, herbs, potato flour and other questionable 1960s ingredients (including weirdly orange breadcrumb coating) that most people would now recognize.[2]

Fast forward to the present day and a modern fishcake packet which promised me this:

GASTRO POETRY FROM THE FREEZER SECTION

'Smoked haddock, cod and salmon mixed with mashed potato and vintage Cheddar cheese topped with a mature Cheddar cheese, cream and white wine sauce in a sourdough breadcrumb coating.'[3]

It's still just a fishcake. Now substitute the word 'fishcake' for 'grid' and you have the conversation that I had with one of the finest people analytics technology minds about their SWP product.

To be clear, I was the one waxing lyrical about what I thought this product could do. The great mind was essentially telling me that the product was a Software as a Service (SaaS) version of a spreadsheet (hence the name grid). I was adamant that there was so much more to it than that and it took me four years before I wrote to concede that they were, after all, completely right. Which begs the question:

Are SWP technologies strategic?

So the premise for many SWP modules – they are often modules of something more substantial rather than standalone products – is that currently most people do SWP using spreadsheets. But hang on a minute: is what they're doing SWP at all?

SPREADSHEET HEAVEN – OR HABIT

I'm a spreadsheet geek, by the way. I was enthralled when I first saw Visicalc in 1984 on a Commodore CBM 8032 – packing a whopping 32 kilobytes of RAM.[4] My phone is now several million times more powerful, as are the machines that sit on my desk; yet the spreadsheet remains ubiquitous. We plead with our IT departments for a download facility that lets us manipulate carefully curated application data in our own Excel-based End-User Developed Application (EUDA). There's comfort in using those 15 or so functions (out of the 500+ that are available) to deliver a graph that we can then shovel across to PowerPoint.

So I shouldn't have been surprised that, when I asked a colleague to explain how they had reached an odd-looking outcome in our SaaS SWP system, the first thing they did was to share the spreadsheet they had used to calculate the input. Staring back at me were pretty much the same SaaS system inputs.

This told me two things: first, that our group system was perceived to offer nothing much that couldn't be done in a more comfortable Excel setting; and second, that it was being used almost entirely for short-term operational workforce planning, with lots of tiny detail spread across the following 12 months, with individual columns for the following two years. While I wouldn't wish to over-generalize, I suspect that this is the reality for the majority of people charged with workforce planning within their units. There's nothing wrong with OWP, I might add, but an extended OWP does not an SWP make.

It speaks, perhaps, to a greater truth: that true strategic thinking at a unit level is an unaffordable luxury; like Steve Hackett in Chapter 8, people are trying to play the right notes and the sheet music in front of them has been written by those who need to get through the next quarter, the next year.

The other truth might then be that technology vendors are giving people what they want – a systematized approach to spreadsheet building that aggregates things more easily – rather than what they should perhaps be asking for. Maybe people just need to be weaned off the old and coaxed to love the new.

REASONS TO LOVE WHAT WE'VE ALREADY GOT

> '*People crave a magic bullet, so tech vendors bolt SWP onto whatever they already sell. Got an org-chart tool? – "Cool, let's call that SWP." Holding a big skills database? – "Sweet, SWP!" Fancy spreadsheets in the cloud? – "Bang, SWP platform!"*
>
> *It's easier for them because folk recognize a chart or a spreadsheet, but it totally confuses the market. HR buys a shiny labour-market dashboard and thinks, "Job done". Then we show up and say, "That's one input, not the discipline".*
>
> *Add the US angle: over there they can fire Tuesday, hire Thursday, so a head-count graph feels like planning. Europe can't do that, Australia can't, Asia often can't, so they need real planning – but the sales noise is coming from that US mindset.*
>
> *Net result: noisy market, wrong expectations, and we spend half our life explaining what SWP isn't before we can show what it is.*' – Necessarily Anonymous Consulting Leader

I can picture various technology CEOs making an effigy of me and looking for a box of sharp pins: please don't, because there are a good many things to like about what's available. We just need to be clear about their SWP-enabling capability.

SWP is an eclecticism; a bringing-together of a variety of different functions, activities and disciplines that tries to unify them behind a more holistic purpose. I'm not altogether surprised, therefore, to see SWP modules emerging from a variety of core technology products.

So, before I'm mistaken for a grumpy old Luddite (two of these three things are true), here are some of the things the best tools can actually do.

IMPORTANT POSITIVES

- **Data aggregation.** The Sapient Insights Annual Systems Survey from 2021–22[5] lists around 90 separate HR systems. These systems can be ingested by analytics and planning tools to provide incredible analytical potential and depth. As Oliver Shaw of Orgvue put it: 'If I have a digital twin of the organization – the full position view – I can pull in skills data, labour-market risk, talent-succession outputs. I don't want to mandate your tools; my job is to unlock the data you already have and assemble a solution around the problem you're trying to solve.'

- **Predictive attrition.** Taking past people movements – in, out, across, up, down – and associating them with people attributes – demographics, tenure, location, unit, manager, etc. – to draw inferences about what movements are likely to happen in the future. This can be surprisingly accurate and can help identify future risk.

- **Organizational complexity and roll-ups.** Anyone who has ever issued a spreadsheet template to 50 separate units will know only too well just how many exotic ways each unit can respond in ways you didn't want and which can't be aligned to what anyone else sent you. These systems are great at bringing order to such chaos.

- **Dimensional flexibility.** Plotting future changes by cross-reference to other dimensions available in the people data, e.g. I want to grow our team by 50 per cent in Japan, but I want the grade mix to be skewed towards lower grades because of AI and we have an ageing workforce issue there that's predominantly male, so we'd like to increase the number of women under 35. Great for Bend planning.

- **Feasibility what-ifs.** Taking a specific attribute or selection and then running some desired outcomes against them can highlight what's possible and what's not, e.g. discovering that a company which aims to have a 50-50 gender balance by the end of next year would need 116 per cent of its hires to be female to achieve it.

- **Skills mapping.** Being able to calculate, mostly through inference (which will only improve), likely future skills needs which can then be compared against the current inventory to identify reskilling and upskilling options. Handy, but still a bit inference-heavy.

- **Talent and market intelligence.** Different modules to SWP, but by scraping the internet for anything in the job and skills market that moves (new patents, laws, job advertisements), you can make comparisons between different companies, benchmark them against their rivals and flag those areas where your plans are off-trend or likely to be harder and more costly because of market realities.

- **Organizational hypotheses.** Modelling the effect of organizational change to illustrate future shapes that may bring about risk or rapid attrition, e.g. bringing together two teams of different cultural and age backgrounds could stoke tensions without careful handling.

- **Outflow.** SWP systems are not the centre of everything. What they tell us needs to be shared with other systems too.

Other features are available. The big issue here is that, as David Green put it to me, 'The amount of times I'm asked, "What should we use for work-force planning?"… there still isn't one system to rule them all… Vendors bolt SWP onto org-design, or spreadsheets in the cloud, or labour-market scraping, and it just muddies the water… People are genuinely confused about which bit does what.'[6]

So what might that 'one system to rule them all' look like?

Future SWP technology

I'll start with a contradiction: I don't think there's a need for a future SWP technology, in the sense that everything that's needed to create that future already exists (apart from the ability to adapt to constant hierarchy changes – that would be nice); it's just that we don't currently connect what we have in a way that we could: we need a secret sauce.

Current technologies excel at projection, calculation and extraction – but that's not the same as planning. In Chapter 5's re-imagined Dowding system diagram, the SWP Practitioner is receiving a diverse collection of different indicators and processing them into something that is consumable by leaders.

All of the positive features that I've listed in this chapter help me to form a picture of what might happen to my workforce supply, either in managing it, projecting it or adding to it. The digital equivalent of the Ghost of Christmas Yet to Come, if you like. Ton van Dijk of Capgemini says:

> 'You buy [such] a tool in the market and then you implement it and then you'll fix the problem… that's not rocket science. The complexity kicks in when you start to look into the demand side.'

We're back to the central question that drives SWP: what do you want to achieve? All of this capability helps but none of it, at least in its current form, will help you determine what you want to achieve. Dirk Jonker, CEO of Crunchr, said that vendors need to '… be more honest and modest. Marketing must not be miles ahead of what the tech delivers. If you over-promise and under-deliver, churn will rebalance the market.' As Figure 15.1 suggests, there is no substitute – yet – for the not-so-secret sauce of human judgement.

FIGURE 15.1 In a world of systems, human judgement is still fundamental

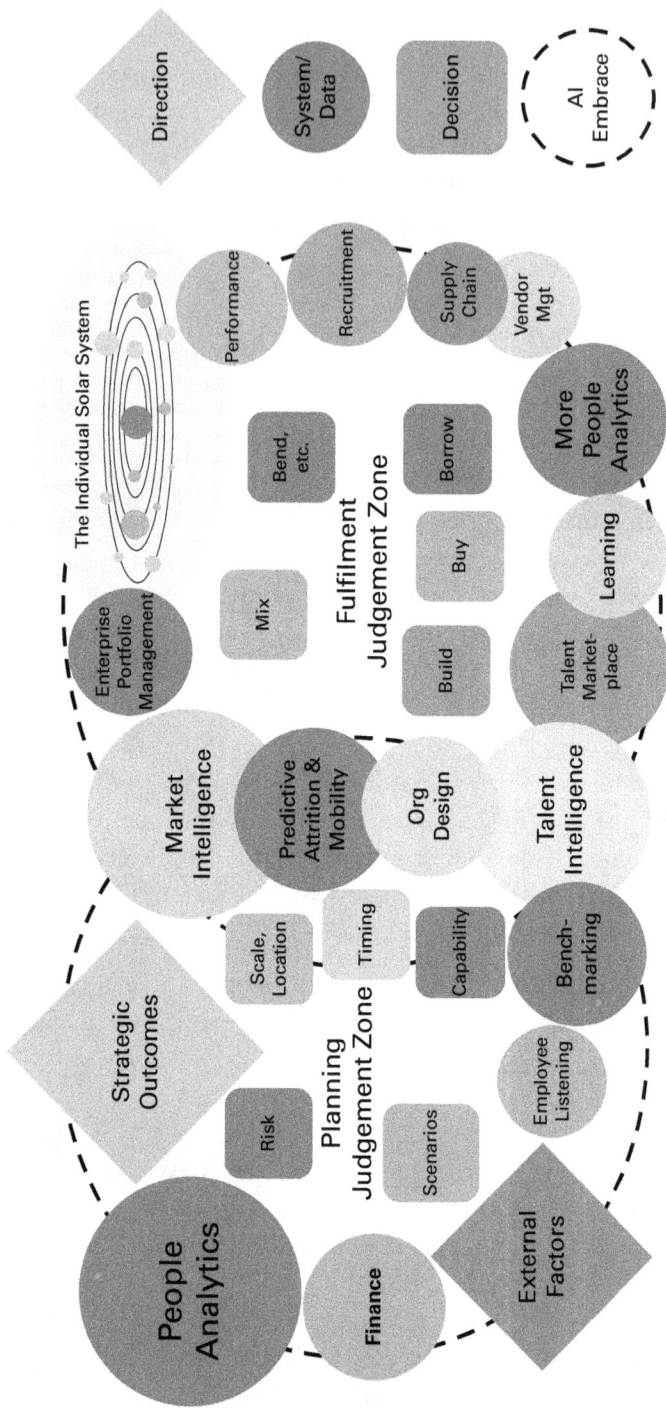

Perhaps there is no such thing as actual, genuine SWP technology at all: it is the synthesis of these different, disparate systems that enables people to work the magic.

But things are beginning to change. Some of these vendors are joining forces, either through joint ventures or through out-and-out mergers, creating solution clusters through which they hope to be able to join previously disconnected dots. We need this, because as Toby Culshaw of Lightcast puts it:

> 'The lack of consistency means you end up with these Franken-systems... bits of everything... imperfect processes drive imperfect systems, which drive all the wrong behaviours and outcomes.'

Something else – although HR is often the primary buyer of SWP tech, it's no longer the only one. 'SWP is a business [process],' says Florian Fleischmann of TalentNeuron, 'so [our system is] mainly bought now by the business and not so much HR anymore.' If that's where we are headed, then the technology needs to head there too.

One or two vendors already are. They are creating wizard-style question sets about desired outcomes that will then assess all of the different factors and pump out answers based on all available data and fulfilment options. I like the sound of this, because this seems to me to be the way in which artificial intelligence could become a secret SWP sauce all of its own.

Fear and loathing? SWP in the age of AI

Nothing new under the sun?

'Science gave man new welfare and new horizons while it took away belief in God and certainty in a scheme of things he knew.' – Barbara Tuchman.[7]

In typically eloquent prose, Tuchman was explaining the emotional impact of technological developments, not in the 20th century, or the 21st, but in the 19th.

'Man,' she said, 'had entered the Nineteenth Century using his own and animal power, supplemented by that of wind and water, much as he had entered the Thirteenth or, for that matter, the First. He entered the Twentieth with his capacities in transportation, communication, production, manufacture and weaponry multiplied a thousandfold by the energy of machines.'

Put another way, we think we haven't been here before when we probably have. Adam Gibson made a similar point in a presentation a couple of years ago, where he persuasively argued that new technologies have a habit of rendering worthless long-prized capabilities overnight, only for them to be supplanted by new ones into which people gradually slotted.

That does not mean that SWP Practitioners should be complacent about this latest step-change in the way we work and the way society operates. Progress does not necessarily mean better and rarely comes along without some negatives. I am not going to give my own Nostradamic prophesies on how work will change; plenty of people are doing that already. But I will try to lay out what I think our practice should be thinking about.

Savings and body parts

The World Economic Forum is an excellent source for considering the impact of AI on jobs (don't become a postal worker)[8] but also makes clear the expectation that, by 2030, there will be 78 million more jobs than there are in 2025, albeit that 92 million jobs will be displaced, meaning a 22 per cent churn rate. The churn rate interests me, because I think this corroborates the notion of continuity I was just talking about.

That continuity is already underway, albeit very quietly. AI did not write this book (why would any machine want to write this way?) but it certainly helped me to fast-track my research, helped to suture the threads of an idea back to something that I could reference. Many of us are already using it, not just as a fairground curiosity but as an integral part of our work. John Simon of Ericsson is pushing out the envelope, using AI agents to develop internal mobility tracks to support people in their careers.[9] It's one example of what's already probably thousands.

I haven't just increased my hours, but I've substituted one set of activities for another, without decreasing my hours either. Yet there seems to be a mindset in some circles that thinks the arrival of generative/agentic/whatever AI will somehow save us thousands of people hours. Legendary practitioner Jen Allen takes up the story:

> '*Immediately someone converts that into "great, we can lose 40,000 [hours] ÷ 37 = X FTE".*
>
> *No, you can't.*
>
> *What you've actually created is 40,000 tiny slivers of time – buckets of fingers and toes.*
>
> *You haven't freed a single whole human you can take off the roster; you've shaved three minutes off everyone's day so they can finally take a sandwich break...*
>
> *Incremental productivity is brilliant for service quality and staff wellbeing – but if you instantly bank it as a payroll cut, you destroy the very benefit you just created.*
>
> *That's why SWP has to start with demand and task: what work genuinely has to be done? Which tasks can tech absorb? Where does a human add irreplaceable value?*
>
> *If you lead with "how many people can we lose?", you're salami-slicing buckets of body parts and wondering why service collapses.*
>
> *Better business, not cheaper business should be the headline. Savings come later, through retention, reduced burnout and smarter demand handling – not through fantasy arithmetic on a spreadsheet.*'[10]

SWP pointers

This exemplifies the core competencies the SWP Practitioner needs; assessing the likely impact of AI on the workforce is no different to assessing the workforce impact of a more traditional transformation programme: the work's going to change, so let's talk about how. The pretty clear implication for me is that work redesign has to accompany any planning assumptions around AI – a redistribution of the work and not just a 'reduce headcount by x and make that work'. Dave Ulrich wrote about Worktask planning as long ago as 2019:[11] it could just be that its time has now come.

Which is not to say that any of this is an easy projection to make. McKinsey recently put it thus:

> '*Employers do not know how many AI experts they will need with what type of skills, whether that talent bench even exists, how quickly they can source people, and how they can remain an attractive employer for in-demand hires after they come aboard. On the other hand, they do not know how fast AI may depress demand for other skills and thus require workforce rebalancing and retraining.*'[12]

So we know there will be 170 million new jobs and 92 million lost jobs by 2030, but we can't be terribly sure what any of them are or how quickly they will come. McKinsey's response is that organizations will need to invest heavily in on-the-job training and 'human-centric development'.[13] I'm not so sure. Perhaps AI-related technology is currently developing so quickly that perhaps it's impossible for internal learning to keep up. Could this – in the short-term at least – lead to employers defensively engaging more RA in the knowledge that the vendor proposition is to provide people with the latest skills. I don't see how that could work in the longer term, but it may herald the infiltration of the gig economy into large enterprises.

'If 15 per cent of a job's tasks are automatable,' says David Wilkins again, 'tell me *which* tasks go, *what* skills remain, and what it costs to fill the rest by build, buy, bot or bend – that's a metric executives use.'

One last thing to think about here. Talk about AI is now so all-pervasive that my friend David Shontz calls it 'a weapon of mass distraction'. It is but one input on the re-imagined Dowding model we assembled in Chapter 5: an important one, but not the only one.

Saviour or...?

> 'AI will help when it gives a more sophisticated view of what a person can do – not when we stamp "with added AI" on another skills database and call it strategic.'
> – Tech vendor CEO

In Figure 15.1, I drew a dotted-line circle around each judgement zone, calling each an 'AI Embrace'. I did that because I believe that AI has the potential to help us make better judgements by synthesizing all those disparate systems much better and faster than we mere humans could ever do.

But there are drawbacks:

1 AI is known to hallucinate an answer when it can't compute a rational one. With so many moving parts to consider, is there not a risk that it might happen here?

2 Old fairground machines would promise to read your palm for a penny, spitting out a printed ticket that was supposedly tailored to you: is an AI 'black box' any more trustworthy or verifiable?

3 If AI is that good – and it could be – what's to stop it from doing what all these different systems currently do? Do you need a people analytics solution if you can tell AI to write an application that does very similar things?

This is still an early-stage game. A vendor CEO paints an interesting proposition though:

> 'When it comes to AI, I think it's going to level the playing field within the lower ranks. For example, my CMO probably would have needed an intern to do all the content we're producing. She doesn't have to because she's very proficient with AI and content writing. It's about quality, not quantity.'

Chris Hare, co-CEO of eQ8, agrees but adds an important caveat:

> 'I think AI will fundamentally change how quickly novices can do SWP. They don't need five years of training, maybe two months with the right AI coaching. But it won't solve everything – there's still nuance, intangible decisions, synergy. We might see real leaps in a year or two, but as of right now, the space is new enough that vendors haven't fully leveraged it.'

Is the customer always right?

> 'The biggest barrier is rarely technology; it's the maturity of the customer. Even if you give them the perfect tool, the perfect system, if the organization isn't ready internally – if they haven't got the mindset, the governance, and clarity around what workforce planning is supposed to deliver – they won't succeed. SWP tools don't solve organizational readiness.' – Vincent Barat, CEO, Albert

There is no shortcut that avoids having to think. A lot. This doesn't invalidate Jill Dobbe's Chapter 10 exhortation to 'do something', but it does mean that you need to know what you want to do and, roughly, how you're going to do it. 'Half of the problem is governance and muscle-memory,' says David Wilkins of TalentNeuron, 'You need people who can champion processes, not just tech. Without that, the moment the charismatic sponsor leaves, the whole thing collapses… Trying to tackle global skills, job architecture and SWP in one go is a Kafka-esque nightmare. Start with a sliver of the business, prove value, and replicate.'

Technology should enhance and turbocharge what your company has already embraced as the right thing to do.

REFLECTIONS

- No matter how advanced the tech, the essence of SWP remains stubbornly human.

- Technology can do incredible things: process faster, see further, connect more dots than we ever could on our own. But it still can't answer the only question that matters: *what is it we're trying to achieve?*

- Systems can help us scale our thinking. They cannot do the thinking. They can simulate, infer, estimate and forecast but they cannot choose. And if we let them substitute for judgement, we risk losing that which gives SWP its value.

- Ask what we're trying to achieve first. Then decide which buttons are worth pressing.

Notes

1 Draycott, J (2009) *Apicius: A critical edition with an introduction and English translation,* Totnes: Prospect Books

2 Davidson, A (2014) *The Oxford Companion to Food,* Oxford: Oxford University Press

3 Waitrose & Partners (2025) Waitrose No.1 2 Fish Pie Fishcakes [pack label] Bracknell: Waitrose & Partners. Back of pack

4 Jakobsen, R (2018) Commodore CBM 8032, Remi's Classic Computers, https://rclassiccomputers.com/2018/11/19/commodore-cbm-8032/ (archived at https://perma.cc/AT3J-3FJT)

5 Sapient Insights Group (2021) 24th Annual HR Systems Survey: 2021–2022. Sapient Insights Group.

6 Edwards, D (2025) Conversation with David Green, Insight222, conducted on 22 May 2025

7 Tuchman, B W (1966) *The Proud Tower: A portrait of the world before the war, 1890–1914,* New York: Macmillan

8   World Economic Forum (2025) The Future of Jobs Report 2025 Geneva: World Economic Forum, January 7, 2025, https://www.weforum.org/reports/the-future-of-jobs-report-2025/ (archived at https://perma.cc/2U4Z-R4FL)

9   Simon, J (2025) WALL-E was wrong: AI won't make us lazy, it'll make us limitless, LinkedIn. 21 July, https://www.linkedin.com/pulse/wall-e-wrong-ai-wont-make-us-lazy-itll-limitless-john-simon-yi4bc/?trackingId=HH%2F2MOkeRuSZ22buHik GcA%3D%3D (archived at https://perma.cc/NDG7-G76C)

10   Edwards, D (2025) Conversation with Jen Allen, conducted on 20 May 2025

11   Ulrich, D (2019) From workforce to worktask planning, LinkedIn, 12 March, https://www.linkedin.com/pulse/from-workforce-worktask-planning-dave-ulrich/ (archived at https://perma.cc/6W5H-49ZH)

12   Mayer, H, Yee, L, Chui, M and Roberts, R (2025) Superagency in the workplace: Empowering people to unlock AI's full potential, San Francisco, CA: McKinsey & Company, https://www.mckinsey.com/capabilities/mckinsey-digital/our-insights/superagency-in-the-workplace-empowering-people-to-unlock-ais-full-potential-at-work (archived at https://perma.cc/6W5H-49ZH)

13   Ibid.

PART FOUR

Where it's heading

16

Future perfect

If you were setting up a new org, I think SWP should be a required skill for any HR director ... No conversation about workforce strategy should happen without that SWP lens. People think they can do it, but you need that independent, expert mirror in the room to shine the reality back. That's what prevents SWP from realizing its benefits, across any organization – someone at the top must see it as integral, not an afterthought.

PRACTITIONER LINDSEY CLARKE

I see so many people-project teams – transformation, strategy, skill initiatives – that are basically SWP by another name. If we realize it's all about influencing decisions on the workforce, then SWP is a core part of how HR is set up.

ALEJANDRO GIORDANELLI, MERCK KGAA

Throughout most of this book, I've written about SWP as – well, as SWP, actually, although the sharp-eyed among you might have noticed that I have occasionally talked about calling it SWP – 'for now'. I've also written about SWP as something inherently belonging to HR. When I first mapped out this chapter, I wanted to focus on who should own it, but I now see that there is something bigger to talk about. The thing is that SWP doesn't always have a good press. It doesn't always work. Given the degree and pace of change in business, you would surely think of it as being a business essential, but it isn't seen that way in all businesses.

Why is that, and what has to change? Let's start with a premise and see if it holds up.

> SWP doesn't succeed because it's rarely positioned at the right level or in the right part of the business to resonate. Moreover, much of HR is not perceived as being sufficiently business-savvy for SWP to be taken at all seriously under their ownership, despite that being where it's probably best placed.

After the last few chapters, that should have relieved me of any friends I might have left. But let's start dissecting what I've just said.

Should we call it SWP at all?

Let me remind you of part of a quote I used in Chapter 12:

> *I remember somebody saying if you're going to [anonymous], do not use that terminology, strategic software plan. They will throw up on you before you get out the door.*

Just in case you think that's an isolated example, here are a few others (I had so many that I had to use some of them).

> WHAT'S IN A NAME? QUITE A LOT.
>
> *'Everyone I've spoken to – their shoulders go down when you mention it.'* – Viv Meredith
> *'I'd love to see us consider getting rid of the name strategic workforce planning because it comes with such emotion around complexity or issues around data.'* – Chris Woodward
> *'Sometimes we just call it "workforce strategy". Because if we say "SWP" from the centre, in a federated org[anization], folks switch off.'* – Paul Habgood
> *'I realized I had a branding issue to manage before I had any chance of getting this thing off the ground.'* – David Boyle
> *'Until we rebrand what this is, we'll always struggle to get buy-in from the business. Leaders don't care about HR speak, they want us to mitigate risks to the business strategy and find opportunities to seize.'* – Viv (again)

> 'We don't need to be wedded to calling it SWP, especially if the brand is damaged. It's just the third leg of the business planning process which, for whatever reason, has fallen out of the nest on a branch halfway down the tree.' – Nick Kemsley

I am struck by that word – process – and I wonder if that is a part of the problem (even though that's how I've also described it): that it's seen as a set of procedural steps designed to produce a truckload of output which then ...well, which then does what?

SHOULDERS UP

Viv Meredith (from Chapter 13, who implemented SWP at AstraZeneca, GlaxoSmithKline and Anglo American) recalls one of her own experiences: 'A company I'd worked with had had a massive failure of SWP – all spreadsheets, the wrong conversations. So I told the HRLT, "First job: we're killing it. We're never going to call it SWP again." From now on we'll only do work where shoulders go up. We'll find people we can truly help, energize them, and create passion – because passion follows passion.

We will never show you a process, never lead with a template. If anyone accredited to drive this starts waving a template, we've failed. This has to be a strategic play.'

She's pivoting the activity away from something that is hard and fast, baked into a set of instructions somewhere, and instead she's offering help, but not on her terms.

The truth is that a number of things that we do in HR are, if you care to peel away the logos, forms of SWP: we just choose not to call them that.

TABLE 16.1 A taxonomy of SWP avoidance

Public label	What it might actually be
Workforce of the Future	Capability-based planning
Talent Strategy	Supply-side forecasting
Skills Transformation	Demand translation
Organizational Design	Organizational scenario work
Cost Reduction	Demand-side restructuring

I'm not trying to suggest that everything we do is SWP at its heart – of course not – yet there is a strategic angle to a lot of what gets done in HR. But if we could rebadge SWP from scratch, what naming might open doors that it currently does not?

I'd suggest the following:

- it should align with a business rhythm
- it should feel like it solves a problem people already know they have
- it should imply action, not merely analysis

Everyone will have their own take on what name might appear, but I like the idea of Workforce Strategy, Risk and Solutions. Looking to the future, recognizing challenges and dealing with them. You could call it Strategy, Opportunities and Solutions of course, but that would be Workforce SOS and I don't know if that's a good message.

If SWP disappeared from your organization tomorrow, who would notice?

'Strategic workforce planners are still being wiped out when the company changes direction. Two of the out-and-out industry-leading experts have just had their roles evaporated in the latest enterprise cost-cut. That tells you how fragile the profession still is ... I don't sleep well yet with a warm, fuzzy feeling that SWP is on the corporate safe list.' – Nick Kennedy, Workforce Planning Institute CEO

There is a world in which the value of SWP has been realized and cascaded through the organization, such that it has become a way of life, rather than an unwelcome interloper. It is certainly not enough for it to simply exist, regardless of whether or not it is delivering value. There will be a constant carousel of new managers who need to be persuaded and cajoled into seeing the value of surrendering some of their erstwhile sovereignty over their decision-making and ownership. This is magnified several hundredfold if or when a champion or charismatic leader moves on. All too often, the momentum leaves with them and, like an elastic band that has been stretched, it snaps back to its original state.

Here's a quote I introduced in Chapter 12, to which I said I would return:

> *'Culture gets in the way. People might want to keep doing it the old way, or they have to weigh short-run goals. Then you ask if they truly want SWP solutions, or if they just want to keep the old system. That's an underlying political dynamic – how the org is structured, how leaders are rewarded – it's not malicious, it's the system.'* – Jordan Pettman

Notice that phrase, 'how leaders are rewarded' … We've already considered the topic of manager reward in Chapter 6, but only in the context of external staff. We need to ask if this is something more fundamental. It was on this topic of reward – or, to be more precise, accountability for people's actions and decisions – that John Boudreau of USC spoke at length: it bears repeating.

JOHN BOUDREAU: WE DON'T VALUE THE TREATMENT OF PEOPLE LIKE WE VALUE THE TREATMENT OF MONEY

It's unlike finance, where leaders are expected to be held accountable for the way they make decisions about money... they're trained to do that and their careers reflect gates, where, if you don't understand this much about finance, then you don't get to be a leader.

I think leaders are relatively seldom held accountable for their effects on people at work. So if a business leader is reporting to the C-suite team or the board as part of the... annual cycle... several of them will be called in because they're relevant or the board would like to hear from them, something like that. And when they do that report, let's say every year or so, it's understood that they will report on the results of how money was used and it's the leader [who does that]. Yes, they have a controller. Yes, there is a finance function. Yes, there is a CFO. But the way money was used in your unit is your responsibility, and it's yours to report.

You will also be held accountable for it, unlike HR, where if you say to someone, 'Well, we're going to take your retention numbers and we're going to hold you accountable: you're going to report on why people aren't staying in your unit.' Well, that's very rare. I think most business leaders are allowed to say, 'Oh, why? I just do what HR tells me. It's HR's fault if everybody's leaving. I don't know why they can't get enough people. You know, talk to the head of HR about that.' And I think the same thing would be potentially true about strategic workforce planning if you said, 'Are you held accountable for thinking about the workforce of today and how you need to shape it for the needs of tomorrow?'

Our feeling was that there wasn't enough understanding about the value proposition of the human resource profession as decision support; its value to decision support is often vastly both misunderstood and undervalued, let's say, or under-emphasized.

I think the comparison to finance is useful, both for analytics and planning, because you can ask, *How is it that finance became so prominent?* There are lots of reasons – generally accepted accounting principles, etc. – but if you look at the history of accounting and finance, it's not as if finance came to us with the first businesses. For decades and decades finance was misunderstood, under-represented – it was all about sales, etc.

It was a massive breakthrough when Sloan undertook the idea of running units by return on investment instead of the amount of sales or the size, and it created a competitive advantage because General Motors was using ROI to allocate its capital while others were allocating capital to the highest sales. So it isn't as if finance had some magical aspect that makes a parallel impossible; finance matured exactly the way HR is maturing – only far more quickly than HR has in the 40 years I've been watching.

That maturity curve includes articulating very clearly what the value propositions are for a function. Pete [Ramstad] and I divide them into:

1 **compliance and governance** – mostly legal standards and risk mitigation;

2 **service delivery**, which is where most strategic workforce planning and people analytics still sit ('we're doing wonderful work: we hope you like our models'); and

3 **decision support**, which finance does brilliantly and HR does poorly.

In a nutshell, I ask: *Are leaders outside HR actually thinking better about their decisions on people because of HR?* If someone asks me whether an HR system is effective, I won't look inside HR. I'll evaluate the depth and sophistication of leaders' thinking about people. If I ask a leader 'What's motivation?' and they say, 'Motivation means I pay people to do things I tell them to do', that's a very naïve, myopic view – akin to saying cash-flow equals sales. They'd never get away with carrying along the idea that cash-flow and sales are the same, yet the organization lets them carry naïve ideas about people.

Now those are pretty big statements to make, but they're hard to argue against and entirely consistent with an overarching premise of this book; namely that HR can, through SWP in its extended form of risk identification and feasibility assessment, contribute to strategic decision-making and not merely react to it – if only it would. That's the latent frustration in what Boudreau says here – Finance has pushed itself forward while HR has not, to its detriment. You can almost hear him saying, *'If only they would do something about it'*. But what?

What does HR need to do?

Put the HRBP at the centre of everything

> 'We ran a scenario workshop for a customer's marketing function. The model showed that to deliver their shiny new operating model they actually needed head-count growth, big time.
>
> The CMO sits there stunned – "We're not growing at all". His direct reports go, "Well then we can't deliver what you just signed up to".
>
> They'd never had that conversation: strategy, operating model, workforce – all finally on the table together. The business leaders walk out saying, "Wow, we've never talked like this before". We're on a high.
>
> The HRBP [HR Business Partner] pulls us aside and says, deadpan, "That was a waste of time; I've still got 600 roles to recruit". Same data, same meeting, two realities. And that is SWP in a nutshell: you can surface gold, but if someone is wed to the hire-and-fire treadmill they'll call gold mud.' – Alicia Roach, co-CEO eQ8

In a hotel, the Director of Guest Relations is a relatively senior position – not as senior as, say, the Director of Food and Beverages, or the Director of Rooms. Yet the Head of Guest Relations is one of the most important people in the hotel. Why? Because customers who are happy talk to them (so do customers who are really unhappy). DGRs convey that intelligence to everyone else in the place, and if they say that something needs to be done in response, it happens. They are the living, breathing customer interface, combining data with that crucial human element – sentiment – to judge whether there is a situation here. They are the Voice of the Customer.

In the HR function, surely it is the HR Business Partner who should be that voice. There's plenty of belief that they should be more strategic and that, currently, they aren't.

Examples include the 'Wannabe Hero – aspiring to be a strategic player and make an impact, these HR professionals often talk about driving change but tend to revert to operational tasks.'[1] Surveys that suggest 79 per cent of HR professionals say 51 per cent or more of their typical workweek is spent on transactional activities while just 20 per cent say the same about time spent on strategic HR planning and implementations.[2] As long ago as 2018, Dave Ulrich advanced the need for HRBPs to pivot towards the business and value – 'HR is not about HR but the business'[3] – and, in an email to me this year, said something quite stark: 'I think business partner is continuing to evolve. Those who use 90s models for 2020 problems misunderstand business partnering.'[4]

There's plenty more where this comes from. All told, they yearn for a point when HRBPs are taken seriously as strategic partners. I believe two things are needed for that to happen:

1   HRBPs, People Analytics and SWP Practitioners must form a much more symbiotic and strategic relationship.

2   If they are to be effective, we need to re-orient the rest of the HR function around the businesses HRBPs represent.

Let's stick together

It's already the case that People Analytics and SWP are often found in the same function. According to David Green, 'Half the 348 firms in our most recent annual Insight222 People Analytics Trends (2024) survey now put workforce planning inside people analytics. The two disciplines are merging.'[5] Amit Mohindra, however, has come to the view that you can focus:

> '... on People Analytics to get the outcomes of workforce planning without the blood, sweat and tears. Arm decision makers with the right information at the right time and let them make "local" optimal decisions that add up to a "global" optimum in the way that the free market works. Central planning for countries died a while ago with socialism – Mongolia may be the last stronghold of the five-year plan.'

I think that's hopeful, unless the People Analytics function itself is strategic and more business-oriented in its thinking. At the moment though, it feels as if too much of it doesn't identify issues the business cares about in a language that it understands. David Green again:

> *'If the data doesn't land in the language of the audience, it's wasted. Analytics is great – translation is the value.'*

And this is where the symbiosis is possible. If the HRBP holds the business context, the SWP Practitioner sees the strategy, the risks and the solutions, the people analyst can, to begin with at least, be directed towards the kind of insights to divine. But we all of us need to understand that none of us have the answer to everything, whereas together, we can become an immense force, not only solving specific business problems that we identify but also solving with a growing confidence and sophistication problems we're asked to look at.

It happens already at times. The commercially minded HRBP takes a problem to SWP, they liaise with People Analytics to generate appropriate correlations, indicators and risks and then build a business case from available fulfilment solutions before handing it across to fulfilment partners.

I saw a demonstration recently from a high-end luxury goods company in which people analytics and sales performance were brought together to illustrate people characteristics that correlated to outstanding sales achievement. What I didn't hear was how SWP could then be used to replicate that performance through laying down tracks for other people to reach the same level of performance, although I strongly suspect they're using it. As Viv Meredith says:

> *'People analytics gave us the flashlight, but SWP gave us the map. You need both to navigate.'*

Now it may seem a bit presumptuous of me to suggest re-orienting the whole of HR; after all, it's been around a lot longer than I have. But we need to ask ourselves nevertheless:

Does HR's traditional structure help itself?

> 'It became very decentralized. Workforce Transformation sat as a separate
> organization in HR, People Analytics sat under HR Ops, and the business-unit
> [workforce] planners reported to Business Unit Operations. Each claimed, "We own
> the plan". In reality nobody owned it as a central, strategic plan. Then P&L power
> shifted back to the business groups; HR central organizations shrank to a thin
> concept layer and the "All for One" narrative quickly evaporated. From that moment
> SWP was multiple disconnected conversations – site strategy, transformation and
> analytics – none of which spoke the same language in the same circles.' – David
> Shontz, ex-Nokia

The phrase 'what goes around comes around' is very appropriate for business organizations and their tendency to flip-flop between centralized and decentralized operating models. What doesn't seem to change that much through any of these upheavals is the essential construct of the HR function. Through everything, they sail on regardless – Reward, Talent Acquisition, Talent Management, L&D, plus the more recent additions. This can be exasperating for some, such as Oliver Shaw, Orgvue CEO:

> 'What we've seen, rather than an integrated view of the organization as a system
> and how that evolves, is a tendency for the capabilities that have to be integrated to
> exist in silos. You'll have somebody talking about org-design, somebody else talking
> about resourcing, somebody else on strategic workforce planning, somebody else on
> analytics, each in a completely separate column of the organization... although you
> can also read it as an opportunity. One archetype of the behaviour we see is people
> rushing into a "skills" project, gathering huge amounts of skills data, and then the
> conversation turns into: "So what are you actually going to do with that?" The
> answer quite often is "not very much", because nothing links back together. It's
> reductionist; everyone's looking for a single magic bullet.'

I spoke recently to an SWP Practitioner who's been constantly pushing out the envelope and two things that they said made me sit up:

- First, that SWP now sits as the directional hub to which the executional spokes – those traditional functional silos – respond.

- Second, that their CHRO holds a call every WEEK with all of those heads and the SWP Lead to check on progress being made against the plans in place for the business.

I don't know if a specific HR function needs to be at the centre of the hub, but the business needs absolutely do. Anyone in HR can be an advocate for those needs, on a case-by-case basis. The critical thing is that they are need-driven: project teams of individuals, with standards set, operated and measured against by small Centres of Excellence – the teams being multi-functional in nature, with some standing members (HRBP, Analytics, SWP) calling in resources to join problem-oriented teams as and when needed. And why keep this to just HR? Let's make sure that these teams draw on all the talents from Finance, Real Estate and anywhere else that is relevant. After a while, you no longer belong to a specific function; you simply work for the good of the company.

This may seem fanciful, yet I have seen in my own SWP journey the possibilities brought about by multi-disciplinary project teams driven by delivering a business outcome, and I believe it not only to work, but to enrich everyone who participates in them. In that respect, SWP has been catalytic.

For me, two questions remain: what is it about SWP then that has been catalytic, and how should it therefore be managed and led in a company?

Strategic workforce – well, what exactly?

I'm wrestling with what it actually is that makes SWP somehow distinctive and which qualities constitute something more than just another process. You may have other ideas, but this is what stands out for me.

STRATEGIC WORKFORCE…

- **Thinking.** Eliot Jaques first introduced the concept of levels of Work in 1956[6] and kept building on it thereafter.[7] Essentially, this is the notion that, as complexity, ambiguity, time horizons and delivery breadth increase, so does the work required to deal with them necessarily broaden in its scale and scope. Drawing on the work of Jaques and Gillian Stamp,[8] Professor Nick Kemsley of Henley Business School adds a strategic workforce planning interpretation:

FIGURE 16.1 SWP and levels of work[9]

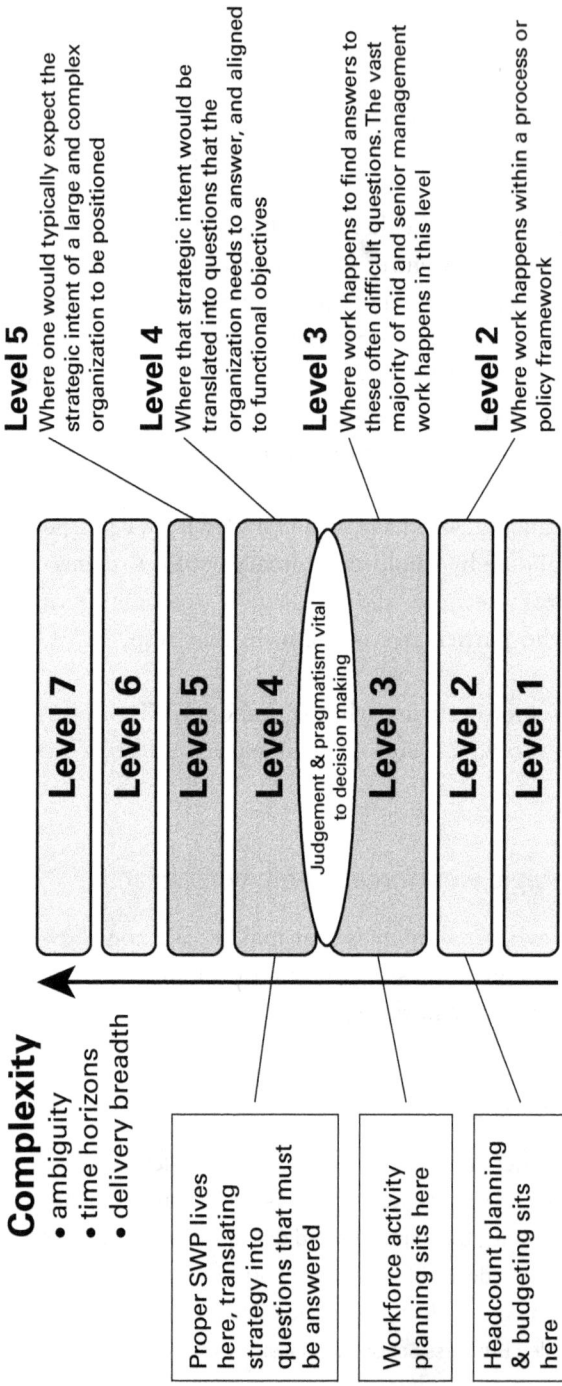

Complexity
- ambiguity
- time horizons
- delivery breadth

Level 7	
Level 6	
Level 5	
Level 4	
	Judgement & pragmatism vital to decision making
Level 3	
Level 2	
Level 1	

Level 5
Where one would typically expect the strategic intent of a large and complex organization to be positioned

Level 4
Where that strategic intent would be translated into questions that the organization needs to answer, and aligned to functional objectives

Level 3
Where work happens to find answers to these often difficult questions. The vast majority of mid and senior management work happens in this level

Level 2
Where work happens within a process or policy framework

Proper SWP lives here, translating strategy into questions that must be answered

Workforce activity planning sits here

Headcount planning & budgeting sits here

It's where he takes this next that interests me. He argues that our modern-day VUCA environment (one of Volatility, Uncertainty, Complexity and Ambiguity) has significantly increased the need for Level 4 translators of strategic ambition into Level 3 procedural direction.

In his original demand curve, Nick recognizes the effect of technology on reducing demand for Level 1/2 work. The advent of AI suggests, at least to me in Figure 16.2, that demand for Level 3 work (and, to some extent Level 4) will also be depressed, but that the need for thinking will still be met by largely human contributors.

- **Collaboration.** None of us have all the answers. A strategic approach to the workforce is necessarily collaborative, because no single individual could possibly be able to handle this alone. But it needs to be institutionally collaborative and this still feels far off to me.

- **Risk.** 'The only way to combat... resistance,' says Amit Mohindra (who put People Analytics into Apple), 'is to wrap everything in a risk wrapper – that's the burning-platform argument that works.' The combination of people analytics and business strategy awareness and understanding of the dynamics of talent acquisition, mobility and development creates an incredibly powerful capability that HR does not presently use as it could.

- **Fulfilment.** Do we need to hire everybody individually? Companies are not like armies, yet there are economies of scale in cost and onboarding speed to be had from high-volume roles that many companies fail to explore. By focusing on generating a high-quality pipeline of recruits, we can build managerial trust in the recruits we're inviting them to take on.

- **Responsibility.** Despite the short-term pressures, managers have a responsibility for the stewardship of an organization's future; a failure to exercise it will lead inexorably to the organization's decline and ultimate fall. It applies also to taking in someone who may not yet be the finished product and developing them to full proficiency. It's not just a responsibility that comes with being a manager: it's an obligation.

- **Management.** As John Boudreau has said here (not a lone voice), Human Capital must mean something more than a mere label on a suite of software products. It is not the case that you can just hire more people or different people anymore, yet we seem to have few qualms about losing people to avoid losing money. Until manager performance is judged on the safe curation of people as much as of finance, the former will always be treated less seriously than the latter.

FIGURE 16.2 Levels of work and strategy translation[10]

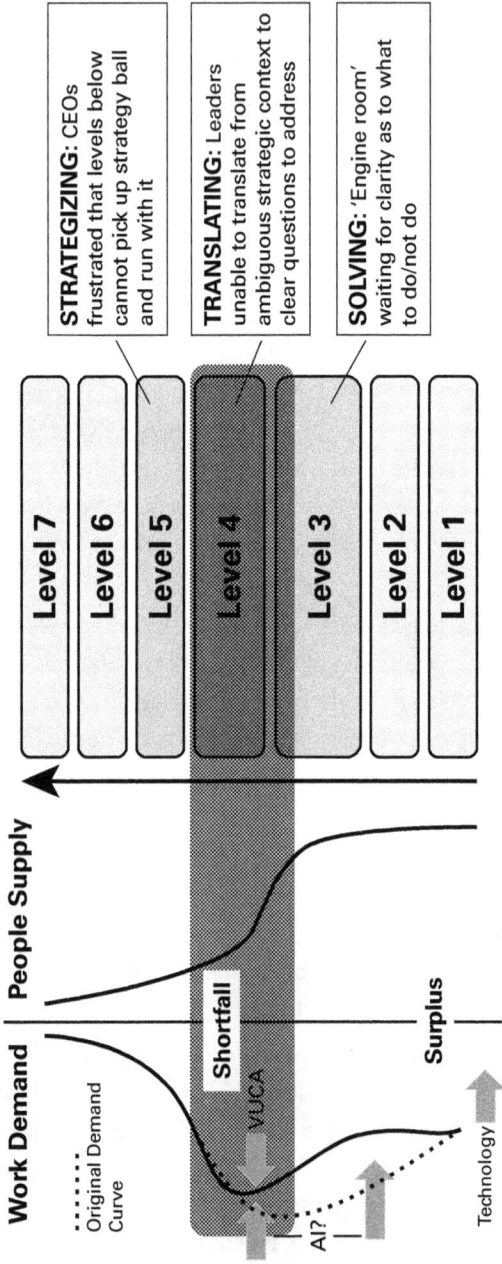

Work Demand | **People Supply**

STRATEGIZING: CEOs frustrated that levels below cannot pick up strategy ball and run with it

TRANSLATING: Leaders unable to translate from ambiguous strategic context to clear questions to address

SOLVING: 'Engine room' waiting for clarity as to what to do/not do

Level 7
Level 6
Level 5
Level 4
Level 3
Level 2
Level 1

Shortfall

Surplus

Original Demand Curve

VUCA

AI?

Technology

> - **Ecosystem.** We all recognize that the management of people is more like an organism than a series of separate components. Yet we seem to insist upon slicing that organism into sections and wonder why it doesn't work so well.

SWP is a shorthand for multiple SW Somethings. It's a way of being, a mindset, an outlook, a collective responsibility. Perhaps that's why it's so hard to pin down.

What about ownership?

I asked a lot of people a lot of questions about this, but I now think that they are slightly superfluous. If what I've said here means anything at all, then it doesn't matter who owns it. What matters is that they *care*. Whoever is responsible for Strategic Workforce Somethings should sit alongside the Chief Architect, Principal Designer and Chief Engineer, as indispensable to the CEO as the US Army's Sergeant Major of the Army is to its Chief of Staff.

So the answer to the question: if SWP disappeared tomorrow, who would notice? Well, you won't be surprised to hear me say that, if we get this right, the answer should be: *everyone.*

Notes

1   Cuel, R, Ravarini, A., Imperatori, B, Antonelli, G and Torre, T (2025) Have HR strategic partners left the building? The (new) role of HR professionals from a social-symbolic perspective, *Personnel Review*, 54(2), pp. 722–39, https://doi.org/10.1108/PR-11-2023-0929 (archived at https://perma.cc/N3MK-A6GN), https://www.emerald.com/insight/content/doi/10.1108/pr-11-2023-0929/full/html#sec005 (archived at https://perma.cc/N3MK-A6GN)

2   HR.com (2025) *Future of HR skills and strategies 2025: Transform HR with essential skills for strategic impact*, HR Research Institute, https://www.multiratersurveys.com/blog_files/19/1740522345-Future-of-HR-Skills-and-Strategies-2025-Research-Report-Peoplogica.pdf (archived at https://perma.cc/NC9F-4C92)

3   Ulrich, D (2018) HR Business Partner 2.0, *HRD Connect*, 21 August, https://www.hrdconnect.com/2018/08/21/dave-ulrich-hr-business-partner-2-0/ (archived at https://perma.cc/A2EJ-K7JF)

4 Ulrich, D (2025) Email to David Edwards, 6 July

5 Edwards, D (2025) Conversation with David Green, Insight222, conducted on 22 May 2025

6 Jaques, E (1956) *Measurement of Responsibility: A study of work, payment, and individual capacity,* London: Tavistock Publications

7 Jaques, E (1989) *Requisite Organisation: A total system for effective managerial organisation and managerial leadership for the 21st century,* Arlington, VA: Cason Hall

8 Stamp, G P (1988) *Longitudinal research into methods of assessing managerial potential,* Technical Report 819, Alexandria, VA: U.S. Army Research Institute for the Behavioral and Social Sciences

9 Kemsley, N (2024) Levels-of-Work diagrams [unpublished diagrams] Henley Business School, University of Reading, reproduced with permission

10 Ibid.

17

A painful passion

SWP is not an easy thing to do and anyone tasked with bringing it to life needs a large portfolio of experiences and skills – yes, skills – to do so. They also need to be able to cope with those twin imposters, triumph and disaster. If people are the product of SWP, then SWP Practitioners are its people by-product.

No organization or part thereof is immune from stress, and no one working for it is immune from stress either. However, there seems to be something about what it takes to get SWP to work and about the people who take it on that is especially challenging. My good friend Paul would tell me that this all sounds terribly 'poor me' to him. He wouldn't say stuff like 'suck it up' or anything else similarly unsympathetic, but he'd argue that it's not unusual. You, the reader, will decide.

The many practitioners I've spoken to are hugely intelligent, thoughtful, reasoned people. Their observations are driven by the hard realities of the work that they've taken on. Their stories are not just tales of woe, far from it. They are resilient – well, most of the time. Too often, though, they don't get heard and they believe they should be, because they believe that what they're trying to do is fundamentally good for an organization and for its people.

What follows then is what practitioners have to say, in their own words, about coping. They are all verbatim but, for obvious reasons, anonymous.

But where's the support?

I think this has been one of the hardest. It's exceptionally stimulating. I've never been a particular HR person who stays in their lane. I've always been much more interested in the wider interplay of the business, which I think is really good. From a personal perspective, I think probably the five years I've been full time, fully immersed in SWP have been the hardest personal and professional challenge I think I've ever faced.

Ultimately, I'm just trying to help, and the kind of reaction I mentioned about the leadership team was a fairly typical one. It is perhaps naivety on my part that you're expecting someone to go, 'Oh, this is great,' and having to unpick that. It's not that the data is wrong, or that I don't understand or believe the data, it's 'You are wrong. You don't know what you're talking about'. It's never a conversation about the data – it's a conversation about you as an individual. And I find that really difficult to negotiate around, because I can go in and be clear on the shortcomings of the data and the assumptions that are made, and say, 'Actually it's still valuable to be talking about this'.

But a lot of the time it's your bad data I'm playing back to you, so I am the messenger. It's very much that the nature of the news often infects the teller. That can be dispiriting. You're dealing with people who don't see you as an ally, or at times, your own HR colleagues can be the most toxic if they think you're trying to usurp their relationship with the business.

So you can feel really lonely and unsupported, and that's what I've really struggled with in this. Doing new stuff doesn't faze me; being the only person in the room, trailblazing, is fine. It's not having that base of support anywhere. But I keep going because I do believe if we get SWP right, it delivers serious value – not just for the bottom line, but for the people. And one day, I hope we'll see that pay off.

Hopeful but attritional

It's questionable. So, this year is supposed to be a big year for strategic workforce planning, so as of a few weeks ago, I would say yes and I'm very hopeful for the trajectory from hereon out.

What I've experienced in the last three years is complete turnover of my team and an extreme lack of direction, buy-in and support. When I started three years ago, we were a team of six, and we have slowly lost headcount. Whether folks have been let go or found different employment, I'm the only original member.

I think it all stemmed from differences in philosophies – trying to build a textbook SWP practice for all business units, pushing too hard and burning out HRBPs. The next CHRO never really got behind it, so we had no clear sponsorship. There were times when I wondered, 'Is this still worth it?' But I stuck it out because I see the potential if we ever get the traction we need.

The challenge is, it's so far into the future; our business case is lacking because we can't prove immediate value. We can't say, 'Look, we saved x millions this quarter'. You've got to play the long game, and that makes it harder to get quick wins that change minds. We also fight an element of 'I told you so' – if leaders ignore us, we can't prove them wrong until the future arrives, by which point it's too late for an easy fix.

At the same time, I'm excited for what's supposed to happen this year. I've seen signs that top leadership might finally take SWP more seriously. Maybe we'll get enough budget or at least the freedom to do deeper analysis, especially if they realize how it ties into talent acquisition, L&D and broader people initiatives. And whenever I do talk to people who really get it, that motivates me to keep going. Ultimately, I believe in this, because when I've seen SWP click in certain pockets, it truly impacts cost savings, retention and overall strategy.

Not what I expected

No joke – it has made me, in certain times, completely reevaluate my professional career. It seems like, as an I-O psychologist who has a background in these various talent CoEs, that SWP kind of represents the culmination of all that. Take what I was doing before, then also add strategy and add more business relationships and partnerships – and, you know, it seemed like it would just propel me to the next level. That was kind of the promise, and it's been a bit of a bait and switch, honestly.

Because it's caused me to say, you know, 'Should I give up on I-O psychology? Should I give up on this company? Should I give up on corporate life? Screw it, because this was supposed to be the next thing, and it's just not panning out.' And I'm at this point – kind of midlife – where I've got some time on my hands and I'm constantly thinking about how we can do this better because you have to be so intentional in SWP.

I think that's why, as a psychologist, you're like, 'Well, what's the point in even going back to earlier CoE work? If there's no point, what's the point in sticking with a company that can't resource SWP properly or doesn't want to?' And it has really gotten me down, to where I'm thinking maybe I'll just become a teacher, or maybe I'll just become a truck driver or something – in my lowest moments, I'm like, screw this whole knowledge work.

And I don't feel, like, if I were in a different CoE that's well-established, I'd be second-guessing all of my life's decisions. But with SWP, you kind of have to figure so many things out, dealing with hurdles, and it can be lonely. Sometimes you think, 'Am I the right person? Is this the right role? Does the business even want it?' But I keep on because I know the payoff could be huge if we actually get the traction we need.

Hard but so rewarding

It's been really, really exciting and really, really hard. The really exciting bit is the North Star. I know where we want to get to, and I know if we do some of the things that I'm trying to influence, we will see massive change and we will see a complete systemic change in how we upskill.

But it is a one-man band, I'm a one-man band who hasn't been given an open chequebook. Everything I've done is just me, and that's been through not only coming in and learning a new business, trying to make connections. There've been times where I'm thinking, 'Am I the right person? Is this the right thing?'

Also, is anyone the right person? Is it ever the right time? There've been times I've gone, 'This feels like trudging through mud', and I've got a little Post-it Note in my office that says, 'The call can change everything'. What I mean by that is I could be having a day where I'm just in PowerPoint, trying to create a deck, or writing a white paper. I could be feeling quite stuck, thinking, 'I'm just not getting anywhere'.

And then I can have an external call or have a catch-up with a colleague who just gives me a lightbulb moment and it completely changes my mood or my trajectory or my thinking, and it makes me feel empowered to get forward. Sometimes I'll speak to one person in the business that says, 'This is awesome – I'm going to speak to my team of 100 about this and let me help you pilot that', and I'll go, 'Brilliant, one step closer'.

And it's finding those little steps that absolutely keep you motivated. Sometimes it feels like pulling an oil tanker, and then one conversation makes it all worthwhile.

Thrilling

It has been thrilling, and here's why. Because I think workforce planning has forced me over the years to become the best strategist I could be. I came into workforce planning 10 years ago, thinking I could do everything in the world, thinking big value strategy, but I didn't really understand how you build small wins. I had to learn those things. And so I think the past few years, especially combining analytics with workforce planning, have been thrilling, and I don't want to change jobs – I don't want to go do something else. I want to keep doing this because it's so fun to be able to help people connect the dots and see value.

People think I'm crazy, but I love it. It's really interesting. There's a dopamine hit to it. As a business partner, I never felt that when running org effectiveness or more core HR stuff. I didn't feel it like this. With SWP, I feel like there are wins, there's strategy, there's connections, and you have to have patience, see the broad picture, and execute closely. But if you do those things, you're moving mountains – even though maybe you barely make that move sometimes.

So I'm constantly excited about this work, and that's how I cope on the personal side. Sometimes it's lonely, sometimes it's tricky to coordinate with finance or the product teams, but the bigger the challenge, the more rewarding it feels when you get a pilot or a 'lightbulb moment' for someone else. That's my recipe: building trust, bridging silos and focusing on the next step that helps the business. There's a pained passion, sure, but also a real buzz in cracking these problems.

Conflicted

There are days in this job when I don't want to do anything else, and then there are days when I would rather do anything else but this. When you see something fall into place, or when you see that lightbulb moment in someone as they grasp the possibilities, it's great because you know just how much has gone into that happening. But all too often, you're left feeling frustrated by the scepticism or by having to repeat the message you've given someone for the umpteenth time or discovering yet another blocker that you have to negotiate away.

It's like, 'What is wrong with you people, can't you see what I can see?' And then you beat yourself up because you convince yourself that the problem isn't them: it's you and your failure to explain things properly or to line up what you're trying to do with what your leadership actually cares about. People don't want to think about the long term because that's not what they get rewarded for.

I feel lonely more days than I don't and I can feel myself shrinking behind the barricades I've erected for myself because I don't want to charge out into that inferno of indifference yet again only to be beaten back, yet again. I don't want to do that because one of these days I worry I won't just get beaten back, but I'll be all burned up instead.

But you hang on because you believe that the next lightbulb moment might be just around the corner and that will give you the mental strength to climb out of the trenches once again.

Reasons to be cheerful

I have three main professional areas: talent acquisition, talent management and SWP. But there is no SWP team – I'm basically on my own with a model for the corporation, trying to show them what we could achieve if we do it right. Stakeholder engagement is everything. Our technical function is top of the tree – if they're not in, you can't get anything through. The data and scenario planning stuff is probably the easy bit compared to winning them over.

It hasn't been easy. Last year, I tried to push an SWP model onto all four of our businesses at once, but two of them just weren't ready. That was on me – I shouldn't have forced it. They didn't have a five-year strategy, and if you're only doing in-year resource management, then what I'm asking for isn't going to land. So that was a stress point: feeling like I was pushing something that couldn't succeed.

And of course, there's the question of ownership. Some parts of the business see SWP as more than 'just HR' – like it affects facilities or IP – and they ask, 'Why are HR treading on my turf?' So I've learned it's easier on me if I let them feel they own the direction, and I'm here to enable them with the people lens. That reduces conflict and honestly reduces my stress – I don't want to be the lone champion in battles all the time.

I cope by celebrating the smaller successes when they happen. When I see even one business unit actually apply SWP principles or have a big 'aha!' moment about how people strategy shapes everything, it reminds me, 'Yes, the concept works. I'm not wasting my time'. It keeps me going in this environment where no one else is dedicated to SWP. Sometimes that's all I need to balance out the frustration.

There must be some misunderstanding

I think it's a really hard job to do in any organization, mainly because it's a bit of an unknown. Not many people have done it, and they don't necessarily know what SWP really is. So you end up having to explain, 'It's not just resource management, it's thinking about future skills, building up capabilities, and being flexible about who leads the conversation.' Then there's the big challenge outside of HR. You've got these larger operational teams and finance people who think they're doing it already. They have spreadsheets with job codes, or they say, 'We know how to forecast for the next financial year, so we don't need your help'. But that's not what SWP is. They might call it workforce planning, but it's mostly short-term resourcing – and that can be frustrating, because you know there's a bigger, more strategic conversation to be had.

I can see how they feel about me coming in with a plan or a model, especially if they think, 'We've got this, why is he from HR telling us something new?' So it can feel lonely, and at times, I have to keep repeating, 'I'm here to help. We don't have to do it my way. Let's find common ground for what's best for the business.'

If I just push it on them when they don't have a longer-term strategy, it can fail. I learned that the hard way when I tried to roll out SWP across business areas that didn't have a five-year horizon view. You want SWP to show its worth, but they weren't ready, so it came across like I was forcing something they couldn't use.

So from a personal perspective, the stress is in balancing this unknown – people not really understanding it – and the fact that I'm often the lone driver. But I stay motivated when I see one or two people in the business get that 'aha!' moment about future capabilities or bridging a skills gap in a more thoughtful way. Then I think, 'Okay, we're making progress'. And that small progress helps me put up with the frustrations, because I know SWP can save a lot of headache when the business is eventually ready.

Box-ticking

Then we say, 'Actually, here's the reality', and overnight it's, 'Wait a minute, you were here to fix everything and now you're just pointing out the bloody obvious!'

That's exactly what happened to me. They hired me because Audit said they had to show a workforce-planning capability. Top-cover, nothing more. The moment I'd written the first plan they shoved me in a cupboard: 'You're not allowed to talk to anyone, you're not allowed in meetings.' They literally blocked stakeholders from speaking to me.

So you're one tiny team – sometimes one person – told to transplant a brand-new organ into a host body that's determined to reject you. You can see the system's on fire, but the brief is 'write a spreadsheet of how many people we need and don't rock the boat.'

It almost completely broke me. I ended up off with stress for about eight months. Not because the theory's hard – the theory's easy – but because you're set up to fail before you walk through the door. They want the badge that says 'SWP done', yet they're actively invested in denying every problem you surface.

That's the personal cost: you go from golden child to nobody's child in five minutes flat, carrying the weight of a discipline nobody understands and few really want. And if the organization's only motivation is an audit tick-box, the trench warfare will eat you alive.

Dogs, holidays... and hanging tough

I love HR and SWP, or I wouldn't do them. Day-to-day life is no joy ride for me, but I keep going because I enjoy adding value.

There's also a lack of respect for SWP – people think it's just an HR add-on. I keep an audit trail, so if they say, 'You took too long to issue a plan', I can show them exactly when I flagged it. I also refuse to provide half-baked data – I have to be confident that it is accurate or can caveat its limitations. It can offend leadership if I say no and they think I'm being difficult, but if I give them something incomplete, it leads to the wrong outcomes.

It's not that I love conflict – I hate it – but I'd rather have it than produce a worthless plan that impacts future outcomes. Sometimes it's draining, though, because the pace of change is slow, and there can be a resistant environment. But if I'm not pushing forward, it's not me. I might move on eventually – unless I win the lottery, in which case I'm retiring with a lot of dogs and going on holiday!

But truly, if we don't speak up, who will? That's how I cope: I remind myself that my 'tough' questions are what strategic workforce planning is meant to do, even if it causes friction.

Being kinder to myself

I recall so many vacations where I came back *unrested* because I was so exhausted from the change management work, all the stakeholder drama, and the, you know, *being drained* by working in these environments where everything is such a big struggle. Then you realize they don't actually want to put in the real discipline. It can be so deflating.

I had to do a *ton* of self-work. I started adopting that growth mindset – like, 'A setback is part of the process; we'll get there eventually' – and also just being kinder to myself. It sounds basic, but if you don't do that, you end up miserable. Actually, my hot take is: if your psychological makeup needs a lot of control, if you can't handle flux, don't go into SWP. Because everything's always in flux, they might ignore the entire analysis you put together. You can't take that personally – technically you *did* your job. But it's definitely draining when you see them do the exact opposite of your recommendations.

And it's frustration on top of frustration unless you accept that's how it goes. If you need total control, *don't* do SWP. It's too fluid; it'll drive you mad. You have to just say, 'OK, we gave our best guidance, they chose something else, we move on.' And that's why being kinder to yourself and building a support network helps a lot. At least you know *you're not alone* in feeling that stress.

It's worth it

Yes, it can be exhausting at times. We'll get new tasks from finance or enterprise HR, all wanting the data in a specific format, while managers keep shifting seats internally. It feels like you're forever explaining the same issues: 'No, we're not adding heads, we're reusing them.' It's not an easy place to be; sometimes I think I'm a full-time translator, and that's on top of my actual day job! Each side has unrealistic assumptions – finance wants a standard approach, ignoring internal mobility. Managers are opening requisitions left and right.

We also spent the first few years just handling the basics – like, purely 'who's on budget, who's off budget'. So any deeper strategic workforce thinking, like big skill transformations, took a back seat. That was frustrating, because you see big needs – like the agile shift in Cyber – but you're stuck re-validating data with finance. It's mentally draining not to have a good system or synergy from the start.

Once we averted that big $2 million budget error, though, it was a reminder that all this bridging matters. Suddenly finance was like, 'Oh, your clarifications saved us from overshooting!' That gave me a personal lift, because you see direct impact. But it's still a constant push: different leaders want solutions in silos, or enterprise HR is slow on comp changes, or finance tries to apply the same formula to everything. You do need resilience – a thick skin – to keep bridging them, especially when each side thinks you're messing with their territory. I just keep telling myself, 'As soon as they see real benefit, it's worth it'. And so far it is.

REFLECTIONS

- **It's a deeply personal mission.** There is an evangelistic spirit about this.

- **Personal credibility can be at stake.** Yet many accept this reality and have made peace with it.

- **This can be draining.** The multiple sources of obstacle and setback can be exhausting, debilitating.

- **It can be lonely.** No wonder we go to conferences for therapy.

- **Opposition can be from within.** There can be unlikely sources of resistance.

- **Bring some resilience.** Don't expect the job to create it for you.

- **One of these contributions was mine.** Which one? Not telling.

- **This can be exhilarating.** The 'dopamine hit' you get from making meaningful, tangible change is wonderful.

- **Baby steps.** Little wins, lightbulb moments: that's how you succeed.

- **It's still worth it.**

18

Reflections

Everybody's stuck reacting to the consequences – ironically of not doing it two years earlier. What gets in the way of thinking long term is the amount of time the short term takes up, and every year you spend focusing just on the short term is another year you'll have to spend focusing on the short term because you didn't think 5 per cent about the long term... It's a self-perpetuating cycle and an inevitable symptom of the complexity of work versus the relatively unchanging way we develop people.

NICK KEMSLEY

Ghosts

In 1978, I went to the southern Kenya coast to work as a volunteer teacher in a small, village-funded secondary school. Aged just 18, it was one of my life's most formative years and the memories of that time endure. I lived with Niall, a fellow volunteer, in one of the four small, simple whitewashed houses provided for teachers. They stood apart from the village just 100 metres from a deserted beach of sun-drenched palm trees and coral reef. There was running water but no electricity, phones or any other means of communication. The long, unmade and tree-shaded road from the nearest highway I had walked on my first day with Niall (because we didn't know we should have stayed on the bus for another two miles) led to the tiny village of wattle and daub houses and shops, where freshly made chapatis and green bananas were our lunchtime staple and Ramadan evenings on this Muslim coastline were vibrant, heady events.

Thirty-five years later, I was in a minibus heading down the same road to revisit my former home. But the trees had gone, replaced instead by multiple homes along the route, so much so that I was convinced we were on the wrong road. Even when we arrived at the village itself, nothing felt the same. Finony and I walked the final half mile of what I was sure was the right way, passing the stained hospital walls and shops selling SIM cards, to a place that felt like mine. I stood, the memories flooding back – laughs, loneliness, exuberance – until I realized that I was at the wrong place. For there, a short walk away, the four houses stood. No longer standing alone, but crowded by other houses and broken picket fences, their walls blackened, windows cracked and broken, gardens overgrown. The beach was still there of course, but the palm trees were mostly gone, replaced by giant holiday villas doubtless belonging to the rich and well-connected.

It was raining.

Nothing remains the same. The hundred or more oak trees that were planted around 1805 by a Lady Mildmay in my home village were in response to an appeal from the British Admiral Collingwood, who wrote, after the Battle of Trafalgar, 'What I am most anxious about is the plantation of oak in this country. We shall never cease to be a great people while we have ships and we cannot have ships without timber.'[1] This very early example of Strategic Workforce Planning turned out to be unnecessary with the arrival of ironclad ships, leaving the village with a magnificent common of huge oak trees. Yet sometimes the fruits of foresight endure in unexpected ways.

I am a child of the 1970s and a weekly TV staple for my brother and my sisters was always *Top of the Pops*. In the first half of that decade, The Drifters were a regular feature, with timeless favourites like 'Under the Boardwalk'. Well, The Drifters are themselves seemingly timeless, having formed in 1953 and still, 72 years and 60 singers later,[2] performing to packed houses. Change can be transformative and catastrophic; it can also be evolutionary, enduring and gratifying.

Change agency

Change, like memory, has no single shape. For the SWP practitioner, the challenge is often to distinguish the enduring from the transient – to understand what must adapt and what must stay as is.

At its heart, this book is about change agents – practitioners introducing operational change to help others manage changes of their own. SWP just happens to be the vehicle. But it's a sprawling and seemingly cumbersome one, a little like the infamous *Spruce Goose* built by the billionaire recluse Howard Hughes, a colossal eight-engined aircraft designed to transport enormous quantities of freight but which achieved a single one-mile test flight in 1947, never to be used again.[3]

Perhaps that's the misconception. That this one giant entity can swoop in and transform things for everybody, when everybody else is looking at it and saying it's never going to fly.

The 1948 Berlin Airlift – in which the US, British and French sectors of Berlin were kept supplied after road links were severed – was serviced by thousands of flights of aircraft with one-twentieth of the Goose's capacity. Small contributions making small differences which, when accumulated, made a very big difference. Each contribution was united by the idea that we could do things differently and for a good cause.

SWP – or whatever we should now call it – is not a crusade in the same way, of course. But in addition to the other things I called it in Chapter 16, it is a belief system, forged in an accumulated broad exposure to aspects of work and the workforce, that it's possible to do things differently, better.

Throughout this book, I've tried to give this belief system practical expression: things to consider, things to say and things to do. The intention has been to de-mystify and re-orient around a more accessible viewpoint, one which I hope is now visible.

Perhaps Professor Nick Kemsley is right: we practitioners exist as cheerleaders for a different, more inclusive and collaborative way of working which, when properly established, may not even need us. To use the viewpoint analogy, once you can see the sea, you no longer need someone to tell you what the sea looks like, or how to find it. Like The Cheshire Cat, we slowly fade until only our smile is left.

A call to care more

Yet I don't see us vanishing any time soon. Positive outcomes are emerging – we've seen some of them throughout this book – but they don't yet seem to outweigh the upsets and the perception in some quarters.

For that to happen, there needs to be greater care:

- **From leadership,** who need to understand how workforce risk and its mitigation can impact their organization for better or worse.

- **From managers,** who need to believe that this is relevant and valuable to them and therefore worth the effort.

- **From HR,** who need to accept the need to place the business imperative at the heart of everything they do and orient around that.

- **From fulfilment functions,** who need to see themselves as a single engine for delivering the business the talent it needs — and for improving both cost and speed.

- **From anyone** who needs reminding that people are neither machines nor dispensable commodities.

None of this will be perfectly realized, in part or in its entirety. A need to care more does not mean indifference; the pace of change robs us of opportunities for reflection, in which we may see other, better ways to do things. SWP Practitioners are but one, themselves imperfect, means of helping others to see them.

A few years ago, I visited one of the last working tin mines in Cornwall, except it hadn't been working for several decades. Among the many sights was the mine's administration office, left untouched since the mine had closed. There, laid before me, were all the things that I recalled from my first days as an office worker: the analogue telephones, the pin-up wall planners, the basic drinks vending machine, the adding machine with its till roll output, the total absence of screens, speakers and devices.

Those ghosts inform my past, but they did not define my future, just as today's future of work will one day become its past, a Loriner for its time. People who can keep laying down the tracks for others to continue their personal and professional journeys will never be short of things to do. Whether they are called SWP Practitioners or something entirely different, they will still be doing the work – and doing it with the same passion and enthusiasm that marks them out today.

> 'It's difficult, but I get such a sense of purpose knowing I can help the business avoid unnecessary layoffs, prepare the workforce for the future, and uncover internal mobility opportunities for employees. Even with all the uphill battles, even if the impact is years down the line, I know I'm helping prevent unwanted redundancies and preparing the business for what's ahead, and that's what keeps me going.' – A proud SWP Practitioner

Notes

1 Hartley Wintney Parish Council. (n.d.). The Commons, https://www.hartleywintney-pc.gov.uk/the-commons/ (archived at https://perma.cc/5QXE-TLQJ)

2 Last.fm. (2025) The Drifters – Biography, https://www.last.fm/music/The+Drifters/+wiki (archived at https://perma.cc/KM77-W8H2)

3 Evergreen Aviation & Space Museum (n.d.) 'The Spruce Goose lives on! The largest wooden airplane ever built', https://www.evergreenmuseum.org/exhibit/the-spruce-goose/ (archived at https://perma.cc/UM8N-QGTC)

INDEX

Numbers in *italic* refer to a figure.

Looking for another book?

Explore our award-winning
books from global business
experts in Human Resources,
Learning and Development

Scan the code to browse

More from Kogan Page

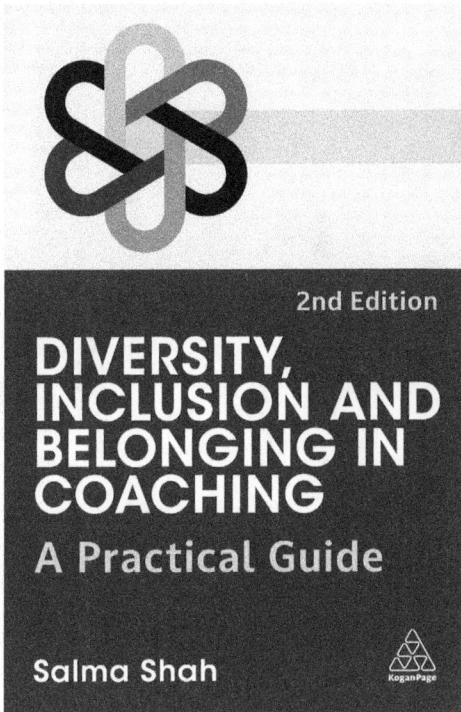

2nd Edition

DIVERSITY, INCLUSION AND BELONGING IN COACHING

A Practical Guide

Salma Shah

ISBN: 9781398623644

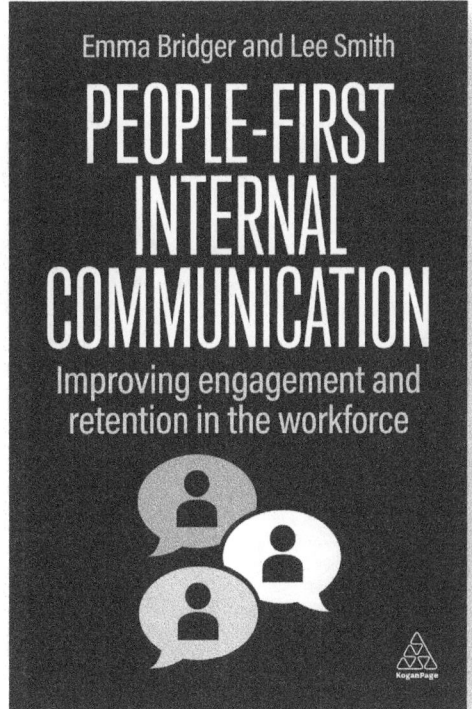

Emma Bridger and Lee Smith

PEOPLE-FIRST INTERNAL COMMUNICATION

Improving engagement and retention in the workforce

ISBN: 9781398623064

www.koganpage.com

From 4 December 2025 the EU Responsible Person (GPSR) is:
eucomply oÜ, Pärnu mnt. 139b – 14, 11317 Tallinn, Estonia
www.eucompliancepartner.com

www.ingramcontent.com/pod-product-compliance
Lightning Source LLC
Chambersburg PA
CBHW071546210326
41597CB00019B/3133